# The Power of Speech

## Leadership Speeches 2002 - 2006
## Graham Watson MEP

*Compiled and edited by Christine Gilmore*

To Katherine Adams,

with thanks for your help in
making all of this possible.

Graham Watson

Published by Bagehot Publishing

The Power of Speech
Compiled and edited by Christine Gilmore

ISBN 0-9545745-4-0

Published in December 2006 by:
Bagehot Publishing
Bagehot's Foundry
Beard's Yard
Langport
Somerset TA10 9PS
United Kingdom

Printed by:
Contract Printing
1 St James Road
St James Industrial Estate
Corby
Northants NN18 8AL
United Kingdom

Previous books by Graham Watson:

The Liberals in the North-South Dialogue (ed.)
FNS, Bonn 1980

To the Power of Ten - essays from the European Parliament (ed.)
CfR, London 2000

2020 Vision - Liberalism & Globalisation (ed.)
CfR, London 2001

Liberal Language - speeches & essays 1998-2003
Bagehot Publishing, 2003

EU've got mail! - Liberal Letters from the European Parliament
Bagehot Publishing, 2004

Liberal Democracy and Globalisation (ed.)
Bagehot Publishing, 2005

Liberalism - something to shout about (ed.)
Bagehot Publishing, 2006

# Contents

**Introduction**
*Foreword by Graham Watson MEP*     9
*About Graham Watson*     13
*About the Editor*     15

**Liberal Leadership**     17
*All Liberals Are Leaders - Speech to the ELDR Group upon Graham Watson's election as leader, 2002*     17
*Freeing Europe's Potential - Speech to ELDR Conference upon agreement of its European election manifesto, 2003*     21
*Britain Needs Brussels - UK constituency campaign speech for the European elections, 2004*     27
*European Democracy Has Everything Other Than Voters - Speech to the ELDR group on priorities following the 2004 European elections*     33
*Ready To Launch - Speech commemorating the launch of the ALDE Group, 2004*     36
*The Birthday Present Gibraltar Deserves - Speech marking Gibraltar's 300th Anniversary, 2004*     39
*A Platform For Progress - Speech to the Centre for European Policy Studies on ALDE priorities for the new parliamentary term, 2004*     41
*An Invisible Elephant In The House - Speech to the European Parliament on democratisation of the EU, 2004*     48
*Building The EU Is Like Making Sausages - Speech to the Liberal Democrat Autumn Conference, 2005*     51
*Imitation Is The Worst Form Of Politics - Speech to the Liberal Democrat Western Counties Conference on the dangers of political opportunism, 2005*     57
*An Immortal Memory - Burns Supper Speech, Brussels, 2006*     60
*30 Years Old But Still Young At Heart - Speech commemorating LYMEC's 30th Anniversary, 2006*     66
*Energising Europe - Speech commemorating the ELDR's 30th Anniversary, 2006*     70
*Build Your Rock Upon This House - Speech to Gibraltar's National Day Celebrations, 2006*     75

## Building An Enlarged European Union 77

*Breaking Down The Berlin Wall* - Speech to the European Parliament
on EU enlargement, 2002 78

*Success Has Many Fathers* - Speech to the European Parliament on the
draft EU Constitution, 2003 81

*Divided They Stood, Divided They Fell* - Speech to the European
Parliament on the failure of the Annan Plan to reunify Cyprus, 2004 84

*Vote For An Ideal, Not Simply A Text* - Speech in Barcelona
campaigning for a yes vote in the Constitutional Referendum, 2005 86

*A Little Rebellion Now And Then Is A Good Thing* - Speech on the
failure of France and the Netherlands to ratify the Constitution, 2005 91

*You Only Get Out What You Put In* - Speech to the European
Parliament on the long-term EU Budget proposals, 2005 94

*A Single Market For A Successful Future* - Speech to the European
Parliament on the Services Directive, 2006 96

*Never Be Afraid Of Telling The Truth* - Speech to a European
Parliament Seminar on Turkey in Europe, 2006 98

*Kosovo Lies Firmly At The Heart Of Europe* - Speech to an ELDR
Congress on the future status of Kosovo, 2006 102

*More Democracy, Please* - Speech to the European Parliament in
advance of June's European Council, 2006 106

*Treat Your Neighbour As Yourself* - Speech to the European
Parliament on Romania and Bulgaria's progress towards accession, 2006 109

## Liberty And Security 113

*Global Laws For A Global Village* - Speech to the European Parliament
on the establishment of the International Criminal Court, 2002 113

*Europe's Defence Deficiencies* - Speech to the European Parliament
on Europe's joint defence capabilities, 2002 116

*The Road To Hell Is Paved With Good Intentions* - Speech to the
European Parliament on the EU-US Extradition Agreement, 2003 119

*An Unlikely Experiment In Global Governance* - Speech to the
European Parliament on the UN's receipt of the Sakharov Prize, 2004 121

*Is 'Big Brother' Watching Us?* - Speech to a biometrics seminar in
Brussels, 2004 123

*Eurocop* - Speech to the European Confederation of Police detailing the
Liberal Perspective on Justice and Home Affairs, 2004 126

*A Deal Too Far* - Speech to the European Parliament on a proposal to
store records of air travellers between the EU and the US, 2004 130

*Tough On Terrorism Yet True To The Treaties* - Speech to the
European Parliament on the proposed Passenger Name Record, 2004    132
*Civilisation And Its Discontents* - Speech to the European Parliament
on the conduct of the War on Terror, 2005    134
*Criminals Can No Longer Outrun The Law* - Speech to the European
Parliament on the European Arrest Warrant, 2005    137
*Tackling Crisis On A Wing And A Prayer* - Speech to the European
Parliament on the Common Foreign and Security Policy, 2006    139

**The Future Of Europe In The World**    **143**
*All Roads Lead To Lisbon* - Speech to a Social Affairs Seminar on the
need for European economic reform, 2004    143
*A New Deal For Europe* - Speech to an EU-Politix Seminar on the need
for a revised institutional framework for Europe, 2004    148
*Unity Through Diversity* - Speech to a European Parliament Seminar on
European Integration Policy, 2004    154
*The Future Of Europe Sixty Years After The Second World War* -
Speech to the European Parliament on the achievements and purpose of
the EU, 2005    159
*Britain Can Teach Europe A Thing Or Two* - Speech to the European
Parliament on the UK's priorities for its EU Presidency, 2005    163
*Migrations Are Necessary* - Speech to the European Parliament on the
need for a common EU migration policy, 2005    166
*Redefining The Purpose Of Europe* - Speech to the College of
Europe in Bruges on the EU's purpose in a globalised world, 2005    168
*Eastern Promise Versus Western Wisdom* - Speech to a European
Parliament seminar on the EU's 7th Research and Development
Framework, 2005    180
*Don't Turn Back The Clock* - Speech to the European Parliament on
the dangers of economic protectionism, 2006    183
*Nuclear Peril And Potential* - Speech to the European Parliament on
the 20th Anniversary of the Chernobyl disaster, 2006    186
*'Finlandia' Is Music To Liberal Ears* - Speech to the European
Parliament on the priorities for Finland's EU Presidency, 2006    189

**Strengthening A Liberal World Order**    **193**
*Religion Doesn't Have To Be A Political Conversation Stopper* -
Speech to a Liberal International Congress in Senegal on 'Islam and the
West', 2003    193

*Pride And Prejudice: The Problem With Transatlantic Relations -* Speech to the American Chamber of Commerce in Brussels on transatlantic relations, 2003    *199*

*The Emperor's New Clothes -* Speech to the European Parliament on EU-Russia relations, 2003    *205*

*Life In The Global City -* Speech to students at Sofia University on Liberalism and Globalisation, 2004    *207*

*Applied Liberalism -* Speech to a CALD Conference in Malaysia on the adaptability of Liberalism to global challenges, 2004    *218*

*Understanding The East Is A Career In Itself -* Speech to a CALD Conference on EU-Asia relations, 2004    *226*

*The Semblance Of Reform Must Not Be Allowed To Mislead Us -* Speech to a European Parliament hearing on the Chinese Arms Embargo, 2005    *231*

*Gender Equality Is A Liberal Challenge -* Speech to an Arab International Women's Forum in Cairo on gender equality and democracy, 2005    *235*

*Turning Peace On Paper Into Peace On The Ground -* Speech to a European Parliament Seminar on the prospects for peace in the Great Lakes region of Africa, 2005    *241*

*Promoting Europe's Values In The World -* Speech to the European Parliament on the need for a common foreign and security policy, 2006    *245*

*Viruses Don't Respect Borders -* Speech to a European Parliament Seminar on plugging the gaps in global health security, 2006    *248*

**Appendix**

*UDF Referendum Speech - French*    *250*

*FDP Congress Speech - German*    *255*

*Margherita Congress Speech - Italian*    *262*

*Information and Addresses*    *269*

# Foreword

There is something dangerously arrogant about compiling a book of one's own speeches. Not only the 'look at me' - or more precisely 'listen to me' - factor but the belief that the politically-minded reader will find interest in ploughing through a series of disparate and sometimes repetitive contributions of varying import to public discourse. Many of these speeches can be found elsewhere, for example on the excellent European Parliament website - www.europarl.eu - or my own - www.grahamwatsonmep.org. Nonetheless the essentially ephemeral nature of political debate and the level of interest in my first such volume ('Liberal Language', Bagehot Publishing, 2003) persuaded me to repeat the exercise for my speeches as Leader of the Liberal Democrats in the European Parliament during the years 2003 to 2006.

It is an immense privilege to be able to speak on behalf of Liberal Democrats from across our continent in the crucible of debate which is our Parliament. The period covered by this book was a difficult period for the institutions of the European Union. The large member states, resenting the self-imposed limits on their freedom which their EU commitments implied, sought to put a brake on European integration, weaken the institutions of EU government and reassert their own rights. Ten more countries joined the Union, putting a strain on its administrative capacity. The draft EU Constitution, which fifteen countries had elaborated painstakingly in an effort to improve governance and prepare for a Union of 25 was rejected in referendums in two of the founding member states, France and the Netherlands. The politics of energy supply became more divisive. The US-led invasion of Iraq divided the Union into two camps. Terrorism and migration often featured prominently in the news headlines.

This, then, was a fascinating period in which to have privileged access to the debates, mingle with the actors and absorb the mood music of a continent in the making. However damp the enthusiasm of national governments or their people, events were driving them inexorably closer together. If Europe was no longer being pulled together from the centre, it was being pushed together by the centripetal forces of world developments. Increasingly, European citizens demanded of their governments policies which could only be provided by a stronger, more effective EU. I hope the speeches in this book succeed in giving the reader some flavour of these challenges.

I am indebted to Christine Gilmore, an adviser during 2005 and 2006, for her work in sifting through the many candidates for inclusion in this collection of speeches; in researching and introducing each speech selected and in devising a logical framework for their presentation. She has also, inevitably but good-naturedly, had to fit the nuts and bolts to an operation involving photographers, printer and publisher. This book is as much her work as mine.

A political speech has a life of its own. The content, the choice of language and the structure (both grammatical and the order of themes) are often determined by the imperatives of the occasion. Speeches made in the European Parliament's hemicycle, or debating chamber - which make up the majority of those in this compendium - inevitably follow the statements of Commission and Council representatives and the replies by the leaders of the two largest political groups; in many senses they are a response to these. They are also a commentary on current events, disclosing how Liberals interpreted and analysed them at the time. I hope too that they reflect a Liberal philosophy of life.

As Leader of a parliamentary group one speaks on behalf of its members. Thus a speech in the hemicycle may be informed by a debate with colleagues a day or two beforehand since, if it fails to reflect the balance of opinion among MEPs in one's own political family, there may be a political price to pay. Such is the intrigue of parliamentary politics, it is often said that a party leader is only as strong as his or her most recent speech on the floor of the House. A Leader has to choose his or her words with care and stand by them.

Though I have consulted whenever possible, I rarely circulate to colleagues a draft of my speech beforehand. They receive a transcript shortly afterwards and - if they have not given vent to enthusiasm or lack of it in the Chamber - they frequently react. I am particularly grateful to those who regularly send me text messages of approval via my mobile phone: it does wonders for morale. Where there is little consensus in a political party, a leader seeks refuge in unifying themes. In my case, eagerness for the further and faster construction of the EU (since 2004 my Group's name as been *'The Alliance of Liberals and Democrats for Europe'*): in the case of Hans-Gert Poettering, Leader of the mainly christian democratic European People's Party, support for His Holiness the Pope. The hapless Leader of the European Socialists is frequently in great difficulty due to the sharp differences of opinion within his ranks and the frequent lack of points of consensus.

Some of the pleasure in being invited to make a speech beyond Parliament is that it permits me greater freedom. Speeches to outside audiences are less influenced by the need to react to earlier speakers (a political leader's diary is such that too often one arrives just in time, speaks, and departs). Engagements are normally taken further in advance so the speech can be better prepared and the likely mood of the audience is easier to predict. Despite alleged public dislike of politicians, non-political audiences are often more appreciative. Most of all, a speech beyond Parliament often provides the opportunity for a comprehensive presentation of one's ideas, as shown here by my speech to the College of Europe in Bruges, entitled 'Redefining the Purpose of Europe'.

Though the casual observer might imagine otherwise, very little of a politician's time is spent making formal speeches. Of the fifteen hours I work each day I am likely to be 'on my feet' performing for fewer than one and a half. Nonetheless, apart from formal speeches to the Chamber or outside bodies, rarely a day goes by without a couple of visitors groups to address in an 'introduction, question and answer' format; and inevitably these occasions require more adrenaline than most other aspects of my work. Interviews on radio or television, to meet the needs of broadcasters serving nearly 500 million people over 25 countries, might account for another thirty minutes. But most of my working day consists of reading, writing, correspondence, meetings and - inevitably for a European Union politician - travelling.

Nonetheless the speech is perceived as the apogee of political activity. Few political careers can survive an inability to speak fluently and convincingly. In the European Parliament, the ability to speak fluently in the four major languages - English, French, German and Italian - is almost a sine qua non for leadership of a major political group; I have included examples of speeches I have made in languages other than English in the appendix to this collection.

Students shadowing me on 'work experience' schemes often ask how I prepare for a speech. Yet politics is such a 'fly by the seat of your pants' type of profession that preparedness varies widely. A good speech frequently bears the hallmarks of different authors. I am fortunate to have been assisted during the period covered in this volume by Philip Tod, Sarah Kent, Stephen Adams, Neil Corlett, Christine Gilmore and many others. On occasion, my speeches have been almost entirely their work. Sometimes I have jettisoned their carefully crafted prose and chosen a different tack. Currently, my preference is to be less heavily 'scripted' for debates in the hemicycle. A few salient facts, an appropriate literary allusion and a shot of adrenaline are often the best cocktail.

I have enjoyed the privilege of leading my parliamentary group for five years. Within that time I have opined on countless occasions on behalf of Liberal Democrats from Famagusta to the Faroe Islands and from Helsinki to Horta. If my interventions have inspired it is due in large measure to those who have assisted and inspired me. Where they have failed, the fault has been mine. In this selection there are speeches which have electrified my audience and some which have gassed them. Nonetheless I hope they make interesting and varied reading for anyone kind enough to purchase a copy or fortunate enough to receive it with my compliments.

Graham Watson
Langport, Somerset
December 2006

# About Graham Watson

Graham Watson was born in March 1956 in Rothesay, Scotland, the son of a Royal Naval officer and a teacher. He was educated at the City of Bath Boys' School and at Heriot Watt University, Edinburgh, where he gained an Honours degree in Modern Languages. He is a qualified interpreter who speaks four European languages and is currently learning Mandarin Chinese.

From 1983 to 1987 he served as Head of the Private Office of the Rt. Hon Sir David Steel MP, the then Leader of the Liberal Party and subsequent Presiding Officer of the Scottish Parliament. He had previously been politically active as General Secretary of the Liberal International's Youth Movement, and was a founder of the European Communities' Youth Forum.

Before entering Parliament, Graham Watson worked for the Hong Kong and Shanghai Banking Corporation in both their London and Hong Kong offices, encompassing a three-month stint with the European Bank for Reconstruction and Development.

He maintains an active interest in the Far East as a member of European Parliament Delegation for relations with China and Korea whilst promoting Liberal Democratic ideals in Asia through his work with the Council Of Asian Liberals and Democrats. He is an Adviser to the Asia-Pacific Public Affairs Forum

Graham Watson was the first British Liberal Democrat to be elected to the European Parliament, winning the Somerset and North Devon constituency in 1994 with a majority of over 22,500. In June 1999 Graham was elected to represent the new enlarged South West of England constituency, which covers Bristol, Gloucestershire, Somerset, Dorset, Wiltshire, Devon and Cornwall.

From 1994 to 1999 Graham was a member of the Committee for Economic and Monetary Affairs and Industrial Policy and of the

Budgets Committee. From July 1999 to 2002 he served as Chairman of the Committee on Citizens' Freedoms and Rights, Justice and Home Affairs.

On 15 January 2002 Graham Watson was elected Leader of the 53 strong group of the European Liberal, Democratic and Reform Group in the European Parliament. After the European Elections in 2004, Graham was re-elected as President of the newly formed Alliance of Liberals and Democrats for Europe, which comprises 89 MEPs from 20 different countries as well as Observer MEPs from Romania and Bulgaria.

Graham lives with his wife and two children in the small market town of Langport in Somerset.

He has published 7 books, the most recent being 'Liberalism - something to shout about.'

# About the Editor

Christine Gilmore was born in Edinburgh, Scotland, where she attended George Heriot's School. She gained an Honours degree in English Language and Literature from Oxford University before turning her back on Europe to teach in China. Upon her return, she decided to pursue a long-time interest in politics and has worked for the Liberal Democrats since 2003: firstly as political adviser to the Liberal Democrat Group in the Scottish Parliament and subsequently as Editorial Adviser to Graham Watson in the European Parliament. She is currently studying for a Masters Degree in Political Philosophy at the University of York.

# Liberal Leadership

*Entitled 'Liberal Leadership', this Chapter charts Graham Watson's political career from taking over the reins of the European Liberal Democrat and Reform Group in the European Parliament in January 2002, through his election as leader of the Alliance of Liberals and Democrats for Europe in 2002, to seeking re-election in the Autumn of 2006. Ranging from reflections on his constituency work as MEP for the South West of England and Gibraltar, to the formation of the new political Alliance following the last European Elections, this collection of speeches is intended to shed light on the internal politics of the European Parliament and life behind the scenes of its third largest political group. From both a political and a media perspective Group Leaders are judged largely on the strength of their performances in the Chamber which showcase the party's position on the issue of the day. However they are also called upon to deliver a number of other major addresses, from set-piece speeches at Party Conferences, to Liberal International and ELDR Events and lectures to think tanks, universities and NGOs, a selection of which are laid out in this chapter.*

\*\*\*\*\*\*\*\*\*\*\*\*\*\*\*\*\*\*\*\*\*\*\*\*\*\*\*\*\*\*\*\*\*\*\*\*\*\*\*\*\*\*\*\*\*\*\*\*\*\*\*\*\*\*\*\*\*\*\*\*\*\*\*

## All Liberals Are Leaders

*Address to the European Liberal Democrat and Reform Group upon Graham's election as leader on the 15th of January 2002. He had succeeded Pat Cox as head of what was then a 53-strong Group of Liberal Democrat Members of the European Parliament when, with EPP-ED support, Pat became the first Liberal President of the European Parliament in twenty two years. Here Graham sets out his priorities for the year ahead - and gives colleagues a taste of his future leadership style. Following 2004's European Elections ELDR numbers swelled to 62 MEPs, who then teamed up with the French UDF and Italian Margherita parties to form the 88-strong Alliance of Liberals and Democrats for Europe and the largest 3rd force the European Parliament has ever known.*

*15th January 2002, Strasbourg.*

'Colleagues, thank you for the confidence you have shown in me. There have been many speeches today, but I hope you will allow me to say a few words more.

Until I joined you seven years ago there had been no UK Liberal Democrat member ever in the directly elected European Parliament. I had the honour of being the first member of my Party to be declared elected here. In assuming the honour you now bestow upon me I do so not only in my own right but also on behalf of the Party of John Stuart Mill, Walter Bagehot and William Gladstone, of Grimond and Jenkins and Steel.

I succeed Pat Cox as Leader of this Group. Pat, we are proud to have elected you as President of the European Parliament. Thank you for all you have done for the ELDR Group in your four years as our Leader.

Pat, this speech is in no way a valedictory address. You remain a member of our Group and our political family. Moreover you carry the standard of Liberal Democracy to the summit of our institution. If we see less of you at the meetings of our Group over the next thirty months we will however understand; the work you will be doing in leading our House will be hugely demanding.

Colleagues, Liberal Democrats are growing in strength across Europe. Werner Hoyer, the ELDR President who we are pleased to have with us today, presides over a Party which runs governments in Belgium, Denmark, Slovenia and Latvia and plays an important role as a coalition partner in several other European countries. Moreover it now counts in its ranks the President of the European Commission and the President of the European Parliament. Our Group is part of that strength. The combination of the talents and energies of our MEPs and staff, matured over two and a half years of working together, is a powerful kinetic force.

So permit me a word on style. I have the good fortune to take over a Group whose MEPs work well. Organisations such as this are often better sailed than driven. Team work will be essential to get the best out of our ship. I will not fail on my watch, but I will normally seek only to use a light hand on the tiller to guide and amplify the forces of nature.

I want to use the skills of all Members to help to grow our Group: to carry on Pat's work in central and eastern Europe and to look for new recruits from current EU member states.

I want to hone our energies to concentrate on issues where the European Parliament has legal powers, to show our electors how Liberal Democrats make the difference.

I want us to tell every Liberal Democrat across our continent - every member of every member party, especially those in elected office - about what we are up to here.

Together with our new Secretary General, Alexander Beels, I look forward to making proposals on objectives and working methods to achieve these and other goals. I hope we can agree these within a month.

We have one immediate task. Parliament is to establish a temporary committee on Foot and Mouth Disease. With your agreement I should like to ask Jan Mulder to bring his expertise to bear in drawing up a draft ELDR position paper so that our members of the committee can hit the ground running.

I hope too that our Group will look outwards more. The enlargement of the EU is a huge and important dossier. Pat's Presidency will be an enlargement presidency. But while the Union is fussing over its own kailyard there are massive changes taking place in the world outside; changes which contributors to the book '2020 Vision - Liberalism and Globalisation', published recently, have exposed with commendable clarity.

We have the great fortune to live at a time replete with opportunity for Liberalism; not only at home but in Asia, in Africa, in the Hispanic world. For Liberal Democrats in a supranational parliament not to grasp those opportunities would be to betray our unique ideological heritage.

Colleagues, today is a day for rejoicing. The Christian Democrats have been true to their word. In return for our support for Nicole Fontaine two and a half years ago, the EPP-ED group has helped us elect one of our number as President of the European Parliament. A Liberal Democrat Presidency, which both reflects and contributes to our growing strength across the continent, is long overdue. We needed to break the cynical 'old pals act' between left and right and we have done so through successful cooperation with another political party. We can and we must remain open to further cooperation in areas where we find common ground with others. That way we maximise Liberal Democrat influence. But let us be clear: there will be no blank cheque of Liberal Democrat support for any one party. If we work with others it is to promote our cause, which is a Liberal Democrat agenda for Europe.

There is a movement afoot for democracy, human rights and preferment uniquely on the basis of merit. For what the poet Robert Burns called 'pith of sense and pride of worth'. It may yet hasten the advent of the world Burns described, where 'man to man the world over shall brothers be for all that'.'

## Freeing Europe's Potential

*Speech to the European Liberal Democrat and Reform Party's Annual Congress in Amsterdam. This had been dedicated largely to agreeing the platform for the manifesto in advance of the 2004 European elections. Here Graham congratulates the gathering on a fruitful and democratic discussion - something of a rarity in an age of managerial politics - and reflects on the achievements and future direction of Liberalism in Europe. D66 and VVD, referred to below, are the two Dutch Liberal parties belonging to the ALDE Group.*

*November 14th 2003, Amsterdam*

'Fellow Liberal Democrats, fellow Europeans. Thank you for an excellent congress. To our hosts from VVD and D66, may I extend on behalf of all of us our warm thanks for their hospitality. To all of you, thank you for a lively, intelligent, good-natured debate.

This week's debate on our manifesto for next year's European elections confirms one thing for me. That we are the European political alternative. In this party, you can have a sensible discussion about the kind of Europe we want. You can talk about the issues without prejudice or caricature. You stand and you fall on the power of your argument. It's a characteristic of this party that serves us very well in Brussels and Strasbourg.

Liberals hold the balance of power in the European Parliament, where our arguments command respect. Studies by the London School of Economics show that the ELDR wields influence in the European Parliament out of all proportion to its size. As my predecessor Pat Cox used to put it: we punch above our weight. It is the Liberal Democrats and Reformers who make the difference.

In this parliament we made the difference on public health. We voted to make Europe's cigarette manufacturers cut tar and nicotine levels and put clear health warnings on all their packaging. In the face of fierce lobbying, we made the difference on consumer safety. Genetically modified food in Europe is now subject to the world's strictest labelling requirements. That means choice for customers. We made the difference on the environment. We voted to force EU governments to honour new targets for renewable energy.

We made the difference on enlargement. When the time came to welcome the new member states, only European Liberals voted unanimously to do so. We made the difference on economic reform. We demanded a more open and accountable Commission and European Central Bank. We voted to further open the European market in services. That means new investment, more competition and more choice. We made the difference on the Convention on the Future of Europe. We demanded a Bill of Rights - the Charter of Fundamental Freedoms - at the heart of our new political contract. We got it. We made the difference in democratic accountability. We helped produce a European Constitution that would dramatically increase the power over policy-making of elected representatives in the European Parliament. In Pat Cox we gave that Parliament its first Liberal President in over twenty years. Pat has carried our Liberal message to the highest levels of the European Union. These are our achievements. But what of our future?

For Liberals, history is a succession of struggles against prejudice - religious, ethnic, racial, gender or other. For Liberals the European Union is a weapon in this struggle. With each enlargement we get collectively stronger, even as the weight of our national divisions diminishes. In the new Europe we are all minorities, even if some of our larger nations haven't grasped this yet. From now on we can think only in terms of coexistence and co-operation. Proceed only in concert.

Next year's European elections have to be about Europe's added value. For far too long European elections have been simply another chance to deliver punches in domestic politics. Next year we all have a responsibility to raise the level of debate about Europe. It is sometimes said that the EU has no "demos". No electorate. Brits are Brits, Greeks are Greeks and Finns are Finns. But there is a European 'street'. How do we know? Because this year Europeans poured into it and spoke with one voice, over the heads of their squabbling governments, about the war in Iraq.

The Convention on the Future of Europe may not have caught the imagination of Europeans. But the Constitution it produced has. Eurobarometer figures released this week show that almost 70% of Europeans believe Europe needs such a constitution. Four out of five want a say in this process through a referendum. This public sense of Europeanness must be grasped and nurtured. If Europeans want a say on the Constitution, there should be an advisory referendum, held on the same day as the European elections. The German writer Gunther Grass once said that the job of a citizen is to keep his mouth open. We must encourage Europeans to think and talk and argue about Europe.

More than ever, we must all be activists now. Why now more than ever? Because the European Union is about to get bigger, and as it gets bigger the importance of connecting it to Europeans becomes more crucial than ever. Why now more than ever? Because globalisation and increasing interdependence are raising the stakes for all of us. The world outside Europe is pushing against us insistently. Europe faces new threats and new challenges. New challenges like a growing world population, where more and more leave their homes to escape from war or hunger or sheer hopelessness. Or challenges like easing the tensions where the tectonic plates of Islam and Judaism and Christianity grind against each other. New threats like internationally organised crime, where some criminal gangs are more powerful than some national governments. Or threats like climate change, and our impact on our shared planet. New realities, like the way money and information move faster than ever before.

These are challenges that no one country can tackle alone. They can only be confronted by countries with common values, working together. So we lock our economies together to provide stability and prosperity. We work side by side in search of security. We insist on a fairer world and a society that takes sustainability seriously. We translate our combined weight into influence where it matters most: in the UN, the WTO, the corridors of the White House.

When the European Union fails we all fail. Europe failed to live up to its own economic rules. France and Germany preached allegiance to the Growth and Stability Pact. And then practised contempt. Contempt for Europe's credibility. Contempt for those who play by the rules. Contempt for the need to make convergence work. Sweden's voters were decidedly unimpressed. Who can blame them?

Europe failed in Cancun, where its indefensible Common Agricultural Policy continued to make a mockery of our grand words about helping the third world rise out of poverty. One billion people on this planet get by on one euro a day. Every European cow gets a subsidy of two. Where is the success in that kind of injustice?

Europe failed to find a common approach in Iraq. It stood sidelined as Britain and the United States and their coalition of the willing blundered into war and occupation. The cost of building democracy in Iraq will be high, as Italy tragically discovered this week. The cost to Europe of failure would be infinitely higher.

Too often Europe's potential is squandered by vested interests and bad national habits. If Europe is to move on from these failures to a more successful future we have to learn from them. Learn that if we don't stand together on foreign affairs, we will fall apart. Without the force of argument, the argument of force will prevail. Learn that we cannot make free trade work for the poor unless we practice what we preach. Learn that while we jealously guard our own police and judicial traditions, the criminals will run rings around us.

Fellow Liberals, we live in an age replete with political opportunity. I believe the twenty-first century will be a Liberal century. Because ours is the message of the moment for humankind. That's why Europe now has 5 Liberal Prime Ministers. Liberals are in government in 11 European states, including here in the Netherlands. Liberals head the European Parliament and the European Commission. Liberals hold the balance of power in the European Parliament. We are a growing family and a growing movement. Next year we stand to win twenty new seats in the expanded European Parliament. Maybe more.

We need to make this momentum work for us. By making sure that the new rules on European political parties do not weaken the link between the party and the group in the European Parliament. In fact, by strengthening the links between group and party, and between national MPs and European MEPs. By working to ensure the maximum number of Liberal Democrat Commissioners when the new Commission is appointed next year. By making one of Europe's exceptional Liberal leaders our candidate for President of the Commission and campaigning to see them appointed. And perhaps most of all, by being clear about why our message works, and how to make it work better.

Our Liberalism is a modern creed, but it has long traditions. We draw on the Classical Liberalism of Locke and Rousseau and John Stuart Mill. We understand that the only measure of humanity is the individual. No society, no culture, no government, is sovereign over the mind or body of any one of us. We understand the insights of Economic Liberalism. Of Adam Smith and David Riccardo. We believe that if you grant men and women the freedom to buy and sell at a free market then their hundred small enterprises will enrich our common enterprise. Smith called this 'our most sacred property...the property that every man has in his own labour'. Yet we also know that Liberals who speak only of free individuals and free trade will never long enjoy success. Because freedom means nothing without fraternity.

It is not enough to emancipate. We must also empower. If we cannot argue for solidarity and social justice then we do not deserve to be in power, and we never will be. This part of our inheritance is the Social Liberalism of the great New Liberal tradition. Of Gladstone and Grundtvig and Karl-Herman Flach, who understood that in a democratic society, true freedom is not the absence of fetters, but the presence of fairness.

The twentieth century was the century in which war and intolerance and ethnic cleansing soaked our soil in blood. It was the century that added to our languages the words, 'totalitarian', 'genocide', and 'crime against humanity'. This will be the century of Liberal democracy. What will our words be? Freedom. Tolerance. Democracy. Reform. Human Rights. These are words to transform our lives.

Words to free Europe's potential.

We can free the potential of Europe's people by making their political contract the envy of the world. By insisting on diversity. And celebrating it.

We can free the potential of Europe's political institutions by making them more open and democratic. By forcing a revolution in accountability at every level of European government so that people trust and respect the European Union.

We can free the potential of Europe's economy by unleashing the job-creating, prosperity-producing power of the world's largest single market. Europe needs a dynamic economy to prosper. We must cut away the red tape that hampers innovation and ties down Europe's entrepreneurs and small businesses. We must free people to buy and sell and move and work from Belfast to Budapest.

We can free the potential of Europe's sustainable technologies and lifestyles by making Europe the world leader in environmental enhancement. By committing to cleaner, safer forms of energy and embracing the world's highest standards of pollution control and renewable resource use.

We can free the potential of globalisation by making it work for everyone. We must insist on sustainable development and free and fair trade. We must open our own markets to the trade that can help the world's poorest escape the trap of poverty.

We can free the potential of Europe's global influence by speaking with a single voice. We must speak as one to give that voice credibility where it counts most. That is why, Liberal Friends, our message for these elections is a simple but powerful one.: European Liberal Democrats - freeing Europe's Potential.'

## Britain Needs Brussels

*Campaigning for the European Elections in Britain is never an easy task, particularly given the media is dominated by a populist euroscepticism scarcely seen elsewhere. In this speech to the annual preconference Liberal Democrat rally - with public attention focussed on the Madrid Bombings - Graham criticises Tony Blair for dragging his feet on the European Constitution and abandoning the field to the 'No' camp at a time when more, not less, EU co-operation is necessary to guarantee security and prosperity. In the event, the anti-European UK Independence Party made significant gains in the European Parliament elections, while turnout plummeted to 37.6%, prompting a heartfelt reexamination of Britain's future in Europe.*

*19th March 2004, Southport*

'I want to start by telling you about Fred, an elderly neighbour of my mine in Somerset. Fred was born and grew up in Somerset. He's never been further afield than London. But last year he decided he'd drive over to France, to visit his daughter and son-in-law who have moved to live there. "Be careful, Fred", I warned him: "you know they drive on the other side of the road in France." "Oh, I hadn't thought about that", he said.

I saw Fred again some weeks later. "How did you get on in France, Fred?" I asked him. "Oh, I didn't go in the end", he replied: "You know what you told I about driving on the other side of the road? Well, I thought I'd better try it before I went over there - and I can tell 'ee it's darn dangerous!"

Fred's daughter can buy a house in France because of the European Union. He could buy a low cost airline ticket to visit her because of laws passed in Brussels. If he'd driven and had an accident he would get first class hospital treatment in France. Because of the European Union.

But here's the rub. Fred may not bother to vote in the European elections in June. And his children almost certainly will not. Fred's children don't do politics.

Fred's son is a dairy and beef farmer. The people who herd his cows are Lithuanian. This year, the factory in Chard which processes his meat took on 200 workers from Portugal. You cannot get local people for those kinds of work.

But what do you imagine Fred thinks about immigration? Or about Lithuania and the nine other countries joining the EU in May? Too often, Fred thinks what the Daily Mail tells him to think.

We are about to fight an election about Europe. Let's be clear about that. This European election will not save your local hospital or lower your Council tax, however important they are, and however tempted we might be to campaign for them. This European election is not about top-up fees or affordable homes. It is about Europe. And yet it is still a local election. Why? Because Europe is the environment. It is security. It is jobs. It is investment. It is your rights as a citizen.

To get drugs off our streets we need Europe-wide action. Cleaner air is a common concern. Large lorries cross borders. Companies are now owned and trade and decisions about local jobs are made elsewhere.

Our party's euro manifesto this year - one of the best we've had - points out that government at EU level is no different from government at local or national level. Where it's broken we have to fix it. Where it works we have to say so.

It says Government at European level is good, and it's here to stay. And we can and must be there. And we can and do make the difference.

In this parliament the votes of Liberal Democrat MEPs made the difference on public health. We voted to make Europe's cigarette manufacturers cut tar and nicotine levels and put clear health warnings on all their packaging.

In the face of fierce lobbying, our MEPs made the difference on consumer safety. Genetically modified food in Europe is now subject to the world's strictest labelling requirements. That means choice for shoppers.

We made the difference on the environment. We voted to force EU governments - including this Labour government - to honour new targets for renewable energy.

We played a key role in freedom of information legislation and moves to open up the European Central Bank and the Commission to greater public scrutiny.

Just like here in Britain, it was Liberal Democrats in Europe who spoke out against a cavalier Blair-Bush policy in Iraq: our call for a UN role won the day.

And we're out to build a stronger Centrist force in the next Parliament to give us even more clout in Europe.

A Liberal Democrat vote in the euro election brings the same as voting for us at national level. A change from the closed political worlds of the left and right. A vision for Europe to match its size. A 450 million person vision.

The Liberal Democrat Europe is not something that happens somewhere else. It is as much about Birmingham and Bangor and Bristol as Brussels. Why? Because the European Union is our guarantee. Our guarantee of prosperity in the largest single market on earth. Our guarantee of security in an unprecedentedly dangerous world. Our guarantee of sustainability in a world where the damage we are doing to the environment puts our planet's eco-systems at stake!

Don't expect the European election campaign to be easy. Don't waste your energy on the doorstep trying to undo the poison of a generation of anti-European propaganda.

But don't hide your colours.

It would be all too easy for Liberal Democrats to adopt a cautious approach, at odds with our Party's national appeal; to play the Europe issue like the hare in winter, turning white and vanishing against the snow.

Rather we must be, to borrow from the poet Tom Paulin, like the juniper tree. Tougher than the wind. Rugged, fecund, with resined spines, our springy resistance skirting the warped polities of other trees bent in the Atlantic wind.

Our opponents are still hopelessly confused on Europe.

The Tories are in favour of staying in the EU. They just want to repatriate the fisheries policy, the farm policy, the regional policy, the development policy, the aid policy, the security policy and the defence policy. But then they'll be ready to lead Britain in Europe!

Even by Tory standards, this is astonishing testimony to the invincibility of ignorance. In thirty years the Tory party still has not cottoned on that Britain is stronger in Europe than out.

Like Labour they prefer the facade of influence in Washington to the reality of power in Brussels.

Liberal Democrats say better a strong European pillar than a creaking Atlantic bridge.

And Tony Blair needs to realise that being a European is not about pasta lunches and schoolboy French: it means thinking as a European. Not at the expense of Britain, but because Britain cannot be strong in a weak Europe.

On the Constitution, on asylum, on social cohesion and on crime, the man who pledged to take on the eurosceptics is now one of the biggest foot-draggers in the EU.

Even the Euro Roadshow had to be canned, because Gordon Brown kept letting the tyres down.

It's taken seven years for Labour policy to go from the heart of Europe to the middle of nowhere!

Six weeks from now, the European Union will welcome 10 new countries. That sounds a lot, but proportionally it is no bigger than when the UK and Denmark and Ireland joined 30 years ago. I recall we were welcomed by existing members at the time. Welcomed for the new ideas and the new energy we would bring.

When I meet Lithuanians and Latvians and Poles and Hungarians I don't see welfare scroungers and benefit tourists. I see people who want to work, people with a hunger for a new life. People who want to rebuild societies grappling with the changed realities of the world. I welcome them. And to those in this country who would say otherwise - I say shame on you! Shame on your prejudice and shame on your hatred!

Fellow Liberal Democrats, last week's terrible events in Madrid reminded us that Europe is built on solidarity - and they demand a response.

But will Europe's governments put aside their national prerogatives to make us safer? Or will they allow the illusion of national sovereignty to assist in global anarchy?

They should use the tools of co-operation we already have, left idle by national inflexibility, not just create another job in Brussels!

In the latest budget round the Council wanted to limit spending on anti-terrorism intelligence to 1 million euros. The European Commission had asked for 15 million.

The European Parliament had to fight - fight! - to raise it to 9 million, the minimum we need.

This year we finally got a European Arrest Warrant balanced with strong procedural safeguards. Finally got the tools to help European authorities work together to catch criminals who flee across national borders.

But don't thank the Tories - they voted against it!

In Europe there is no more safety in sovereignty.

There is no dignity in an island mentality that trades on a proud history rather than a formidable future.

And there's no freedom and no prosperity in a parish-pump politics that closes doors and carps from the sidelines.

The different approaches of the Tories, Labour and ourselves were summed up by Victor Hugo, "The future has several names. For the weak, it is called the impossible, for the timid, it is called the unknown, but for thinkers and the valiant, it is called the ideal."

Europe is our future. That's the case we have to make. We need to be there. So let's go and get out our voters.'

## European Democracy Has Everything Other Than Voters

*Opening Remarks to the first ELDR Bureau meeting after the 2004 European elections, the first since enlargement. The Bureau, which is made up of the delegation leaders of every member party, meets monthly to discuss major policy decisions and move initiatives forward. Here Graham welcomes new MEPs and underlines the need to maintain the Group's internal cohesion if it is to maximise its impact on the new Parliament, where it held 9% of the 732 seats. However, he points to poor turnout at the elections - which dropped from 49% in 1999 to 44% in 2004 - as a sign that all is not well with European democracy and cautions Bureau Members to raise their rhetorical game and bring the EU closer to their citizens - or risk a rising tide of Euro-scepticism in their national political arenas.*

*25th June 2004, Brussels*

'Election night told us a lot about this institution; the people who would build and serve it and the people who would - in their own words - wreck it. If it is true that an institution survives not by bricks and mortar but by successfully expressing the aspirations and values of a society then the low turnout and the wreckers and the withdrawalists reminded us that we have not yet convinced the sceptics that this particular pile of bricks and mortar speaks for them, or that it belongs to them, or that it is - as every durable institution must be - a mirror of their hopes and values. Sometimes it seems that half the people do not know what we do and many of the rest resent us for trying to do it. As the American Democratic Senator Robert Byrd once quipped: "it seems the approval figures for Congress go up every time it goes into recess." That is what makes this the toughest, the most rewarding and challenging job that most of us will ever have.

And I say 'we have not yet convinced the sceptics' because in European politics I think Liberal Democrats have always been optimists. Can we see the European constitution ratified in all 25 European states; can we somehow reverse the trend of declining participation in European Elections; can we send Jean Marie le Pen and the Vlaams Blok packing? We can and we must.

And can we rally the forces who want to build the EU into a new front against the sceptics? We have no choice. Remember that 85-90% of voters cast their vote for pro-European parties. We have to keep driving that message home. Eurosceptics are quick to paint their political movements as a return to democratic principles but that argument is, and must be said to be, an affront to the overwhelming majority who voted for a healthy functioning European Union with a strong democratic European Parliament.

And for that reason it is crucial that we do not confuse the symptom with the disease. The refusenik glamour of many our new sceptic colleagues will fade and the press interest will wane. Despite their expressed intention of wrecking the European Parliament, they are more likely to be the abstainers and the absentees.

But say as much to a journalist and they will probably accuse you of complacency, because they see the symptom not the disease. The danger lies not in UKIP or the MEPs of the June movement or Self Defence or the rest. It lies in allowing their arguments to go unrebutted out there, and in the well of misconception and prejudice on which they feed. A journalist from *The Guardian* newspaper in London went up to our press people after the UKIP press conference last week and said "looks like you guys need to raise your rhetorical game". He was right.

One of our stated aims as a political group is the establishment of "a genuine parliamentary democracy at the European level". Sunday June 13 suggested that the distance between us and achieving this aim lies not in the bricks and mortar and the ballot boxes but in the voters who come in between. As one of the papers put it on election night: 'European democracy has everything but voters'. If any European politician doubted the importance of making the work we do here relevant to the people who elect us, we have our corrective.

And that's another reason for optimism - because we have the people and the will to change things. The ELDR had a good night on June 13. We held old ground and we broke exciting new ground. We increased our size in the Parliament from 8% to over 9%. After 10 years we can welcome the FDP back to Brussels. We have new colleagues from Poland. In Britain, the Liberal Democrats were the only major political party to increase their share of the vote, gaining two new MEPs despite the reduction in the overall number of seats. Throughout the new Member States we held our ground or won new ground.

We remain the third largest group in the Parliament and we retain the crucial balance of power. In my estimation, we have never been better equipped to make an impact.

Colleagues, this is the first Parliament of the enlarged European Union. It was elected by the largest democratic election ever conducted in European history. We are a stiff but winnable fight away from a European Constitution that will give this House wide new powers in its next mandate.

Hard work is going to mattter. This group had the strongest record on reform in the last Parliament. It had the strongest record on green issues of any major group. It had the best record of group cohesion and the best attendance rates at votes. That wins us respect.

Group cohesion is going to matter. Not at the cost of a diversity of opinions or a vote of conscience, but overall, on the whole, it is going to define us as an effective political force in this Parliament. We are going to need to work hard to hold to a common course.

Political power is going to matter, not for its own sake, but because as a growing group every increment in size, every new resource that extra members bring us, weights the punch we throw in our favour. As the coalition around our political platform gets stronger we can only become a more attractive ally to those who would work with us.

In the presence of both outgoing and incoming delegation leaders allow me to say that I am exceptionally proud of what we achieved in the last mandate and I relish the chance to do it all again. It is a privilege to have led you at this important time.'

## Ready To Launch

*Speech given to a Press Conference alongside François Bayrou, leader of the French centre-right UDF party, to announce the formation of a new political group - and the largest 3rd force in the European Parliament's history - the Alliance of Liberals and Democrats for Europe. Here Graham, who led the drive for ALDE's formation, details the new group's membership, goals and political platform. Setting out its 10-point political programme he explains how Europe should harness the power of centrism to move beyond twentieth century ideological boundaries separating left from right to make a stronger, more integrated and more prosperous EU the new reality. The deal alluded to in this speech was that made between the PSE and EPP to share control of the five-year legislature, propelling Josep Borrell to the Presidency of the European Parliament.*

*14th July 2004, Brussels*

'The Group of the Alliance of Liberals and Democrats for Europe is born. I am proud to announce that the new Group of the Alliance of Liberals and Democrats for Europe was formally created last night and that I have the honour to lead this group.

Yesterday the MEPs of the former ELDR Group voted unanimously to merge with French MEPs from the UDF and Italian MEPs from the Margherita to create the foundation of a new centre force in the Parliament. This new group assembles 88 MEPs from the democratic and liberal traditions and will form a pivotal force in the new Parliament.

At the foundation of the ALDE Group, we have assembled 88 MEPs from the liberal and democratic traditions. In addition to the MEPs of the former ELDR, the UDF and La Margherita, we are pleased to count in our ranks 5 MEPs from the Lithuanian Labour Party, 2 Italian Radicals, Gérard Deprez (MR/BE) and Jose Ortuondo (PNV/ES). As we anticipated, the creation of this new Group has created a dynamic which has already attracted others, and we expect other MEPs to join us in the course of this legislature. Indeed, we invite all those who share our values and are disillusioned in their groups to join us.

The new Group is the largest third force in the history of the European Parliament. We have begun to uncover the power that lies latent in the political centre. Our message will continue to attract those uncomfortable in their current political homes on the left and right. It will draw those looking for an unequivocally pro-European home. It will appeal to those who saw Bronislaw Geremek debating last night and saw the best man for the job of President of the European Parliament. As Mr Bayrou has put it, this is an idea much bigger than the sum of its parts. We expect to grow further during this legislature.

As the name suggests, the Alliance of Liberals and Democrats for Europe has a deeply pro-European philosophy. We are committed to building an effective, open, European Union, better able to act in the world and secure the prosperity of the people it represents. The first of the ten points on the programme that we launch today commits us to a genuine democracy of the European peoples through a European Union in the Federal tradition. We will be championing and campaigning for the European Constitution. We are an unequivocal rejection of euroscepticism's claim to have captured the spirit of the times.

All of the MEPs of the ALDE are keen to get down to business. We have a huge amount to do and deep reserves of ambition and energy. The Alliance of Liberals and Democrats for Europe is the tool, it is not the job. This new group must be measured by its ability to indelibly imprint Liberal and Democratic values on the legislation of the European Union. We will be campaigning together for the application of our ten point programme and most immediately, we will be fighting to see Bronislaw Geremek elected President of the European Parliament.

Our ten point programme sets out a vision for Europe and is our point of departure for this mandate. It describes a Europe that would be economically stronger. A Europe that would be stronger and more influential abroad. A greener Europe. A Europe that would be more accountable and open to its citizens. A Europe that invests better in research and development. A Europe that takes regional government seriously.

It will also be the basis for any and all co-operation with other political groups. We will be seeking open and constructive relationships with both large groups based on the advancement of this programme, but there will be no blank cheques. This group will surrender its independence of mind to nobody.

For too long politics in the European Parliament has been fenced off by the two big groups - witness yesterday's statement of understanding between the PPE and the PSE. The two big groups have happily ploughed the deep, and frankly cynical, furrows of left and right. Yesterday we gave formal notice that from now on there will be rocks in that particular field.'

## The Birthday Present Gibraltar Deserves

*Speech given on the 300th anniversary of the settlement of the Rock of Gibraltar. The people of Gibraltar had been part of the European Union since 1973 but until 2004 they were unable to vote in European elections, due to obstructions by the Spanish government and a lack of political will on the part of the British Government and the European Commission. Here Graham reflects on the Liberal Democrat campaign to enfranchise Gibraltar and praises the recent European Court of Justice decision giving its citizens the vote for the very first time.*

*August 5th 2004, Gibraltar*

'This year marks the three hundredth anniversary of the current settlement on the rock of Gibraltar. Captured by English sailors and marines during the War of the Spanish Succession in 1704 and ceded to England by Spain in 1713, Gibraltar has been peopled by a combination of immigrants from all over the Mediteranean ever since. These people have become the Gibraltarians of today and they were on the rock when America was still English and Europeans had yet to sail to Australia.

This tercentenary coincides with the first time the people of Gibraltar will be able to vote in European elections. This enfranchisement, the result of a long campaign, corrects an historic injustice. Since 1973 the people of Gibraltar have been part of the European Union through their connection with Britain, but they have not been able to elect their own representatives to the European Parliament. Despite a bad-tempered campaign of obstruction from the Spanish government and a European Commission far too willing to avoid antagonising Madrid, the rights of the people of Gibraltar have won the day. Gibraltar has become part of the South West of England constituency, with which it has strong historical and maritime links. There are few sailors in Plymouth who haven't spent a bit of time on the Rock.

I have no doubt Gibraltarians will be the most politically engaged of Europeans. Liberal European election candidates Tony Welch and I have busied ourselves in the business of Gibraltar and are looking forward to campaigning here. When Gibraltar throws itself a three hundredth birthday party on National Day in September both of us hope to be in attendance as two of its first elected MEPs.

These elections in Gibraltar will mark the end of an important fight for Liberals in Britain and Europe. The European Liberal Democrats were the first and only European political party to have actively campaigned for the restoration of Gibraltar's democratic rights in European Elections. At our Congress in Amsterdam last November we adopted a resolution calling on Spain to drop its proposed legal action against Britain over the enfranchisement. The Liberal Democrats at Westminster have been strongly critical of a Labour government far too willing to make a quick deal with Spain over the heads of Gibraltarians. For their part, the Tories have somewhat characteristically been quick to stress the imperial connection but far too slow in making sure that the rights of Gibraltarians are protected.

Gibraltar has to have its own place in the new Europe of 2004. The new Spanish government has said they will try to use the new European Constitutional Treaty to advance their claim again and they will press on with their action at the ECJ. This is to be regretted. Spain is a proud country, but there is no shame in a dignified concession to history and actuality. We have to start building a twenty-first century relationship across the line at La Línea.

Gibraltar itself will press ahead with constitutional reform of its own and is seeking a new relationship with Britain. Gibraltar has expressed the desire to lose its colonial status without severing its strong British links. What will not change is the fundamental right of Gibraltarians to determine their own future, as laid out in the United Nations Charter. Liberals in Brussels and Westminster will continue to take the strongest line on a prosperous and self-determined Gibraltar. That is the birthday present Gibraltar deserves.

## A Platform For Progress

*Speech made to the Centre for European Policy Studies, a leading Brussels think-tank, on ALDE's priorities for the five year mandate of the Barroso Commission, which took office on 18th November 2004, and the new European Parliamentary term. By setting out the Liberal Democratic stall, Graham hoped to influence the Commission's direction of travel - and stimulate public debate on key issues for reform - since under EU Treaty rules, the European Parliament cannot propose legislation, but only approve it. In the event, ALDE priorities have been largely reflected in the Commission's work to date, particularly in terms of building a more flexible, competitive economy and cutting red-tape.*

*28th September 2004, Brussels*

'I have been asked to say a few words about the political priorities of the Alliance of Liberals and Democrats for Europe in the next session of the European Parliament. I want to say a little about the creation of my new group and the Group's take on the Barroso Commission. Then I will talk a little about what the ALDE hopes to achieve in this Parliament.

The Alliance of Liberals and Democrats for Europe was formed in June by the merging of the old ELDR group and a large group of French and Italian MEPs from the UDF and La Margherita. It also brought in a number of other MEPs from Italy, Belgium and Lithuania. It combines the liberal tradition of the ELDR with the centrist democratic tradition of the UDF and Margherita. ALDE is the largest third force in the history of the European parliament. It holds the swing vote and the balance of power in the centre of the chamber. When Jose Manuel Barroso was approved as President of the new European Commission in July, it was with Liberal and Democrat votes.

A MORE POLITICAL PARLIAMENT

I'm not sure who said that politics is about 'se servir des conjonctures' - which I suppose translates as taking advantage of the situation - I think it was Louis XIV, who was nothing if he wasn't an opportunist. Too often, 'making the most of the situation' in the European Parliament has involved turning a blind eye to political differences in order to make deals on the distribution of power, and this new Parliament is no exception. Although the Parliament can be highly politicised on an issue by issue basis, the Socialists and the Christian Democrats display an uncanny and strangely apolitical willingness to reach tehnical agreements on sharing out the positions of responsibility in the Parliament, including the Presidency of the Parliament itself. Socialist candidate Josep Borell was elected President of the new Parliament two months ago with Christian Democrat votes. MEPs who campaigned vigorously against Socialist and Christian Democrat opponents in national election campaigns climbed into bed with the same opponents as soon as they got to Brussels. The ALDE candidate for the Presidency of the European Parliament, Bronislaw Geremek - who is a veteran of the Polish Solidarity movement and a hero to many Europeans - ran a genuine campaign and managed to poach more than eighty votes from Christian Democrat MEPs unhappy with the stitch-up. But the stitch-up still won.

A mature European Parliament would not se servir des conjunctures in that way. Politics is about alliance building, and there is no point in partisanship for the sake of partisanship, but without the incentive to campaign for the Presidency we don't get activist Presidents, we get placemen supported by technical and unsympathetic majorities rather than political coalitions. The centre right alliance that shared the Presidency between Nicole Fontaine and Pat Cox between 1999 and 2004 had an ideological dimension - and at least in Pat Cox it delivered a President who used his political majority to campaign for reform of the Member's Statute and MEP allowances. With only the backing of a technical majority, President Borrell will have trouble showing that he is not on a short lead.

So ALDE has spoken out and will continue to speak out against back room deals. We will run another political campaign for the Presidency in 2006, and we will keep pressing for a Parliament that better reflects the political will of European voters. It might sound platitudinous, but connecting the European Parliament to the voters is now an absolute imperative and an important part of that is having a Parliament that has a stronger political profile.

## A STRONG AND LIBERAL-MINDED COMMISSION

As you know, the European Parliament is currently conducting hearings with the Commissioners designate. We supported Commission President Barroso as a moderate of the political centre, and based on my conversations with him I think he will lead that kind of Commission. His college of nominees is liberal in the broadest sense: strongly reform-minded and committed to the renewal of the Lisbon Agenda. It also includes seven actual Liberal Democrats and seven from 25 is not bad for a political movement that had just two Commissioners in the Prodi Commission, including Prodi himself.

The Barroso Commission also has the largest number of women of any Commission college to date, and ALDE was the only political group to make that a condition of our support for Barroso. We also made our support conditional on Barroso refusing to appoint any Super-Commissioners, and this helped him resist the pressure from France and Germany to be awarded high-profile portfolios. Barroso has actually managed to produce a Commission where size doesn't count: the budget Commissioner is a Lithuanian, the Internal Market Commissioner is Irish. Barroso himself has shown that he is not afraid to ruffle a few feathers in Paris and Berlin, which is the absolute bottom line for an genuinely independent Commission.

So there is an important conjunction there: a potentially strong and liberal-minded Commission and a powerful new Liberal and Democrat group in the Parliament, and we are, needless to say, keen to se servir des conjunctures.

## ECONOMIC REFORM

Principally that means a strong new focus on economic reform. Barroso has already shown a welcome focus on better implementation of existing

European legislation rather than new directives, which is something that ALDE wants to prioritise. According to July's Internal Market Scoreboard there were in 2003 134 Single Market directives that have not been implemented in at least one Member State. The Internal Market Strategy 2003-2006 called for a 50% reduction in infringement cases by 2006, but this year there are almost exactly as many infringements as last year. There are some particularly culpable Member States: Italy and France account between the two of them for over 30% of infringement cases. Italy has more infringements than Denmark, Sweden, Finland, Luxembourg and Portugal combined.

This is a political problem as much as anything and it needs a strong Commission with the committed backing of the Parliament. Member States need to internalise the imperative for single market reform and that needs a Commission that can both cajole and coerce. We face a similar problem with the Growth and Stability pact, which has just been re-launched with a few less teeth - although it never had much of a bite. Like single market reform, the Growth and Stability pact comes up against the simple problem of enforceability. As most of Europe's central bankers pointed out, the economics of the pact are sound, but they are hopelessly vulnerable to political abuse. We can write tough rules to control European public finances, but at the end of the day it is up to states to enforce them on themselves. The Stability Pact is essentially a gentleman's agreement, and that is not necessarily a problem, or it wouldn't be if it wasn't so hard to get European Member States to behave like gentlemen.

But in any event, the ALDE will be pushing for the new pact to be respected, because the credibility of the euro-zone and price stability and low interest rates depend on it.

We'll be applying pressure right across the economic reform agenda. We have a liberal Commissioner - Janez Potocnik - at science and research and we will be pushing for even greater investment and coordination in initiatives like the European Research Area. We'll be continuing to work for a more flexible and responsive European labour market that opens up new opportunities for work for older workers, parents and women, while protecting their rights at work. There are still too many restrictions on freedom of movement for workers from the new Member States and we will be working to see them removed. We also need to break the deadlock in Council on key pieces of legislation such as the Community patent and agreement on the mutual recognition of qualifications.

THE EUROPEAN CONSTITUTION

The question of economic reform in Europe matters because it is an acid test of Europe's ability to work as a Union. Without a central political authority to direct economic policy, Europe is the sum of its economic parts. It takes political will on the part of Member States and that political will is often the difference between a Europe that succeeds and a Europe that fails.

At least for ALDE, that is what it means to be pro-European. It means recognising that in a globalised world the ability of European Member States to protect themselves against terrorism or manage environmental change or renew Europe's systems of social protection is directly proportionate to their ability to work together. Europe's ability to project a coherent economic strategy, environmental strategy and security strategy all depend on the same political willingness to work better as a Union. It is also the only way Europe can begin to lay the foundations of a real Common Foreign and Security policy, an important step if Europe is going to project a stronger voice abroad. There is no question that faced with continental partners like Russia and the United States, Europe needs a continental policy of its own. Being pro-European means asking how we do that.

For ALDE the European Constitution is a crucial step. The institutional machinery of the Union is already badly stretched by enlargement and there is no question that it needs to be reformed. The Constitution does this, restructuring the Commission to make it more efficient and streamlining decision-making and voting weights in the European Council. It asks states to pool more decision making in Brussels, but it delivers commensurate benefits in terms of greater efficiency and potential for action. The Constitution also imposes new standards of accountability on all the institutions of the European Union. It strengthens the powers of the democratically elected European Parliament by extending the co-decision procedure into a large number of new areas including oversight of the whole Union budget. This is one area where the Parliament has developed a strong reputation, last year holding the Commission to the most austere budget in a decade.

So ALDE will be campaigning to see the Constitution ratified in all Member States. We expect both the President of the Parliament and the Barroso Commission to undertake to sell the Constitution to Europeans, and we will be doing the same. If the Constitution fails, the costs for the European project are hard to overstate - at least for the next eighteen months, being pro-European means making the case for the European Constitution.

Liberal and Democrat ambitions are of course not limited to these areas. We will be taking a lead on justice and home affairs issues such as migration, on environmental issues and consumer protection issues. These are all things that Europe does well in general. And they are areas where Europeans have said they think Europe could do more.

I stressed the politics of the Parliament and the economic reform agenda and the European Constitution because I think they are issues which help characterise ALDE's outlook and ambitions for the next Parliament.

ALDE wants a more political and more politically representative parliament because we want a more democratic European Union. The European Parliament is growing in power and it should grow commensurately in stature. ALDE wants the European Parliament to be the heart of a genuine Parliamentary democracy at the European level. There are no other European Parliamentary democracies where the left and right find it quite so easy to put aside their convictions for political convenience. Grand coalitions betray the political choices of voters and they have to stop.

ALDE wants a stronger commitment to economic reform because a strong European economy is the only sustainable foundation of Europe's important traditions of social protection. But economic reform matters because it requires that we learn to break the habits of national economic insularity and understand our European responsibilities. We have to learn a similar trick in the area of environmental protection, and in developing the strategies that will keep us safer from terrorism.

ALDE wants to see the European Constitution ratified because it is the key to a more effective and accountable Europe at home and abroad.

It is going to be an intensely interesting and important Parliament. Just in the next year, Europe will face up to its long flirtation with Turkey and set out the European Union's budget for the next seven years, which is an exercise that will define the very scope and ambition of the Union. We need to see the European Constitution ratified and we need to consolidate the dramatic European enlargement of May this year.

If politics is the art of se servir des conjunctures then we are faced with a unique constellation of opportunities. We have a potentially strong and activist Commission. We have a crucial chance to set a budget for the European Union that gives it the resources to do the job. We have an historic shot at EU reform in the form of the European Constitutional treaty. So these are interesting times. For the Alliance of Liberals and Democrats for Europe they are decisive times for the Union. If I had to distil the agenda of ALDE to one single phrase I would simply say that we want to see the European Union emerge from this constellation of opportunities, these interesting times, strong, self-assured and secure, in its prosperity and its values, for the future.'

## An Invisible Elephant In The House

*Sometimes the political process takes precedence over the political programme, and this is one such occasion. Italy had nominated Rocco Buttiglione as the European Union's new commissioner for Justice, Freedom and Security but the Parliament, unimpressed by remarks he had made about the role of women and homosexuals - whose interests he was charged with representing - forced him to withdraw his candidacy. In this speech, which was made in an atmosphere of crisis for the Barroso Commission, Graham reflects on the events of the past months and cautions the Commission President-elect not to treat Parliament as an automatic rubber-stamp for Commission policy. Justus Lipsius, the invisible elephant, is the name of the seat of the European Council whose presence dominates all EU proceedings.*

*26th October 2004, Strasbourg*

'Three months ago, the Alliance of Liberals and Democrats urged the President-designate of the Commission to respect the prerogatives of this Parliament. My Group and this House have offered a sober and considered rejection of his nominee for Commissioner for Justice and Home Affairs.

Mr Barroso, we recognise that you could work only with what you were given. We recognise that your independence is not total. We have, on the whole, offered our support for the other members of your Commission. But our judgement stands, and it will be respected. This Group supported you as President of the Commission; we voted for you; we still support you. But we value the prerogatives of this House too highly to see them taken lightly.

I welcome the package of measures that you have put before this House today. I believe you come here in a genuine search for rapprochement. Some of the measures you propose are bold and all of them are important. I believe that you are committed personally to the promotion of fundamental rights and that this spirit will infuse the Commission you will lead. Liberals and Democrats will consider your proposals carefully. But I am bound to say that they come late in the day and they contain little about Mr Buttiglione's future, a future which may be intimately bound to the future of the Commission-designate.

This House is not asking to be placated or patronised.

We are asking that the other branches of our European government recognise what our Treaties recognise and what the European Constitution recognises: that power in Europe rests in some measure with this Chamber and its elected Members. The approval process is not a rubber stamp and this Parliament should not be treated as one.

It has been said often in the last week that it will be Liberals and Democrats who decide the fate of this Commission. But Liberals and Democrats did not nominate the Commissioners rejected by Parliament's committees. It was not Liberals and Democrats who would not or could not find the compromise that might have put Mr Buttiglione beyond the reach of controversy. Whatever happens tomorrow, the fate of this Commission has more than one architect.

Moreover, I know that I am not the only one in this Chamber who feels that there is an invisible elephant in the room. The elephant is Justus Lipsius. The elephant is in the heads of the governments who gave you a weaker Commission than you deserve, and then refused to come to your aid when our House called their bluff.

How many of Europe's governments would have done what Mr Berlusconi probably did and told you to take their man, basta, even if it left you with a Commission containing a Commissioner whose political feet of clay would probably disqualify him from inclusion in most of the European Union's national governments?

My Group feels that Member States owe Europe their best and their brightest. How many governments have shown their willingness to accept the democratic and legal right of our Parliament to judge the men and women who were proposed? The silence you hear is the sound of Europe's governments leaving you and your new Commission swinging in the wind.

As the defenders of the Community method, the strength of our House is ultimately the strength of yours. Because if the Council can mock the prerogative of this Parliament, then be absolutely sure that it thinks the same of the independence of your Commission.

The Council prefers this Parliament to be weak. Too many in the Council find it convenient for the Commission to be weak. My Group wants this Parliament to be strong, because we cannot conceive of a strong European Union without it. And we want your Commission to be strong because the European Union needs an independent executive of the highest calibre. We have demanded a new framework agreement with your Commission: draft it and sign it, so that we will not be brought to this impasse again.

This House faces a heavy choice. If Liberals and Democrats vote against the Commission-designate, we will not do so lightly. But we cannot, and we will not, diminish the status of this House, the standing of the Civil Liberties Committee or the stature of the post of the European Commissioner for Justice and Home Affairs in the interest of an easy life. You might say - if I can use Mr Buttiglione's own words - that we will not change our principles against our conscience for political convenience.'

## Building The EU Is Like Making Sausages

*Speech to the Liberal Democrat Party's Autumn Conference in Blackpool, 2005. Even in a pro-European party like the Liberal Democrats, there can be some dramatic splits on European issues, as illustrated by a move to veto the EU budget in the absence of immediate reform of the Common Agricultural Policy, that was defeated by a coalition of activists and MEPs and is alluded to below. Following a year of shocks for the European Union Graham uses this opportunity to rally the troops - and the British public at large - to its defence while delivering his 'compte rendu' for a year marked by July's London Bombs and the tragic shooting of Jean Charles de Menezes, an innocent Brazilian, in the city's Stockwell Underground Station. The staccato style of the speech is employed because of the large size of the audience in question.*

*20th September 2005, Blackpool*

'It's always a pleasure to be with people who've chosen to be curious, optimistic and liberal.

The European Union has had a pretty lively year. Its Finance Ministers failed to keep down their deficits. Its people succeeded in voting down the Constitution. And Prime Ministers scrapped over the budget.

But getting Europe together was never easy. Time and again it has been through crisis. Time and again it's been written off. Time and again it's emerged, bloodied but unbowed.

Building the EU is like making sausages. All kinds of things go in there. It's a messy looking affair. But the outcome is wholesome and can taste pretty good. That's why so many countries are queuing to join. First just six, then nine, then twelve. By the turn of the century there were fifteen and now twenty five. Before the decade's out there'll be twenty seven. Many former dictatorships transformed by soft power. Regime change - Europe's way.

And growth is mirrored in maturity. First coal and steel, to keep the peace. Then farming. Trade in goods, for greater wealth. Open borders for freer people. All adding to opportunity and prosperity. It's like a Benjamin Britten opera: better than it sounds. If free movement of money and services could be reached we'd be as wealthy as America or Japan.

We're caring for citizens too. Protecting our people and our planet from poison. I'm Britain's most toxic MEP - WWF tested. I grew up in rural Britain in the chemical crazy 50s and 60s. And like many more men I've had testicular cancer. We're not sure what chemicals do. But we know of falling fertility rates in women. And sinking sperm counts in men. Threatening the ability of our species to reproduce. Rita and I have produced our children. Babies today are poisoned in the womb. That's why we're rooting for a REACH directive to Register, Evaluate and Authorise every CHemical in use. Safer marine fuels, cleaner beaches, action on CFCs: that's Europe too.

Of course the EU needs reform. Continuous change, like all government. Barroso's bonfire of inane proposals is overdue. As is the European Court's commitment to enforce the laws. Europe's farm policy is a disgrace: feeding the greedy, not the needy. But our MEP's don't sit idle. This year's single farm payment is a major reform, with more to come. We've reformed our own pay and expenses. And we've voted out daft ideas like software patents and statutory sun-cream for busty barmaids.

Just as at Westminster, we're the Party of reform. But just as Britain needs Westminster, Britain and its partners need Brussels. Because today's big challenges are supranational. Charles and Sarah Kennedy did their bit for Europe this year. He's called Donald - and he wears the trousers. But fewer Europeans now have babies. Wealth allows freedom to choose.

Elsewhere it's a different story. If you're poor, you need kids. To provide for your old age. And with five billion poor, population is rising dangerously. So we need to pull people out of poverty. Pronto. Liberal

Democrats know that no government can do that. Only markets can. Others disagree. The Left wing wants to close our markets. The Right says close our borders. Both say send home the migrants whose remittances relatives rely on. And whose labour we rely on. To pick our crops, drive our trucks, staff our care homes.

Those policies may appease the popular press but they don't appeal to us because they don't stack up. With developing countries, remember this. The hungry vote with their feet. So either we accept their produce or their migrants. Education, especially for women, micro-credit for business, investment in good governance. Those are all ways we can help. But markets, markets, markets. These are the way forward. And these must be Europe's priorities.

The EU distils our development efforts. But what of other global challenges -

like climate change? If America had heeded the warnings a quarter century ago, we might have prevented it. If Bush acts now we might yet control it. How much more evidence does he need? That's why Europe is committed to Kyoto and my MEPs to alternatives to oil. With prices high, it makes economic sense. We could even move to a hydrogen economy. By pooling our research, bringing together our best brains, Europe can make that leap - but not with a cap on its budget at 1% of GNI.

Think of things we can do with pooled R&D money! Things no country could do alone. Fund research into bio-mimicry. That's inventing processes which mimic life. Water resistant glue without formaldehyde? Some shellfish produce it. Why can't we? We believe we can. We're funding scientists to study how. The Americans have found a butterfly in the desert which strains water from the air through its wings. They've copied its technique for the walls of tents, providing water for refugees. We use enormous energy to heat kilns to fire porcelain but the abalone grows a shell both stronger and finer. And it's made from? Pure sea water. Could we do that? Not if Britain cuts the research budget.

Conference, you voted wisely. Telecommunications and travel have opened up our world. But not only to the curious and the well-meaning. Criminals deal in drugs and guns and sex-slaves. Terrorists foster failing states as training grounds. The once mighty nation state seems powerless to protect. Democracies must pool their power to target terror. But wars are won by cunning, not by force. And peace by understanding, not constraint. Remember the roots of disaffection run deep. In the Holy Wars of our history. Beyond the settlements of the West Bank. In daily discrimination in the job market. In Bedford, Bradford, Leeds or Luton. The language of the 'war on terror' is wrong. New controls create a climate of fear. The justice of Wyatt Earp leaves an innocent Brazilian dead. And citizens can be treated like criminals for their creed.

In Italy, new stop and search powers. In Germany, police surveillance. In France, more CCTV. And here, thrown out or locked up without charge. Breaking the European Convention on Human Rights: who said "This cheapens our right to call ourselves a civilised society"? Cherie Booth! The nub of the problem is this: Government has a dual duty. It must assure our security. But it also must guard our freedom. Get Europe's intelligence services working together. Give our magistrates and police cross-border capability. Give them the powers if they are measured and proportionate. We'll vote for that - but tackle too the hurts and humiliations. The main influence on the last century was not Karl Marx. It was Woodrow Wilson and the politics of identity. That's why the greatest power in the world cannot control a medium sized city like Fallujah. And why our boys are bombed out in Basra. People don't want to be ruled by foreigners.

I'll never forget that fine day after the election. I sat back and thought "Great!" The largest parliamentary group we've ever had. New, young MPs: especially bright young women. Up from 52 - to 88. So I rang Charles Kennedy and said "Charles. Mine's bigger than yours" But Charles's has grown since then - fuelled by new blood including Nick Clegg and Chris Huhne. Our loss but Westminster's gain.

At Westminster, like in the Bundestag and the Assemblée Nationale, we've more MPs than in decades. In the European Parliament, the

Commission and the Council our strength is up. When Europe's LibDems meet before each summit there are six Prime Ministers around the table. It means we pack more punch in policymaking. More than ever, Liberal Democrats make the difference.

But that's not the only reason we are feared. Liberalism's strength is not only in our political presence. It's in the impact of our ideas. For global challenges, we need global responses. Global institutions. Global reach. Liberalism has no problem with that. For us, rights are indivisible. All people equal. Values universal. Freedom for all.

Europe's Right is torn between the claws of the church and the jaws of the secular voter. Between the national sovereignty they crave and the global anarchy it spawns. They want the nation state to become the network state. But still it doesn't work. As we saw at the UN last week. And the left? Do they have answers? Richard Crossman predicted their problem. It's not just that they've no ideological maps. It's their belief that experienced travellers need no maps. They offer only crisis management. So our message to moderates of Right and Left is "Come with us. Construct a coalition of the coherent."

In the European Parliament, where next week our numbers rise to 103 with the arrival of new observer members from Bulgaria and Romania. Or in GLOBE, a global network of lawmakers for a balanced environment, chaired in the UK by Malcolm Bruce MP. Join us in the e-parliament, linking law-makers world-wide in on-line debate. Last week we held our first web-cast hearing On the militarisation of space with a panel of experts including Tim Garden. Come and work with Liberal Democrats the world over for a fair, free and open society. Fighting poverty, ignorance and disease. Turning the page on centuries of self mutilation. Building a millennium of hope.

Europe is central to all this but Britain has reached a juncture. Breathing a sigh of relief as the constitution crashed. Inhaling the innuendo of the antis. Poisoned by propaganda. Hanging in the balance are not just hearts and minds but Britain's part in Europe's liberal agenda. Britain's part in Europe's global reach. Europe can work without a constitution

But if we show it works, they'll vote for it. So face down the faint hearts. Confront the critics. Liberal Democrats must. No-one else will.'

## Imitation Is The Worst Form Of Politics

*Excerpt from a speech to the Liberal Democrat Western Counties annual regional conference in which Graham roundly criticizes his Party for abandoning its beliefs and pursuing an opportunistic election strategy. In the ten years between his arrival in the European Parliament and the 2004 European elections, enthusiasm for European integration had waned both within his party and across the UK as a whole. With a General Election following in twelve months time, the party HQ sought to use the European campaign to feature candidates for the Westminster elections and intervened to remove Graham's election strategist and control the content of campaign literature. Believing that Philip Eavis' local record would prove the best basis for a successful campaign, Graham opposed the move. Subsequently, the party failed to elect a second Liberal Democrat MEP and mismanagement left the regional party with substantial debt. A year later Graham joined other prominent Liberal Democrat 'dissidents' to publish a pamphlet entitled 'Liberalism: something to shout about', urging the party to be bolder in defending its beliefs.*

*12th November 2005, Swindon*

'This is the first regional conference I have attended since the European Election eighteen months ago. At that election, the Group I lead in Brussels and Strasbourg grew from 52 to 89. With our observers from Bulgaria and Romania we are 105. We have more UK Liberal Democrat MEPs than ever before. With our continental colleagues we are the largest third party group in the 25-year history of the European Parliament. It makes a huge difference to what we are able to achieve.

We hold the balance of power convincingly in Strasbourg. We shape new laws. We win parliamentary votes.

I'd like to say a huge "thank you" to the party members who worked to return me safely to Parliament and thus allowed me the privilege to continue leading our troops in the session to come.

But settling down my new colleagues is not the only reason I've missed three regional conferences. I will not hide from you my deep disappointment with the campaign we fought eighteen months ago; nor my anger at the regional party's role.

It is not only because our campaign chiefs caviled when called to show the courage of our convictions about Europe. But also because they abused the freepost facility to promote Westminster candidates in a European parliament campaign: they scorned the advice of our candidates and MEP; and they failed to campaign on the issues, on schedule or on budget.

What was the cost of their choices? It robbed us of a second MEP, when in Tony Welch we had a first class candidate. It left the region in debt running to thousands of pounds. And it killed the consensus on which integrated campaigning depends.

Next time, let us make sure we get it right. In the meantime I've raised nearly two thousand pounds to help pay off the deficit. So I'll be talking to our treasurer.

Things ought to look damn good for us. We have every chance of making a real breakthrough. Not just in Europe, but at Westminster and across the UK. We live in an age replete with opportunity for Liberalism.

Why? Because public attitudes are changing. In May, a survey by the pollsters YouGov showed a massive shift in public opinion over a wide range of issues. The divide in politics is no longer between the right and the left; it is over what the pollsters call 'drawbridge Britain'. Too many of our compatriots want the drawbridge up. Yet a growing number, now over one third of the electorate, want it down. They don't all vote for us, but they're instinctively liberal-minded.

We should be out there, making that constituency of voters ours. Convincing those of a liberal leaning that the Liberal Democrats are the right party for them. Not fighting with Labour and the Tories for votes at the margins. Not pulling so close into Labour's slipstream that on many issues we are indistinguishable from them: on education, the environment, civil liberties to name but a few. Today's political divide is between the open and the closed mind. Let us mind that gap.

## An Immortal Memory

*Speech given on Burns Night 2006 at a supper organised by the Scottish MEPs to mark the 247th anniversary of the bard - who was also a savvy political commentator in his day. Here Graham, a Scot born and bred, gives the traditional 'Immortal Memory' - and draws some pithy analogies between Robert Burns' world and the vagaries of European Politics. He sought advice on the speech from Archie Kirkwood MP, well known as a wit and raconteur. Soon after Burns Night Willie Rennie, Liberal Democrat candidate for the below-mentioned Dunfermline and West Fife by-election, pipped Catherine Stihler MEP to the post on 9th February 2006 to become the former Labour strong-hold's new MP. Graham mischievously changed the Matthew Fitt's poem, below, to include the name of Elspeth Attwooll MEP, the organiser.*

*25th January 2006, Brussels*

'Robert Burns predicted that he would be more respected a hundred years after his death than he was in his lifetime. How right he was! All over the world, the 247th anniversary of his birth is being celebrated. Originally set up by his friends as a way of raising money to support his widow and children, the ritual has grown and grown. And whilst I suspect Burns, with his lively sense of the ridiculous, would have raised an eyebrow or two over anyone proposing his Immortal Memory, I'm sure he'd have entertained serious doubts indeed about the toast being proposed by a politician!

Burns' healthy scepticism of politics was made clear in a letter to a Mr Alexander Cunningham dated February 1793. It included the following passage that I thought I would share with you tonight.

Question - What is politics?

Answer - Politics is a science wherewith by men of nefarious cunning and hypocritical pretence, govern with politics for the emolument of ourselves and our adherents.

In fact, he'd have had us all strung up on the gallows - or, as he called it, that "Tree of France" which he recommended as a remedy for Britain's woes:

"Wi' plenty o' sic trees, I trow,
The warld would live in peace, man;
The sword would help to mak a plough,
The din o' war wad cease man.
Like brethren wi' a common cause,
We'd on each other smile, man;
And equal rights and equal laws
Wad gladden every isle, man."

Were it not for the fact that he was even more beastly about bankers, I might have been forgiven for thinking that I should have stayed with Willie Purves and the band of expatriate Scots at the Hong Kong and Shanghai Banking Corporation. It certainly endowed me with greater emolument than politics! However, perhaps a politician can claim sympathy with what Burns called "the encumbering robe of public notice".A robe whose burdens and whose blessings many of you are well acquainted with - as is one of the recent contenders for the Leadership of my Party at Westminster.

Like the best of counsels, Burns has some sound advice for those who wish to avoid a public dressing-down. It does not involve - as some might think - a brown envelope; an expensive lunch; and several glasses of Malt for the journalist in question! Rather, Burns advised honesty, humanity and humour at all times - save, on occasion, in his romantic relationships! Consider the following stanza, written after he had spotted a pretty young woman flaunting her new hat at church. Unbeknownst to her, a louse was visible on the plumes for all to see.

"O wad some Power the giftie gie us
To see oursels as ithers see us!
It wad frae monie a blunder free us,
An' foolish notion:
What airs in dress an' gait wad lea'e us,
An' ev'n devotion!

"To see oursels as ithers see us" is vital for Europe's politicians and officials - especially after the people of France and the Netherlands said No to the Constitution and showed us what happens when policy-makers and citizens drift too far apart. That's democracy. And it's a far cry from the sinecures and feudal practices Burns described so many years ago. The challenge for 2006 will be reaching out again to citizens and demonstrating our value to their daily lives. Until that mission is accomplished, they may be right to regard the European elite with some suspicion - as Burns did the politicians of his age.

But Burns was no mere satirist. He was a democrat ahead of his time - a true man of independent mind. So ahead of his time, indeed, that it seems he could predict the future of Scottish politics! For proof I turn to his Election Ballad of 1790 in which it is written:

> "For woman's wit and strength o'man,
> Alas! can do but what they can;
> The Tory ranks are broken."

Though, like Nostradamus, his prediction wasn't 100% accurate. He was describing the Dumfries Burgh contest - the only Scottish Westminster seat the Tories hold today!

In defence of liberty, the people and his beloved Caledonia Burns directed his razor-sharp pen against eminences of Kirk, society or state who abused their position or dared flaunt rank or title. He didn't exactly mince his words either!

> "Ye see yon birkie, ca'd a lord
> Who struts an' stares an' a' that,
> Tho hundreds worship at his word,
> He's but a cuif for a' that.
> For a' that an' a' that.
> His ribband star, an a' that
> The man o' independent mind
> He looks and laughs at a' that."

That is perhaps why, when entering the drawing rooms of polite Edinburgh society, his hosts would "welcome" him with a sarcastic "Come in Mr Burns - *you'll have had your tea*".

As a democrat, I suspect that Burns would have appreciated the mix of people in this room tonight. Stalwarts of the Brussels scene and all colours of national politics. Journalists, writers, citizens. People who, once the drink is flowing freely, often let politicians know just how they see us!

So I'll take my own advice and use this opportunity to thank our sponsors. Diageo - for being true to the spirit of Burns night and amply supplying our demand and The Royal Mail, whose representatives have, remarkably, been delivered to us on time! Though, when compared with the horrors of the Belgian postal service, they certainly make us proud to be British!

Given his allegiance to the Union Jack it's surprising to see Roger Helmer here as an honorary Scot - next thing we know he'll be changing his name too. David Cameron has a good Caledonian ring to it! I wish him all the best for his birthday though I hope it is not a poor omen that we are all gathered here to commemorate a death...

Burns' Night is also a time to remember Auld Lang Syne. What, I wonder, could have prevented Catherine Stihler from attending the Brussels Burns Supper? The matter of a small by-election aside, I wish Catherine all the best for the birth of her baby! I'm sure she must be pleased that Gordon Brown has entered the fray by putting his foot down over proposed tolls for the Forth Road Bridge. Perhaps he hasn't noticed that the Scottish Transport Minister is a Liberal Democrat in a devolved government! But then, that's Labour's centralising instincts all over.

Burns, however, was no political partisan like myself - but he'd not always have pleased the Nats. He goes on:

> "Be Briton still to Britain true,
> Amang ourselves united;

For never but by British hands
Maun British wrangs be righted!"

Well educated in the University of Life, his understanding and sympathy
- even for the shortcomings of others - is well-known. He was, above all,
humane, encouraging his readers to:

"gently scan your brother man
Still gentler sister woman,
Tho' they may gang a kennin wrang
To step aside is human"

Burns was a radical thinker by the standards of his age, and rarely a male
chauvinist - though his textile-industry poem "A woman loves a six
inch" is quite a racy read and his indulgence of Tom O'Shanter's failings
is perhaps extreme.

To redress the balance, we're indebted to a contemporary Dundee poet,
Matthew Fitt, for suggesting that Tam's 'wimmin' might have been a
little less forgiving. In "Kate O'Shanters tale" published in 2003 she
shouts:

"well, dinnae gie's it, shanter
juist dinnae gie's it
ye cam in here
fowre in the bliddy moarnan
an ye wur buckled
couldnae staun
couldnae speak
haverin a load ay keech, sae ye wur
tellin us how you'd juist goat back
fae a ceilidh wi the deevil
an how come you'd seen Elspeth Attwooll's belly button...
a bletherin, blusterin, drunken blellum, sae ye ur."

If he were with us today, I doubt that Burns' would have minded the dig.
In fact - as a man of principle who moved with the times - he may even

have agreed with Kate's sentiments. By way of proof, here he is on Europe - and women.

"While Europe's eye is fixed on mighty things
The fate of empires and the fall of kings,
While quacks of state must each produce his plan
And even children lisp the Rights of Man
Amidst this mighty fuss just let me mention
The Rights of Woman merit *some* attention."

His inspiration came from those who had little earthly power - the poor farming folk he grew up with and the - many - women he loved. And - unlike other literary figures of his time - ordinary people can readily identify with his verse. His fundamental belief in human dignity, his joie de vivre and his canny mind - these are surely the reasons that people all over the world still remember Burns with such fondness today. His life was neither easy, nor blameless - but it was, in every respect, human.

That is why, ladies and gentlemen, I ask you to raise your glasses and toast the immortal memory of Robert Burns.'

## 30 Years Old But Still Young At Heart

*Speech to LYMEC's Annual European Congress in 2006 in celebration of the movement's 30th Anniversary. LYMEC, which stands for the Liberal and Radical Youth Movement of the European Community, is an unusual organisation in so far as its membership is growing at a time when political interest amongst young people is generally falling: it currently stands at over 170,000. In this speech Graham reflects on the factors which inspired him, as a student at Heriot-Watt University in Edinburgh, to get involved - and the dangers democracy faces if today's youth do not. IFLRY, referred to below, included members from Council of Europe Member States, as well as those in the European Union*

*10th February 2006, Brussels*

'It is a pleasure to find here tonight so many Liberal Democrats, faces old and new. Many things have changed in the thirty years since LYMEC was founded. Most evidently, most of us have aged. But I can assure you we feel no different. We sympathise with the words of the popular song "Youth, like sex, is wasted on the young".

Perhaps the biggest change is the geographical scope of the EU and therefore also of its political youth organisations. When LYMEC was founded there were only 9 member states; today there are 25, going on 27. I recall an impassioned discussion about the need for contact with young liberals in the candidate countries Greece, Spain and Portugal: and the arrival at the European Youth Centre in 1977 of Paco Rabena, Enrico Bofarull Vilares and Joan Francesc Pont in a Fiat 125 which they had driven for twenty hours from Barcelona.

When I travelled to the Karl Marx University in Leipzig in February 1988 as one of only two exchange students which my university sent there each year - it was hardly an "exchange", since no East German students ever came to Edinburgh, only professors without their families - nobody could imagine that within twelve years the Berlin Wall would be torn down. A few years ago I spoke to young liberals in Sachsen

Anhalt, no longer having to worry that my words to them would be recorded and their families placed under suspicion.

These days however, unless we are vigilant, we may have to worry about <u>our</u> governments snooping on EU citizens. Because the other big change in those thirty years is the scope of the EU's activities. In 1976 there was no co-operation in justice and home affairs: no one dreamed that we might have a Directive on Data Retention on our electronic communications, partly of course because mobile phones did not exist and very few people had computers. There was no single market, no euro, no Schengen border agreement, not even a European Youth Forum. I was involved in the creation of that particular source of money for youth organisations in 1980.

Like you, we all became involved first in national politics. And we helped each other out. I remember hosting ten German Young Democrats in 1979 who came to Scotland to help us try and win a seat in the first elections to the European Parliament. We hired a minibus and toured every seat in Scotland, having hilarious fun but achieving very little: while German liberals won four seats in the Parliament with six percent of the vote, liberals in my country took thirteen percent but failed to win a single seat.

But also, like many of those active in LYMEC today, our national political commitment soon gave way to a primarily supra-national commitment as we recognised that the major challenges faced by humankind are supranational, needing supranational responses. I suppose that is why I went on to become the first British Liberal ever to be elected to the European Parliament, though it took fifteen years before a Brit could join his former LYMEC colleagues like Gijs de Vries in the European Parliament here in Brussels.

At the risk of making myself very unpopular, I must admit that I never actually held elected office in LYMEC. My primary role was with another organisation, IFLRY. I sat on the LYMEC bureau, but only as the IFLRY representative. In fact I have to tell you that there was much opposition to the creation of LYMEC from the Scandinavians and youth organisations of other member countries of the Council of Europe. And the first LYMEC Bureau nearly collapsed in farce when two of its six members - Norb Becker and Rainer Kollner - resigned within a year. Three of us from IFLRY - Rafael Lewental, Pierre Houtmans and I - were asked to step in "to assist in the work of the LYMEC bureau".

Let me share with you just three small reminiscences, three cameos, of a type which I imagine will not be unfamiliar to those active in LYMEC today.

At the ELDR congress just before the European elections in 1979 LYMEC delegates - of which I was one - abstained in the final vote on the election manifesto. Most of our amendments had been defeated and we felt the final text was 'insufficiently radical'. The fact that we had been up all night drinking and fornicating of course had nothing whatsoever to do with our unco-operative mood.

A year later, at our Congress at the Friedrich Naumann Foundation's luxury hideaway in Gummersbach, near the then German capital Bonn, I chaired a LYMEC congress session which - according to my notes - went on until one o'clock in the morning with thousands of points of order and numerous motions to reverse the Chairman's decision. I've no idea how your congresses work today, but it was clearly a good training school, because I'd never allow the MEPs I lead to act like that!

After a seminar in Denmark a prominent Danish young Liberal invited a Scottish girl back to his parents' farm for the weekend. He was quite keen on her and he imagined his feelings might be reciprocated. As they sat on a fence on Saturday afternoon watching the sun go down over the fields of cattle, one of the family's bulls mounted a heifer. Seeing that the girl was watching with interest, the lad plucked up his courage, put his arms around her and said "I think it would be fun to do that". But he had not reckoned with the character of the Scottish women. "You go ahead", she said: "after all, it's your cow".

Not all of us who were active then have remained active in day-to-day politics. But whatever we're now doing, we have all been inspired by the friendships we made, the lessons we learned, the political experience we gained in the misspent days of our youth. In my case my involvement in international Liberal youth politics introduced me to the woman who finally became my wife (after more than a few others who were spared that fate) and to an interest in the development of the EU which I have had the privilege to pursue to the highest levels. I have no doubt today's generation of LYMEC activists will go on to even greater things.'

## Energising Europe

*Speech to the ELDR Congress in Stuttgart which was celebrating its 30th anniversary. In the same town, on the same day, in 1976, the European Liberal Democrat and Reform Party was founded as a pioneering venture in pan-european politics, bringing together parties with common ideals to contest the first European Parliament elections. Today, the ELDR - a political family comprising 49 member parties from across the EU - represents millions of voters and provides an increasingly vital link between citizens and the European Institutions. In this speech Graham reflects on the difference 30 years makes - and how the ELDR can harness its founding principles to respond to the challenges of the twenty-first century. The King in question is Simeon Saxe-Coburg who had returned from exile to become Bulgaria's Liberal Prime Minister in 2001. Poettering and Schulz are leaders of the European People's Party and the European Socialist Group, respectively. Annemie Neyts is President of the ELDR Party, which Graham Watson chaired in the European Parliament.*

*17th March 2006, Stuttgart*

'In 1976 I was a student in Edinburgh. And the International officer of the Scottish Young Liberals, coaxing and cajoling colleagues to come to conferences like this.

The previous year we'd won the campaign to keep Britain in the European Community. Then, here in Stuttgart, we found common cause with our continental counterparts. We strove for success in Scotland in the first direct elections to the European Parliament, with our Leader Russell Johnston flying the flag. I was impressed even then by the campaigning skills of our German Liberal friends - so evident here in Baden Wurttemberg today - when a group of Deutsche Jungdemokraten came over to Scotland to help. They helped us take 14% of the vote, but no seats; while our FDP friends did only half as well and returned 4 MEPs.

What a difference 30 years makes! With five Prime Ministers, seven EU Commissioners and 64 MEPs at the heart of the European Parliament - and even a King, no less - European Liberals, Democrats and Reformers are energising Europe like never before. Not only do we swing the vote on issues of crucial importance. We've put the demos back into democracy. We've exposed backroom deals by Poettering and Schulz designed to put the brakes on free market reform. We've flown the flag of transparency, and successfully challenged the Council on closed-door decision making. And we've radicalised the reform agenda with a political programme that paves the way to European revival.

It's all a far cry from 1976. But Liberal campaigns were always ahead of their time. Indeed we are most feared not for the size of our political presence but for the strength of our ideas.

Let me give three Liberal examples:

1. Gaston Thorn's idea that "Europe's economic problems are solvable only at a European level" was barely believed back then. Now it is taken for granted.

2. Martin Bangemann told us as he left the Commission: "Ich gehe zwar, aber ich verschwinde nicht". How right he was.Martin always larger as life: and I see he still is. His reincarnation, Liberal Commissioner Janez Potocnik, is fighting the very same battle for innovation as he did.

3. My third example is a little known Commissioner who told us that free trade in services is the way forward to renewed economic growth. He's rather better known today! Come back Frits Bolkestein, all is forgiven!

30 years ago, in the introduction to his pamphlet "To be a Liberal" Russell Johnston quoted a constituent who had written to him stating: "I agree with most of what you say, and admire what you do, but I don't vote for you. I want to vote for someone who is a member of a Party which can win power - the power to do things."

30 years ago ELDR took on this challenge. Our numbers were small and our finances frail but we were resolute. We proved the doubters wrong again and again. Today ELDR member parties form national governments in 10 of the 25 EU Member States - and in both of the new Accession Countries, Romania and Bulgaria. Liberalism today is in the ascendant. It has the power to do things, to change and to energise Europe. But as Russell pointed out in his reply to that disgruntled voter, power is not sufficient in and of itself. It has also to have a purpose. And for us, that purpose is clear.

In the Stuttgart declaration of 1976, we resolved to protect and promote people's rights and freedoms. 30 years later we have a European Charter of Fundamental Rights and a nascent Human Rights Agency in Vienna to keep watch lest those rights are undermined. Back then we resolved to create a European polity underpinning a free society. 30 years on we have a European Parliament, whose powers are growing inexorably, a Council which meets regularly and a courageous Court of Justice. 30 years ago we promised a decent life to our citizens. Now the European single market is an engine for growth, prosperity and opportunity for the future.

If we compare the demands of the Stuttgart declaration to the Union of today, we find - in the words of Guy Verhofstadt - "the most liberal Europe that has ever existed". In the end of the Cold War, some saw the inevitable triumph of Liberal democracy. The tragedy of 9-11 and the equally tragic response suggest they were wrong. But they were right about one thing. It is Liberal ideology which provides the tool-box for the break-downs of the modern world. For Liberals recognise that the biggest challenges of the twenty-first century - challenges like population growth and migration, climate change and internationally organised crime - can only be met by concerted action at European level.

So Europe needs the ELDR Party. Unlike the right wing, we have no ideological difficulty with the development of supranational responses to the supranational challenges of our age. And unlike the left, we know the only way to pay for our social policy is by embracing market forces, not protectionist instincts. The EU needs a pro-European force at its centre that is liberal by instinct, democratic to the core and reform-minded by nature. The ELDR brings these principles to the heart of the debate on the future of our common European Union project.

John Stuart Mill wrote of the intellectual superiority of Liberalism back in 1866 when he said in a letter to a Tory MP: "I never meant to say that the Conservatives are generally stupid. I meant to say that stupid people are generally Conservative. That is so obviously and universally admitted a principle that I hardly think any gentleman will deny it."

But we must not rest on our laurels. Nor forget that our programme is far from achieved. To me, success lies in intertwining the three philosophical strands of Liberal thinking: classical liberalism, with its emphasis on the dignity and rights of the individual; economic liberalism, with its belief that the free market is the most powerful tool in the race to eradicate poverty; and social liberalism, which sees a role for government in the case of market failure, to make the world fairer for all its citizens. Annemie, tu as parlé de "générosité" : il faut la rétablir dans nos pensées.

That is why the group I lead in the European Parliament, the Alliance of Liberals and Democrats for Europe, has dedicated itself to a 10-point 'Programme for Europe'. We strive to combine economic dynamism with social justice and environmental responsibility; to enlarge, open up and democratise the European Union; and to use Europe's status as a global strategic player to make globalisation work for all of humankind.

Some say we have a European democracy but no European demos. It's not true. We dress the same way, play the same games, enjoy the same music and feel the same revulsion at Guantanamo and Abu Ghraib. But too often we define ourselves in relation to America - too rarely in our relations to each other. So the EU is seen as imposed from above and poorly explained. The debate on the European Constitution has shown us that. Merkel and De Villepin want to change its name. Not "Constitutional Treaty" but "Institutional Treaty". They've heeded the words of Pat Cox when he said: "It's not the text, it's the context".

Liberals, Democrats and Reformers have much to do to convince our citizens of the need for wider, deeper integration. But we're the only ones who can. There is no 'deus ex machina' in Brussels. Europe is us: every one of us. We need to forge a common defence and security policy: a common policy for justice and freedom; and a Europe capable of promoting European values in the world. And we need to endow the EU with the tools and the resources to do this.

Under the able stewardship of Annemie Neyts, ELDR Members will need to energise policy and debate, continuing to speak out. Radical where necessary. Provocative where appropriate. Honest in our words and our deeds. For 30 years we have argued our case across the continent of Europe and beyond. Sometimes for little reward or electoral gain, but always out of a strong conviction and with firm principle. The seeds of our ideas and our toil are bearing fruit: we now boast parties of government and elected representatives at all levels. As Russell Johnston put it many years ago; "The long slow dream we share is unfolding and the morning can be bright again".'

## Build Your Rock Upon This House

*Speech given at Gibraltar's annual National Day celebrations on September 10th, a date chosen in commemoration of the 1967 Referendum result which established the territory's democratic links with the UK. Graham Watson has represented the people of Gibraltar since 2004, following a ruling by the European Court of Justice that gave them the right to vote in EU elections for the first time. Here he reinforces the importance of the European Union in safeguarding the rights of Gibraltar's citizens. Only two days after this speech was made, the European Court of Justice threw out a complaint by Spain concerning the Rock's electoral laws to help ensure its continuing self-determination.*

*10th September 2006, Gibraltar*

'People of Gibraltar, it is a pleasure to be here with you once again to celebrate your National Day. I bring you greetings from the Liberal Democrats in the United Kingdom and from the European Liberal Democrats that I lead in the European Parliament.

I am proud to represent you in the European Parliament. The European Parliament must uphold your rights in the same way we do for all other Europeans.

This is why a couple of months back Liberals in the European Parliament, with friends from other parties, managed to remove the Gibraltar exclusion clause from a measure affecting your airport. They wanted to leave your airport out and we put it back in again.

We have won this first round. We will put up a fight if the exclusion clause is reinserted by the European Commission or the Council. I promise you that.

I know that Gibraltar has been hard done by in the European Union in the past. We now have to look to the future. Now that you have representatives in the European Parliament we will stand up for you.

A people, no matter how small, have rights too. You are Europeans too.

And so today we celebrate your National Day. We celebrate your self-determination. Stand firm and you will win in the end. Happy National Day Gibraltar!'

# Building An Enlarged European Union

*The fall of the Berlin Wall marked the beginning of a long reunification process that will see the European Union's borders extend to Russia, Ukraine and Turkey when Bulgaria and Romania join in January 2007. However building a Union of 27 members has not been easy task. Public opinion, relatively pro-accession before the countries of the old Communist block joined in 2004, has hardened in recent years resulting in stricter criteria, post-enlargement monitoring, and transitional arrangements for the new accession states. Likewise, the Constitutional debacle has created an institutional impasse for future membership negotiations and Greek Cyprus' rejection of the Annan Plan for reunification jeopardises prospects for Turkish entry. Much will depend on whether the 2007 German Presidency of the EU can put the Constitution back on track and create the conditions for future enlargement.*

*The European Parliament plays a vital part in the accession process through the assent procedure, which means that - although unable to amend the Commission's enlargement proposals - it can accept or reject them. Parliamentary committees also undertake to promote debate and pressure for reform through annual progress reports which measure a candidate country's progress in relation to the Copenhagen Criteria for EU membership. The ALDE Group has unstintingly championed enlargement on the basis that only a strong, integrated, and united Europe can meet the challenges of the future and guarantee liberty, security and prosperity in a globalised age. In this series of speeches Graham Watson examines where Europe's future borders should lie, who is eligible for membership, and what level of constitutional change is required to make a united Europe function effectively.*

\*\*\*\*\*\*\*\*\*\*\*\*\*\*\*\*\*\*\*\*\*\*\*\*\*\*\*\*\*\*\*\*\*\*\*\*\*\*\*\*\*\*\*\*\*\*\*\*\*\*\*\*\*\*\*\*\*\*\*\*

## Breaking Down The Berlin Wall

*Speech to the European Parliament in Brussels on enlarging the European Union. Here Graham welcomes the Commission's conclusion that all candidate countries would be ready to join by the target date of 2004 but stresses the importance of ensuring continued support for the project from Europe's citizens. Less than two years later, 10 countries, the majority from the Cold War's Eastern Block, reunited a divided continent. However, with Bulgaria and Romania set to join in 2007, public support for enlargement has plummeted, prompting politicians to reconsider where Europe's future borders should lie.*

*9th October 2002, Brussels*

'Many of us never thought we would witness in our lifetimes the fall of the Berlin Wall. That event changed the face of Europe and heralded a process of emancipation for our neighbours in central and eastern Europe which is nearing its conclusion. It is worth reminding ourselves of the 13 long years this process has taken as the siren voices of the sceptics seek to dash enlargement on the rocks.

In a previous debate, I described enlargement as a process of continuous assessment, not a one-off exam. I thank Mr Prodi for presenting today the Commission's assessment of the readiness of the applicant states to join the European Union which marks those countries' completion of a major assignment in that process. They are now approaching the final examination at the Copenhagen Summit. The prospects look good although they still have some hard work to do in the months ahead if they are to make the grade.

The Liberal Democrat Group has always sought to apply the Copenhagen criteria and the timetable, not to elevate one above the other. We, therefore, welcome the Commission's conclusion that the ten applicant states will be ready to join the European Union by 2004, but that monitoring of their preparations will continue. A reinforced monitoring system is necessary because the overview provided by the

Commission clearly shows that there are deficiencies in the readiness of those applicant countries and we should be open about this. If we are to convince our own people of the case for enlargement, it must be clear that we are not sweeping problems under the carpet. Openness about those problems and the measures taken to tackle them will make us better able to reassure the doubters.

I therefore call on the Commission to transmit to Parliament all the regular enlargement reports which it will make to Council. If we await the comprehensive monitoring report six months before enlargement, the Commission may have no alternative but to impose safeguards since the nuclear option of suspending enlargement may not be viable. I hope that the threat of those safeguards will be sufficient to ensure that they are not used.

Neither should we forget, however, that it is not only our own voters who have to be convinced. There are referenda to be won in the applicant states. Critics in those countries who compare the European Union to the old Soviet Union are confusing a jacket with a straightjacket. Yet we must show those countries that they will benefit from enlargement from year one. This means a generous financial settlement which precludes them becoming net contributors in the short term. By introducing a secession clause in a new constitutional treaty, we would also assuage any fears that to join the European Union is to throw away the keys to freedom.

My group is deeply worried that corruption remains widespread and that much work must be done to implement the acquis in justice and home affairs. We must be firm on the failings of the candidate countries, yet we must recognise that the report before us today is only a progress report. My own country struggled to meet the criteria 15 months before accession. Thirty years later, some might say that it is still struggling. One thing is clear, however. The monitoring of compliance with EU laws and respect for the Union's values is not a process which should end upon accession.

The Liberal Group welcomes the date of 2007 along with a roadmap for Bulgaria and Romania. The steps which they need to take must be clearly outlined by the Commission in time for Copenhagen, so that they are clear on what needs to be done.

The recent reforms undertaken by the Turkish Government represent a real breakthrough and, while no date can be set for Turkey's accession until the political criteria are met, we will watch with interest the implementation of these reforms. Turkey must be offered a pre-accession strategy accompanied by more financial support and a friendlier political environment. We must show the world that we are not an elite Christian club.

The question of Cyprus will also have to be resolved to smooth the way for Turkey's entry. Here we look to Greece and Turkey to help broker an agreement before the Copenhagen Summit. The prospect of the whole of Cyprus joining the EU would start the Greek Presidency on a positive note which we hope would conclude, in Thessaloniki, with a summit symbolising reconciliation.

In conclusion, the enlargement marathon is nearing the finish line. Despite the exertions thus far, the participants must be prepared for a sprint finish. Once they cross the line in Copenhagen, they will have little time to celebrate, the training for the next marathon begins - the marathon of meeting the acquis communautaire and achieving democratic endorsement of the enlargement process.'

## Success Has Many Fathers

*Speech to the European Parliament in Brussels on the draft Constitutional text that had been agreed by the European Convention, a body of 105 MPs, MEPs, and Commission staff that was set up in 2001 after the failure of the Nice summit to agree wide-ranging reform of the European Union. Here Graham welcomes an acceptable compromise text which places fundamental rights and democratic scrutiny firmly at the heart of the Union. However, he does not refrain from putting the Liberal Democratic case for wider and deeper integration: something unattainable without discarding the requirement for unanimous decision-making. The text of the Constitutional Treaty is currently under reconsideration following 'No' votes in France and the Netherlands in 2005.*

*18th June 2003, Brussels*

'I too thank all those who have represented this House on the Convention. It is said that 'success has many fathers, but failure is an orphan'. The draft Constitution agreed by the Convention last Friday is blessed with many proud parents. Of these, the European Parliament can claim more than its fair share of paternity, since we led the calls for the Convention method to be used to avoid a repeat of the failures of Nice. We owe much to the Belgian Presidency of the European Union, which gave us the visionary Laeken Declaration.

While the birth was difficult and the baby is not as pretty as we hoped, the European Constitution born on Friday 13 June 2003 deserves a long and fruitful life. Liberals everywhere will rejoice that fundamental rights now lie at the heart of the Union's basic law. We welcome the establishment of a single legal personality for the Union, the unification of the pillars and the extension of democratic control by the European Parliament. Crucially, this shorter and simpler treaty should also be more accessible to Europe's citizens since it sets out more clearly who does what.

Of course we would have liked to go further in some respects. We hope that the post of Chairman of the European Council will in time be merged with that of Commission President in an integrated Presidency. We want to see the legitimacy of the Commission strengthened by a real election of its President by the European Parliament. We seek a greater role for regions with constitutional powers. And we would like greater recourse to majority voting, even in a sensitive area like foreign policy, so that the Union can act more decisively abroad.

There is still work to be done. The extension of qualified majority voting needs to be given concrete expression in the policies in part 3 of the constitution. We also urge the Convention to be ambitious in creating a lighter procedure for amending part 3, through voting by super-qualified majority and without recourse to national ratification.

At Thessaloniki, the Heads of State and Government will be granted custody of the new-born constitution and will bring it to maturity in the Intergovernmental Conference. Having been so central to its conception, our governments will not be able to disown the constitution lightly.

The European Council will have to decide the composition and the duration of the IGC. The parliamentary component of the Convention must be fairly represented at the talks - as you, Mr President, have said. Since members of the Liberal caucus under my colleague Andrew Duff have made such a great contribution to the work of the Convention, we insist that Parliament's representation should reflect this.

On the length of the IGC, if Member States seek to unpick one part of the deal, others will pull at it too and the whole fabric risks unravelling. For that reason, we urge that the IGC be kept short and stick to the essentials of the text agreed by the Convention.

This brings me to my final point. The most open and democratic institutional reform in our Union's history deserves to be brought to a fitting conclusion. It is no use making the EU simpler and more accountable if politicians do not then explain it and argue the case for active engagement in Europe

Speaking personally, I hope that my own government will at last shake off its reticence and take the case for Britain's membership of this re-founded European Union to the people in a referendum. Whether they ratify by way of referendum or parliamentary debate, I hope that other countries too will seize the opportunity to have a great debate with their voters. That way, our people can again feel ownership of the European project.'

## Divided They Stood, Divided They Fell

*Speech to the European Parliament in Strasbourg on the reunification of Cyprus. The Annan Plan, which was to be put to a simultaneous referendum between Greek and Turkish Cypriots on 24th April 2004, sought to create a United Cyprus Republic on the basis of loose confederation between the two sides, rather like the system in place in Belgium. Here Graham cautions that rejection could put back the reunification of Cyprus by a generation. In the event, while 65% of Turkish Cypriots voted in favour of the plan, over 75% of Greek Cypriots voted against. When Cyprus acceded to the EU in May 2004 the country remained divided - an issue which is now one of the main stumbling blocks for Turkey's own membership negotiations.*

*21st April 2004, Strasbourg*

'On Saturday, Cyprus votes on the Annan Plan and its future. Cyprus stands at a historic juncture. European Liberal Democrats and Reformers in this House have consistently urged all parties to support the plan and we do so again now.

The Annan Plan offers Cyprus a chance for reconciliation and renewal. It is a door to a better future on an island that has endured too much for too long. The plan makes important concessions to both sides. With goodwill on both sides it could be a first step away from years of partition. My Group thanks Commissioner Verheugen for the leadership he has shown in this matter. We regret that more EU leaders have not expressed the same commitment more volubly. The European Union will underwrite a huge amount of the reunification process and the Court of Justice will provide a legal framework for its resolution. This is the last, best hope for a unified Cyprus to join the European Union on 1 May.

We salute the leaders on both sides in Cyprus who have supported the Annan process and have commended it to their fellow Cypriots. 'No' would have been the simple choice: the answer which rhymed easily with resentment and suited political expediency. 'Yes' took courage.

There are many Cypriots, particularly on the Greek side, who ask what business it is of ours to be having this debate at all. In the face of all our concern and consternation they offer simply the shrug of self-determination. They can and will vote as they please and they have the right to vote 'no'. But I believe it would be a sad and sectarian choice, the wrong choice for the wrong reasons. Moreover, if the purpose of self-determination is the freedom to go on nursing old resentments and the right to weigh the money in your pocket today against reconciliation tomorrow, the Cypriots who have turned their faces against this process are welcome to it. I would just ask them to reflect on this. What if the West Germans had chosen that kind of self-determination in 1990?

On our scarred continent with its crowded history there are some old scores where restitution and compensation can only ever be relative. Only the historically illiterate can believe that we can somehow fix what has happened in Cyprus, anymore than we can fix Kosovo and Serbia or Israel and Palestine. What Cyprus needs is a modus vivendi: some way of living that looks forward rather than backward.

The Annan Plan is a modus vivendi. If it is lost on Saturday it could put back the reunification of Cyprus by a generation. The European Union would have to face up to a new reality on the ground: the possibility for a peaceful transfer of land will be lost; the Turkish army will continue to guard what will remain a militarised border; UN peacekeepers will patrol within the European Union.

The English writer Lawrence Durrell, who lived for many years on Cyprus, recorded a Greek Cypriot proverb that says there is no fire in old ashes. Liberal Democrats and Reformers in this House hope beyond hope that Sunday will not find Cypriots stirring the cold old ashes of a sad history.'

## Vote For An Ideal, Not Simply A Text

*Speech made to the Convergéncia Democrática de Catalunya Party in Barcelona. With a Constitutional referendum fast approaching, Graham uses this opportunity to rally support for the 'yes' vote by illustrating how only reform of an institutional framework that was put in place when six countries signed the Treaty of Rome in 1957 can make Europe more effective, more democratic, more transparent and more capable of influence on the world stage.*

*17th February 2005, Barcelona*

'Estimats amics,

You will be the first Europeans to hold a popular vote on the new EU Constitution. But you are not really voting about a document of 264 pages. You are voting about an idea.

The document is complicated. Few voters will read it. But the idea is simple. Can we build a union of the peoples of Europe, including the new democracies who laboured for fifty years under communism, which is able to defend and promote European values at home and abroad? The EU has grown: from 6 countries in the 1960s to 9 in the 1970s, 12 in the 1980s, 15 in the 1990s and now 25 last year. The Union has also developed: from a coal and steel community to a common market and now, increasingly, into a community of common values.

For 40 years, our values were the same as those of our friends in the United States of America. Because we had the same starting point: 1945. But Europe's starting point is now the tearing down of the Berlin Wall in 1989. For America, it is 9-11, in 2001.

We have far more in common with America than that which divides us. But we will no longer always see eye-to-eye. We disagree with their policies of regime change in countries like Iraq or Iran. We have our own policy of regime change: we are changing the regime in Turkey, for example. And in Croatia. But we are doing it the European way. We use the force of argument, not the argument of force.

If we want the European way to work, we need a European Union which works. And that is what this Constitution is all about.

Walter Bagehot, a 19th century English Liberal economist, once wrote a book called 'The British Constitution'. Actually, my country has never had a Constitution. I can tell you, as a Liberal, we need one. Just as the European Union needs a Constitution which sets out the separation of powers between government at EU level and government at national level: which gives European citizens a Bill of Rights: which gives any country a legal means to leave the Union if they decide to. All these are in the new European Constitution.

You, of all Europeans, have had a proper debate about this Constitution and I salute the leading role which Convergencia - and in particular my friends Carles Gasoliba and Ignasi Guardans - have played in this debate.

Catalonia has been a model of openness, in keeping with your strong international engagement. You set up a Convention in 2002, to debate Catalonia's future in Europe. Your Convention celebrated a political process which enshrines the values of the European Union in a legal document in order for the Union to act more effectively at home as well as abroad. The Catalan Convention also highlighted two important issues for you; first, the role of the regions with legislative powers and the better monitoring of subsidiarity; and second the questions of language and linguistic diversity. I come from Scotland, so those issues are important for me too. They help us bring Europe closer to its citizens.

Cultural diversity is Europe's strength and its unity. That's why Article 5 of the Constitution respects the integrity, identities and constitutions of the Member States. Article 2 requires particular respect for minorities within national boundaries. This is not, as the Partido Popular claims, to say that the Constitution forbids any reorganisation within a Member State. On the contrary, it says it is up to each Member State to work out its own internal constitutional arrangements.

Great Britain has recently given more power to its nations and regions. There is nothing to stop Spain doing the same. And no reason not to support so-called 'non-official' EU languages. Catalan is spoken by 7 million people. Why should it not be used when Maltese spoken by 400,000 is? The Constitution specifies that Member States may translate EU texts into languages which have official status within their country. This may be a small step, but it's an important step in the right direction. The EU is not perfectly balanced, but it is a club where solidarity and mutual respect must prevail.

The debate about language demonstrates the dilemma of the Constitution for many of Europe's citizens. The Constitution is a compromise. Everyone will feel dissatisfied with parts of it. But let us not undermine the Constitution simply because it does not meet all our aspirations, or go far enough in one direction. And do not believe the university professors who tell you that Catalonia can have a free "No" because Spain's majority will vote "Yes". As you say in Barcelona "if you undermine the foundations the house starts to fall down". For the British conservatives the text contains too much of a continental social agenda; French socialists find it too neo-liberal. But it would bring a Europe which works better.

The Constitution modernises the EU; it makes it more effective, more democratic, more transparent and more capable of influence on a world stage.

- MORE EFFECTIVE by simplifying decision-making and slimming down the College of Commissioners;

- MORE DEMOCRATIC by giving the European Parliament more power of codecision, including full scrutiny of the budget, enabling national parliaments to signal their disapproval of draft laws, offering the possibility of a citizen's initiative and including a charter to protect citizens from laws which infringe their rights;

- MORE TRANSPARENT by simplifying decision-making and clarifying which powers can be exercised in Brussels and which are the responsibility of national governments;

- MORE CAPABLE TO ACT ABROAD through an external action service, a European foreign minister and a mutual assistance agreement.

It means recognising that in a globalised world the ability of European Union Member States to protect themselves against terrorism or manage environmental change or to cope with immigration is directly proportionate to their ability to work together.

Faced with continental trading partners like Russia or the United States, Europe needs a continental policy of its own.

A little over 30 years ago, Convergència Democràtica de Catalunya was founded as a democratic, humanist and progressive Catalan nationalist political party. You have remained true to your ideals. Those ideals of progressive humanism also underpin the philosophy of European Liberal Democrats and our vision of the European Union which is encapsulated in the new Constitution.

Co-operation between Europe's Liberals and Democrats also dates back almost 30 years - to the Stuttgart Declaration in 1976. Last year a proper statute for European political parties was agreed for the first time. The clear legal status for European political parties will be instrumental in strengthening the democratic basis of the Union as votes for parties translate into European political programmes. This is already becoming clear in the new enlarged European Parliament. We have the confidence to reject prospective European Commissioners who do not make the grade. We are holding President Barroso to account on his 5-year plan and on the Lisbon Agenda. We are your voice in action when we vote in

Strasbourg or Brussels. We remain accountable to you - and not least in the defence we now are called to make of the European Constitution. As one of your illustrious poets, Salvador Espriu wrote in his poem "They asked me to talk about my Europe":"Quan arribi el dia, haurem fet el primé, i inesborrabla pas vers la suprema, unió i igualtat entre tots els homs." *

Moltas grasias per haver-me convidat y espero un gran reculjament per la Constitució europea.

[*When the day arrives we will have made the first and inexorable step towards a supreme union and equality between all men.]'

## A Little Rebellion Now And Then Is A Good Thing

*Speech to the European Parliament in Strasbourg on the future of the European Union, in the presence of Commission President Jose Manuel Barroso and the Council's representative, the Luxembourg Foreign Minister. 'No' votes in June's Constitutional Referenda in France and the Netherlands threw the ratification process into turmoil. Here Graham expresses his view that an undemocratic, distant EU, combined with the duplicity of Member States, had contributed to this negative result - but that this could yet have positive consequences. Restoring the trust of citizens in the Union, he says, is a key priority - and one which will force it to change for the better, with or without a Constitutional Treaty. VGE 380 refers to the Constitutional Convention chaired by Valery Giscard D'Estaing which was rolled out not long before the completion of the EU Airbus 380 project. Chirac and Balkenende were the President of France and Prime Minister of the Netherlands, respectively.*

*8th June 2005, Strasbourg*

'Thomas Jefferson said in 1787, 'a little rebellion now and then is a good thing'. Beyond the gloom and pessimism about Europe's future, last week's rebellion by our citizens could turn out to have some benefits. Member States are confronted with the outcome of their own duplicity. If you claim the credit for everything that goes right and blame Brussels for everything that goes wrong, then sooner or later your citizens will rumble you - and they have.

When the VGE 380 was rolled out onto the tarmac last summer, we all cheered. But it has features and a name that are scaring away potential passengers. Some complain there are too many foreigners aboard, others that the new French and German specifications for the engines have weakened it. But nobody is completely satisfied with a vehicle in which strategic decisions are taken without proper public debate.

That is a failing not just at EU level, but in our national debates too. For all our grand plans for trans-national cooperation, we have failed to explain to people what we are doing at European level and why, and to address their fears about jobs, careers and a productive retirement in a fast-changing world. Europe is too secretive and too opaque. Too many decisions are still taken behind closed doors and without proper parliamentary scrutiny. Basic parliamentary prerogatives and formal opinions are ignored or dismissed, such as the opposition in this House to heavy-handed proposals on data retention or passenger data transfer. Is it any wonder that big projects like the Constitution are rejected, when even basic institutional respect is lacking?

The British Foreign Secretary has been accused of making funeral arrangements before the coroner has spoken, but he gave voice to what many are saying in private, that the Treaty in its current form is unlikely to survive. It would have been ideal to hear the opinion of all Member States. In future, any such ratification must be put to all European citizens at the same time. But these were votes to reject not a text, but the way our Union operates.

Mr Schmit, Mr Barroso, we do not blame you for getting us into this mess, but we look to you for leadership in getting us out. Of course, there is a limit to how much a small Member State or the Commission can do. A huge responsibility rests on the larger beasts in the European jungle for the economic and social ills plaguing the Union. But since the Franco-German motor is clearly kaput, we want to see you building a new one. More than ever, Europe needs leaders with a sense of purpose and vision, who can inspire our citizens to maximise their potential and opportunity. If not you, then who?

With or without this Constitution, you can improve the way the Union operates and communicates. Here are just three ways: the Council could and should be more open, legislating in public, respecting freedom of information; justice and home affairs policy could and should be decided by the normal Community method, as provided for in the existing treaties; the European Parliament could and should be given a real say on international agreements. Those three steps would help to rebuild confidence in the European project.

At the European Council, you need an answer from Chirac and Balkenende about whether this Constitution will ever be ratifiable in their countries and if not, what kind of text might be. We need a treaty for a Union of 27 Member States, but in the meantime there is much you can do to rebuild on the basis of the current treaties and restore public faith in the European project.'

## You Only Get Out What You Put In

*Speech to the European Parliament in Strasbourg on Europe's long-term financial perspectives and December's European Council meeting. The British Presidency of the EU was responsible for concluding negotiations on the EU budget for 2006-13 but progress had slowed, thanks in part to a reluctance from the UK and five other Member States to commit themselves beyond 1% of Gross National Income. The ten new central and eastern European Member States were likely to be the main losers. Addressing Douglas Alexander, the UK Government's Europe Minister, Graham warns that Europe will only get out of the Union what it puts in - and in a rapidly globalising world we cannot afford to ignore the need for collective solutions to collective problems. The French President, German Prime Minister and British President mentioned in Paragraph Four are, of course, Chirac, Schroeder and Blair.*

*14th December 2005, Strasbourg*

'Two years ago today a letter was written to President Prodi. It bore the signatures of one head of state - President Chirac - and five prime ministers: Balkenende, Blair, Persson, Schröder and Schüssel, four of whom, alas, are still in office today. Signed with poison pens, it is the root of our problems today. That letter called for a limit to EU spending of 1% of gross national income.

Those same heads of state and government simultaneously demanded of the Union policies that they are not prepared to finance. They are Member State leaders who urge on the Union abroad but duck the debate at home; leaders who will the ends, but not the means. Words like 'unacceptable' rarely flow from the very moderate lips of the Commission President, who is reportedly one of Mr Blair's best friends, but the Commission and Parliament must be at one in rejecting a budget that puts the concerns of the accountants above the broader view of the boardroom. I welcome Mr Barroso's letter to the Presidency-in-Office about this week's Council.

For Liberals and Democrats in this House, no deal is better than a bad deal. Liberals and Democrats will not compromise Europe's long-term interests. We will not be implicated in creating a two-tier Europe.

What have the new Member States found in their brave new world? A French President who tells them to shut up, a German Prime Minister who denies them their own tax policies and a British Presidency that moves the goalposts of solidarity. What we expect from the Presidency is a budget that puts long-term strengths and common concerns above individual satisfaction and personal gain. What it seems we will get is a proposal that will paralyse the Union's priorities and satisfy no one.

President-in-Office, 1.03% of gross national income will not pay for our new policies or for enlargement. This House understood that when we estimated the future financial needs at 1.08% of GNI, and that was a conservative estimate. What about money for challenges, such as security? What about the ambitions of the Lisbon Agenda? Five years ago, we said we would raise research spending to 3% of GDP by 2010. It has slipped down even further: to below 2% last year, compared to 2.5% in the USA and over 3% in Japan.

This is not just a budget for tomorrow. It is a framework that will bind us until 2013. It is a budget that must provide for competitiveness and jobs for our young people. It is a budget that must pay for the social solidarity Europe wants. Parliament should reject any Council agreement that does our Union down.

The Presidency has ambitions for a wider Council agenda. I wish you success. My group hopes that you will review the so-called war on terror. Complicity of EU Member States in warfare using depleted uranium and white phosphorous, detention without trial, torture and turning a blind eye to a clampdown on the freedom of millions in countries with whom we cultivate strategic partnerships debases our Union. Two days ago, the General Affairs Council called for a comprehensive approach to combating terrorism while respecting human rights. Liberals and Democrats want the Council to restate the European Union's respect for the rule of law and protection of human rights and fundamental freedoms, and to mean it.'

## A Single Market For A Successful Future

*Speech to the European Parliament in Strasbourg before a crucial vote on the controversial Services Directive to allow more cross-border competition between service providers. Here Graham responds to accusations levelled by the left, particularly their rapporteur Evelyn Gebhardt, that the proposal encourages 'a race to the bottom' - and explains how, instead, it will create more jobs, provide better consumer choice and underpin economic growth in today's competitive climate. In the vote that followed Parliament heavily amended the Commission's draft in a political compromise which, although it fell short of ALDE ideals, represented a satisfactory outcome for most sides. Frits Bolkestein was the Trade Commissioner who proposed the original directive and - in so doing - became the 'bête noire' of the European Socialists, led by Martin Schulz.*

*14th February 2006, Strasbourg*

'I can assure the House that Frits Bolkestein is alive and kicking, and that is why Martin Schulz is looking so bruised these days!

This Parliament must make a choice. Down the route of reform lies a dynamic, competitive Union which creates jobs, wealth and opportunity for its citizens. Down the path of protectionism lies short-term gain for some, and long-term loss for all, especially our 20 million unemployed.

(Applause)

70% of Europe's economy and workforce relies on a healthy service sector, a sector being slowly strangled by a mindless mass of regulation.

Mrs Gebhardt says 'think of small businesses'. It is because we think of them that we want the country of origin principle. 90% of service companies are SMEs. The country of origin principle allows them to assess, and then to test a foreign market. They send people over to do market research. Then they trade to test it before setting up an office or a subsidiary. Doing away with the country of origin principle reduces the growth effects of this measure by half.

Liberals and Democrats favour a search for compromise, but compromise between mutually exclusive policies is no compromise. We call it the 'Berlin blockage'. This directive does not usher in social dumping. If they are in any doubt, Mr Schulz and Mr Rasmussen should read the 1996 directive on the posting of workers. It is still in force. Rather, the draft before us transforms principles like the free market of goods, services, capital and people into reality for 450 million people. These are founding principles of our Union which are simply not compatible with second-class citizenship for our new Member States.

Certainly there will be hard decisions to take, but our task is not to protect one sector over another. It is to legislate for the good of the European economy as a whole. If we can create a single market in services to rival our single market in goods, we can raise GDP by nearly 2% and create up to 2.5 million new jobs. That is what Frits Bolkestein wanted for Europe. To allow Member States to justify barriers to service provision on the basis of social policy and consumer protection would drive a lance through the heart of his proposal. However, we would not be contemplating such an emasculation of draft legislation if Mr Barroso and his Commissioners had defended their draft directive instead of tilting at windmills.

Does Commissioner McCreevy believe that his cabinet's lobbying of Parliament last week advanced the case for Europe's single market? Does he not know that paragraph 3 in compromise amendment 293 is contrary to ECJ jurisprudence and the Treaty's provision on the free movement of services? I hope, Commissioner McCreevy, that you will answer that point in your reply. No, rather than showing the way, this Commission cowers in the shadows of public opinion and Member States' hesitation.

Greater productivity, more jobs, higher wages, stronger companies: these are all within our grasp and that is why I urge the House to vote to make Europe a dynamic marketplace for jobs and services.'

## Never Be Afraid Of Telling The Truth

*Speech to a European Parliament seminar marking International Women's Day. After EU Membership negotiations opened with Turkey in October 2005 Parliament's attention has been focussed on monitoring Human Rights developments in the country. Here Graham examines the progress and challenges confronting Turkish women as they strive for gender equality - and reflects on areas where the EU still lags behind, notably in the promotion of women to the highest positions of the government and legal system.*

*8th March 2006, Brussels*

"Ties between Turkey and Europe have rarely been as close as they are today - nor the prospects for co-operation greater. I am referring not just to October's historic decision to open the EU accession process after decades of negotiation - though that is the greatest concrete symbol of this bond. I am alluding also to Liberal values of freedom, democracy, and Human Rights which are increasingly shared on either side of the Aegean.

For history teaches us that we are "In uno plures" - many in one. Before wars and walls drove our continent asunder Europe's rich and varied mosaic encompassed citizens of the West, the Ottoman and the Austro-Hungarian Empires. What joins us together now are the fundamental values enjoined by the Treaties and demonstrated through fulfilment of the Copenhagen Criteria as opposed to any dominant religion, ethnicity, or culture. Turkey can have a place in this Europe of Values, as Liberals and Democrats have long argued. Perhaps that is because Liberalism is a philosophy capable of straddling cultural difference and embracing plurality by seeking to free individuals from theocracy, oppression, poverty and the social pressure to conform.

In that regard Turkey has come a long way since it first applied for full membership of the EEC in 1987. A virtual tidal wave of legislation has revolutionised the country's legal landscape, from abolition of the death penalty, to establishing a woman's inalienable right to work and perhaps most significantly bringing Turkey's Penal Code and Constitution largely into line with international norms.

However I say largely because I mean largely. Ataturk used to say, "never be afraid of telling the truth." The Turkey that will join the European Union is not the Turkey of today but the Turkey of tomorrow. It will be a nation founded fully on the rule of law, human rights and religious freedom, which has had the courage to break with militarist tradition and to stabilise relations with its ethnic minorities and its neighbours.

While the Government has successfully implemented a number of reforms adopted in 2002 and 2003, reduced incidences of torture and ill-treatment of detainees, and even allowed the start-up of Kurdish language courses and broadcasting - albeit under tight restrictions - there is still a long way to go.

I am particularly concerned about Article 301 of the new Penal Code which prohibits denigration of Turkishness, the Republic, and the foundation and institutions of the State - and poses a serious threat to freedom of expression. Only in December last year an Istanbul Court sentenced Fatih Tas to six months imprisonment for publishing the book 'They Say You are Missing'. And while the case against Orhan Pamuk has finally been dropped I would reiterate Amnesty International's concerns that those of lesser-known individuals like Murat Belge and Ismet Berkan may continue in relative obscurity.

Should Turkey lack the political will to allow intellectuals to analyse and criticise its historical past, reach a comprehensive settlement on the Cyprus issue and fully respect Human Rights - especially the rights of and its Kurdish minority and of women it can never accede to the European Union. The fact that it is International Women's Day should concentrate our minds on the latter.

I sincerely hope we witness no repeat of last year's brutality, when the Istanbul police broke up a demonstration to mark International Women's

Day. There is no place for such violence in Modern Turkey. No state violence and no domestic violence. In this, Turkey's record is a national scandal. Amnesty International estimates that half of all Turkish women may be victims of violence, often perpetrated in the name of family 'honour'. Millions have been beaten in their homes and many others raped, killed and even forced to commit suicide.

Pleased as we must all be that the Turkish government passed legislation mandating tougher penalties for domestic abuse, protection for battered women and the creation of more shelters there is still a major implementation gap. These women have literally nowhere to go. For a population of 70 million, there exist only 13 women's shelters. Add to this the fact that more than half a million girls do not attend school each year and political representation amongst women in Turkey remains at a worryingly low 4.4% and there are serious implications for Turkey's EU dream.

To a Liberal Democrat, gender equality is not a "woman's problem". A freer, society - like that which Turkey is building - is one where every citizen enjoys the maximum scope for self-development, encouraged but not obliged to participate in society, guided but not shepherded by the State. We agree with the Ottoman writer Narik Kemal who - 140 years ago - wrote "women are not inferior to men in their intellectual and physical capacities. In ancient times they shared in all men's activities, including even war. In the countryside they still share in the work of agriculture and trade. Many evil consequences result from their social position, the first being that it leads to a bad upbringing for their children".

That is why today's Hearing 'Women in Turkey - Progress and Challenges' is so important. I am looking forward to learning from our distinguished speakers what role female participation in business and the workplace is playing in elevating the status of women. It may well be that the EU has something to learn from the Turkish experience in this area- especially since it was Turkey that appointed the world's first female Supreme Court justice. Indeed, female emancipation has been one of the major tenets of the Modern Turkish state ever since its inception, when Ataturk's reforms abolished polygamy, recognized the equal rights of women in divorce, custody, and inheritance and made the entire educational system co-educational. A process which culminated in the election of Tansu Ciller as Prime Minister in 1993 - only 14 years after Margaret Thatcher and light years ahead of the USA, which has still never had a female head of executive.

Europe does have a tendency to crow about its achievements even though the wage gap between men and women in Europe is anywhere between 16 and 33%. In fact, on 8th March last year the European Parliament was moved to pass a resolution condemning the total lack of progress in implementing the principle of equal pay for equal work introduced thirty years ago by Directive 75/117/EEC. As someone who has spent much of his life in the corporate world I firmly believe that of the thousand and one areas in which society must learn to give women their due, none is so important as the dignity and independence that comes from freedom to work, and be paid, as equals. And as someone who has spent the remaining portion of his life in politics, I understand that there can be no true democracy without gender equality.

Without women involved in politics we won't get enough of the policies that women want and need. I am sure that the organiser of this event, Karin Riis-Jorgensen MEP (and one of the 3 women Vice Presidents of ALDE) will have more to say on this matter. So without wishing to preserve any longer the stereotype of an older white male dominating proceedings, I will close my introductory remarks by welcoming all the participants and wishing you all a happy and productive International Women's Day. And by recognising publicly that while the cock does the crowing it is invariably the hen who delivers the goods.'

## Kosovo Lies Firmly At The Heart Of Europe

*Speech to an ELDR Conference on the Future Status of Kosovo which involved many senior politicians, embassy staff and journalists from the Balkans and beyond. Kosovo legally forms part of Serbia but - since the war ended in 1999 - has been administered and protected by the United Nations. The EU's main influence to date has been through the Stabilisation and Association Process for integration - however many issues remain outstanding, particularly Visa Facilitation, which was the subject of tense debate at this time. Here Graham makes the case for national self-determination within the context of EU Membership as the most effective way to bring peace and prosperity to this troubled region. However the EU has now effectively put the brakes on further enlargement until a new Constitution is in place.*

*8th April 2006, Council of Europe*

'Je voudrais tout d'abord saluer la présence de tant d'amis du groupe ADLE de l'Association Parlementaire du Conseil de l'Europe dans ce magnifique palais sous le beau soleil printanier de Strasbourg.

History teaches us that Europeans are "In uno plures" - many in one. We are in the process of building a Union of peoples that will run from the Black Sea to the Atlantic and the Arctic Circle to the Mediterranean - maybe even further. The Balkans, more than any other region, reflect this historic diversity of which Kosovo is a potent symbol - Slavic and Albanian peoples have co-existed in Kosovo since the 8th century. It's also a diversity reflected by today's participants who join us from across Europe - many of whom have travelled from Kosovo, Serbia-Montenegro and neighbouring Balkan states to share their experiences and expertise with us.

To our colleagues from Kosovo, as one of the hosts of this conference, I would like to extend a very special welcome and point out that today's conference, interventions, and ideas should be interpreted as nothing more than efforts to understand the developments in your region. And to show Liberal Democratic solidarity with you on the road to EU Membership. We are firm believers in the prospect of eventual EU Membership as the greatest single incentive for peace and reform in the Balkan Region. Including for an independent Kosovo, should that prove the outcome of the talks and the wish of the Kosovar people.

Let me kick off by exposing an emerging myth - many of you may have heard reports that the European Parliament is becoming increasingly hostile to further enlargement. Certainly, some Members of the EPP and Socialists, notably the Germans, have started to wobble on the issue. A German MEP called Elmar Brok, in particular, received far too much media coverage for opinions which do not, and I repeat, do not reflect Parliament's overall view. Indeed, the resolution adopted recently by the EP says little more than that the EU should live up to commitments made and improve its own functional capacity.

Not only does the ALDE Group remain a vocal proponent of the enlargement process, but we are supported by a broad majority within the European Parliament who believe that the EU must honour its commitments to the countries of the Balkans. It is now up to Europe's parliamentarians to overcome internal difficulties and move the agenda forwards in line with the Thessaloniki Process and firmly reject much-publicised German proposals on a new form of a multilateral co-operation with the Western Balkans.

As former leader of the Liberal Democrats Paddy Ashdown warned recently, "the promise of membership in the EU is the "glue" that holds the Balkans to the path of reform and stabilisation". Progress achieved to date is by no means irreversible. Disillusionment with the accession process poses a real risk to the security of the region. Visa facilitation, in particular, has become a burning issue. The EU's credibility is being steadily eroded by the humiliating procedures we demand of our own neighbours - and of the long queues of silent desperation that stand waiting outside our consulates. I personally find it scandalous that the EU is on the verge of starting talks on visa facilitation with Russia, while nothing similar is foreseen for the Western Balkans. My colleagues on the EPs civil liberties committee are currently taking a close look at visa issues and trying to promote progress at inter-governmental level.

It is clear that the European Union must renew its commitment to ensuring long-term peace and security for Kosovo, and the Balkan region as a whole. That is why I am particularly pleased by plans for an ambitious "rule of law" mission in Kosovo, that would provide assistance on the ground from EU police and support a strong and effective justice system. We are already doing this in Bosnia, on a more limited scale, but the draft plans are much more ambitious - with a yearly cost of approximately 80-100 million - compared to the 38 million spent annually on the Bosnia police mission.

However we should recall that ultimate responsibility for reform, progress and prosperity lies not with the EU, nor with the International Community, but with citizens and politicians throughout the region. Europe can provide inspiration and guidance, funding and assistance - but change can only come about locally. In the Kosovan context that means ensuring Minority Rights for the c.100 000 strong Serb population while in the context of the wider region it means improving cross border trade and cooperation. Economic stability is one of the bed-rocks of a successful state. It is an oft-stated fact that Liberal Democracies rarely, if ever, go to war with each other. For free trade helps create reciprocal links between opposing parties and pull people out of poverty - both essential preconditions for a stable and successful future for the Balkans.

Let me share with you a few thoughts on the issue that has brought all of us here today - the future status of Kosovo. Current international thinking indicates that while Serbia irrefutably lost its claim to sovereignty thanks to its terrible treatment of Kosovar Albanians throughout the 1990's, failure to secure basic minority rights for remaining Serbs seriously weakens Kosovan demands for independence.

How to square this circle - without repeating the mistakes of Dayton in Bosnia-Herzegovina - is to my mind the most interesting issue we should consider today. In particular, how do we allow the Serbs around

Mitrovica and the Albanians in the Prejeva valley to maintain links with Belgrade and Pristina respectively, notably in culture and education?

In this context I would like to recall the joint report presented in June last year by Javier Solana and Olli Rehn, which explicitly stated that "Kosovo cannot return to the situation before March 1999 and that Belgrade and Pristina must move on further towards Euro-Atlantic integration". Our aim must be to create a situation where people think of themselves first and foremost not in ethnic terms but as Kosovars - and as citizens of a diverse and plural Europe. That is why I fear that any attempt to deny Kosovo independence puts short-term considerations before long-term aspirations. Kosovan citizens have a legitimate right to live in peace and to aspire to the quality of life enjoyed by their fellow Europeans. This requires pro-European political leadership in Kosovo.

Only the promise of EU Membership can achieve the kind of cultural transformation necessary to realise this dream. The European Union is all about a Union without borders - sweeping away the nationalism and ethnic conflicts of the past. The nation state, while still an important player in EU governance, will matter less and less in a globalised world. Europe's peoples must learn to live side by side without wearing a nationalistic badge on their breasts. That is the future for peace. That is the future for Europe.'

cannot ratify in current circumstances. The Czech Republic and Poland choose not to ratify, and Portugal will find it almost impossible, while committed to a referendum.

So there are two options: renegotiation or oblivion. The sooner we take steps to make structural and substantive improvements to that text and address public concern, the better.

President Barroso, I welcome the vision and determination you are showing today. But I want to hear you say that louder and more often to the Member States. You are right - they are all shareholders in the enterprise, but they have been gripped by a fad for short-termism, and anyway the markets are falling. We need to hammer home to the Member States just how much they need the European Union.

My group thanks the Austrian Presidency for its good work thus far. We wish you success with other important items on your agenda: migration and other aspects of the Hague Programme; social and economic policy; the fundamental rights agency that we so badly need. Make sure too that our Foreign Ministers have aid to Palestine and CIA renditions on their agenda. The fine wines that you served them at Klosterneuburg were a good aperitif. They now need to sit down to the meat.'

## Treat Your Neighbour As Yourself

*Speech made to the European Parliament in Strasbourg on Bulgaria and Romania's progress towards EU Membership. The Commissioner for Enlargement, Olli Rehn, had just presented a progress report stating no final decision on accession in 2007 would be taken until the Autumn, by which time they would be expected to address certain areas of serious concern. Here Graham welcomes this analysis but expresses concern that Romania and Bulgaria be treated no more or less harshly than previous applicants - particularly by those populists pandering to fashionable 'enlargement anxiety'. Boagiu and Kuneva are the EU Affairs Minister and Chief Accession Negotiator for Romania and Bulgaria respectively. Commission President Barroso formally announced that both countries had met the targets for 2007 accession in September 2006. The 'secret services' remark refers to events in Britain and France at that time.*

*16th May 2006, Strasbourg*

'I would like to pay tribute to Commissioner Rehn for his balanced and thorough assessment and his competent handling of this dossier. I also commend Anca Boagiu and Meglena Kuneva and their predecessors as Ministers for EU Integration for their unstinting hard work.

The author Mark Twain observed, 'We can change the world or ourselves, but the latter is more difficult'. Tearing down the Berlin Wall was the easy part. Building a new democratic culture takes much longer. But the bricks of effort and the mortar of persistence are working. The decision to proceed in 2007, with appropriate provisos, is the right one. The Commission should not, in my group's view, revisit its decision in the autumn, except in the gravest of circumstances.

We are concerned that Romania and Bulgaria should be judged no more or less harshly than previous newcomers. Our monitoring must be in line with current treaty provisions and legislation in force. We therefore take very seriously the Commission's expression of serious concern about continuing corruption and failure of the rule of law - areas which need urgent further action. Ill treatment of Romany people, too, continues to offend, which is why the Decade of Roma Inclusion launched by six heads of state and government is so important.

In many other areas the Commission identifies failings. These must be put right without delay. But accession cannot be an examination in which candidates fail. For failure would be at least as much a failure of the Union as of the candidate states. What is most important to the health of a society is the direction in which its face is set. Bulgaria and Romania are looking and moving in the right direction. Can that be said of all current Member States? Imagine, colleagues, that last autumn Romania's Interior Minister had proposed detention of suspects for three months without charge or that the Bulgarian Prime Minister had used the secret services to spy on his colleagues. There would have been outrage.

My group has always been wary of those who would pander to the fashionable anxiety about enlargement, making strangers of peoples who will soon be fellow citizens. I was delighted, therefore, to hear that Mr Poettering has defied some in his own party and thrown his weight firmly behind future enlargement. It gives added salience to his group's decision to meet last week in a city called Split.

I appeal to the faint hearts on the right to look at what has been achieved. Has not enlargement been the European Union's greatest success story, its crown jewels? Commissioner Spidla's report on transitional arrangements shows that enlargement has brought more jobs and higher economic growth, particularly in those countries that gave open access to their labour markets. But far beyond economic considerations, welcoming new Members has enriched the culture of our Union. Bulgaria and Romania will be treasured assets, if only we give them half a chance.

It seems that many of their people believe it is all a matter for government. On the contrary, winning the war against crime and corruption is a matter for each and every citizen. So I urge all Bulgarians and Romanians to work together with government to ensure the best possible outcome and avoid any delay to entry, not least because reform demanded to join the Union is the means to raise standards of living, quality of life, and security at home. I urge all colleagues in this House to show solidarity and demonstrate to the Bulgarians and the Romanians that they do not walk alone.'

July 2004 - With new partners Francois Bayrou (Leader of French UDF) and
Romano Prodi at the launch of the ALDE Group in Brussels

July 2004 - The ALDE Group backing Bronislaw Geremek's campaign for
leadership of the European Paliament.

January 2005 - Graham Watson MEP encounters the robot ASIMO in the
European Parliament.

May 2005 - Graham supporting the UDF's 'YES' Campaign for the
Referendum on the proposed new EU Constitution.

Summer 2005 - Gathering cloud berries on holiday with wife Rita and children
Frederica and Gregory in Sweden.

*Neil Corlett*

June 2005 - With the British Liberal Democrat MEPs in the European Parliament in Strasbourg.

*Neil Corlett*

July 2005 - Graham signs the 'Make Poverty History' ribbon draped around the European Parliament hemicycle, or debating chamber, in Strasbourg.

Autumn 2005 - UK Prime Minister Tony Blair accepts Graham's invitation to hear the Somerset Youth Choir in Strasbourg during the UK Presidency of the EU.

October 2005 - European Agriculture Commissioner Mariann Fischer Boel visits a bio-fuel project in Somerset, a county in Graham's constituency.

# Liberty And Security

*This chapter seeks to link those areas of policy brought into focus by the so-called 'War on Terror', namely liberty, security and justice. Prior to 9-11 the level of international cooperation on such issues was extremely low, due to a lack of political will and popular suspicion about relinquishing any national control over policy decisions. Since 2001's terrorist outrages the climate has changed considerably leading to proliferation of trans-European, transatlantic and global agreements designed to crack down on international terrorism and organised crime. Where these policies lack proportion and violate fundamental values, however, Liberals and Democrats have raised their voices in a debate on the proper limits of power traced through this collection of speeches. Graham Watson was chair of the European Parliament's Justice and Home Affairs Committee from 1999-2002 and, consequently, rapporteur for the package of anti-terrorism measures, including the European Arrest Warrant, which are debated in the speeches that follow.*

\*\*\*\*\*\*\*\*\*\*\*\*\*\*\*\*\*\*\*\*\*\*\*\*\*\*\*\*\*\*\*\*\*\*\*\*\*\*\*\*\*\*\*\*\*\*\*\*\*\*\*\*\*\*\*\*\*\*\*\*

## Global Laws For A Global Village

*Speech to the European Parliament in Strasbourg on the establishment of the International Criminal Court in The Hague. A long-time Liberal Democrat priority, the ICC - which became operational in January 2003 - acts as a permanent tribunal to prosecute individuals for genocide, crimes against humanity, and war crimes. Here Graham praises the step-change in global governance represented by the ICC, but points out that principles are no substitute for political will if it is to obtain results - especially given America's refusal to ratify the Rome Statute alongside Israel, Iran, and China.*

*25th September 2002, Strasbourg*

'The establishment of the ICC marks a huge step forward in enforcing, at a global level, the principle of the rule of law which is fundamental to all liberal democracies. While ad hoc tribunals, such as those for Rwanda and the former Yugoslavia, are doing invaluable work, there is no substitute for a permanent court with the mandate and legitimacy to prosecute criminals wherever they may hide. We need only look at Croatia's refusal to hand over General Bobetko to The Hague on the grounds that Croatia was not the aggressor, to see the problems which can arise.

In negotiations on the Rome Statute, Europe bent over backwards to achieve an outcome which would accommodate American concerns. It is therefore a matter of deep regret to Liberal Democrats in this House that a number of countries have refused to sign the Rome Statute for the ICC. These countries include Iran, Iraq, North Korea and the United States. If we follow the old adage 'you will be judged by the company you keep', what message does the USA's presence in this group of refusniks send to the world? Especially when taken in conjunction with America's disavowal of the Kyoto protocol, the UN Convention on the Rights of the Child and the Biological Weapons Convention. It is bad enough that the USA is refusing to ratify the Rome Statute, but to try to strangle it at birth by reaching bilateral agreements with countries such as Israel and Romania in order to prevent its nationals being surrendered to the ICC is terrible.

UN Security Council Resolution 1422 also sets a dangerous precedent and should not be renewed next July. The European Union should do its utmost to avoid undermining the ICC before it has even begun its work. I therefore urge the President-in-Office of the Council to recognise the storm-clouds gathering over this issue and to pull the EU Member States together under one umbrella. In an age of instability it is understandable that the EU wishes to avoid a breakdown in transatlantic relations, but any agreement with the USA must be supported by all EU countries and be consistent with the Rome Statute. Another failure on our part to show unity would further undermine the EU's credibility in foreign affairs.

We must get our own house in order. The countries wishing to join us, including the Czech Republic, Lithuania and Malta, must understand that the values the ICC represents are fundamental to the European

Union, and that speedy ratification of the Rome Statute would prevent any delay in their accession. We urge Romania not to ratify its bilateral agreement with the USA, and it is also important for the Union to act together within the ICC in terms of financial support and the appointment of judges, the prosecutor and staff. By acting together, Europe can contribute greatly to making the ICC work, and thereby reassure the USA that the Court is serious and poses no threat to their law-abiding nationals. We must work to bring the Americans on board at a later date. Neither government must forget that we are accountable to the court of world public opinion.

In conclusion, Madam President, the ICC is a symbol of the world for which we strive - a world in which human rights and international law will be upheld everywhere, and most of all, a world in which no shelter will be given to those guilty of the vilest crimes. Let us work together to enable the court to get off to a flying start when it becomes operational in January.'

## Europe's Defence Deficiencies

*Speech to the European Parliament in Strasbourg on the priorities for, and deficiencies of, Europe's joint defence capabilities. The Iraq war - which had begun on March 19th - showed up the cracks in Europe's largely make-shift approach to foreign policy, particularly in regard to transatlantic relations, with Germany and France pursuing different strategies to Britain, Spain, Italy and many Eastern European countries. Here Graham reflects on the need for better defence spending and stronger decision making to maximise Europe's influence in matters of global importance.*

*9th April 2003, Strasbourg*

'This report could hardly be more timely. If - as seems likely - US and British Forces are now in control of Baghdad, then the debate on the aftermath of war and its lessons can now commence. Unlike its predecessors, the current American administration shows little interest in a strong and united Europe. Our weakness has been cruelly exposed and the onus is on the EU to develop a security strategy which may help us reshape transatlantic relations. Liberal Democrats in this House welcome the Morillon report as an important contribution to this process.

Europe's divisions over Iraq have been a stark reminder of our failure to speak with one voice on security policy, and yet we should not forget that Europe does have a single trade policy, a common development policy and an embryonic European diplomatic corps in the form of the Commission's offices around the world. These are powerful instruments and would be all the more so if combined as part of an integrated foreign policy.

Our foreign policy is incoherent because it is split between three Commissioners, the Council presidency and a Council High Representative, and because some Member States deny our essential commonality of interests in foreign policy, or forbid the Commission to play a central executive role. Without a common defence policy, Europe will still lack the military muscle needed for a credible common foreign policy. With combined defence spending less than half of that of the USA, it is clear the EU is not spending enough on defence, nor would our citizens be likely to welcome much higher levels of spending.

So it is not enough simply to spend more: we need to spend better, especially on key requirements such as strategic airlift, precision guided weapons and air tankers. That is why the Liberal Group supports the establishment of an armaments and research agency to coordinate defence spending. What we want is to achieve better value for money, and if EU countries agree that military equipment made outside the EU best meets our needs and provides best value for money, we should not choose a European option in a misguided attempt at protectionism. That would be to repeat the mistakes of the common agricultural policy.

Better defence spending must be accompanied by stronger decision-making. By sending to the European Convention, through General Morillon's report, a clear and united message in favour of a strong and effective security and defence policy, Parliament can hope to influence its deliberations. Having one external affairs representative, based in the Commission but supplemented with resources and expertise from the Member States, will go a long way towards connecting the disparate elements of foreign and security policy.

We also need greater flexibility in launching and conducting crisis management operations, if necessary by greater recourse to constructive abstention. While there are clearly reservations about this, introducing a collective defence clause in the new Constitutional Treaty, similar to that under the Western European Union Treaty, also seems a necessary step.

It may be that progress towards these goals cannot be made at once with the 15, let alone with 25 Member States. That is why I welcome the Belgian Government's initiative for a meeting later this month with France, Germany and Luxembourg, on defence policy. Progress in European integration is often only achieved by a group of determined countries pressing ahead, with others joining later. Nonetheless I insist that enhanced cooperation on defence must remain open to all governments who wish to join, and that the British Government in particular, given its military capability and experience, will do so.

A European security and defence policy can usefully complement the collective security provided by NATO as long as there is rationalisation of arms procurement, added value in the form of a doctrine based on conflict prevention and crisis management and backed by the credible threat of military action, and a more coherent and unified approach to security policy. Let our security and defence policy be forged on the anvil of hope from the steel of our embarrassment over Iraq.'

## The Road To Hell Is Paved With Good Intentions

*Speech to the European Parliament in Strasbourg on the EU-USA extradition agreement. While supporting a robust and effective response to terrorism, Graham warns against a slide away from democracy and demands proper parliamentary scrutiny on lop-sided security measures favouring the US, particularly in the absence of any US agreement to abide by the rulings of the International Criminal Court. Later that year the Council concluded two agreements with the US on extradition without further democratic input which have not yet been implemented, pending a decision by the US senate.*

*14th May 2003, Strasbourg*

'18 months ago when I had the honour to serve as chairman of the Committee on Citizens' Freedoms and Rights, Justice and Home Affairs, this House adopted a resolution on judicial cooperation between the Union and the USA. That resolution set out four key requirements for any extradition agreement: full respect for the European Convention on Human Rights; no extradition of persons likely to face military tribunals; no extradition if the accused risks facing the death penalty; and that any measures affecting data protection should be proportionate, effective and time-limited.

The terrorist outrages in Saudi Arabia on Monday night once again remind us that terrorism still poses a deadly serious threat. We need a robust and effective response. However, the Liberal Democrats in this House insist that anti-terrorism measures must always respect fundamental rights and be subject to proper democratic oversight and control. Striking the right balance is essential to success in fighting those who seek to undermine the fabric of democratic societies.

The current draft agreements between the EU and the US on extradition and legal cooperation must not escape the parliamentary scrutiny provided for in our Treaties. They concern 'fundamental choices' within the meaning of Article 21. They fall not only under Article 38 but also under Article 24, and it is scandalous that the Council does not consult this House in advance on all the Article 24 agreements.

In France, the Conseil d'Etat has refused the Assemblée Nationale the right to approve such agreements: so unless the Council consults us, what parliamentary scrutiny exists in the European Union?

These agreements on extradition and legal co-operation are very ambitious. The United States declines to sign the UN conventions on cybercrime, on crime prevention and on the International Criminal Court. In the Union, Member States have not yet ratified our decision on money laundering or the framework directive on terrorism. Yet these proposals cover the whole Palermo agenda. They should at the very least provide for the establishment of bodies to oversee their operation and provide feedback.

I can only regret that this agreement makes no reference to the International Criminal Court. I would urge the Council to rectify this. The Council must seek to reconcile the potential conflict between a request from the ICC to surrender a person to the court and the obligation stemming from this extradition agreement.

The slide away from democracy can start with the best of intentions. The European Union must guard against it. Do not let the Council's haste facilitate it.'

## An Unlikely Experiment In Global Governance

*Speech to the European Parliament on 29 January 2004, in honour of 2003's Sakharov Prize winner - UN Secretary General Kofi Annan. The Prize, which is named after Soviet scientist and dissident Andrei Sakharov, was established in December 1985 by the European Parliament as a means to honour individuals or organizations who had dedicated their lives to the defence of human rights and freedoms. In his valedictory address, Graham concurs with Kofi Annan's demand for a humane migration policy, but stipulates that this must be accompanied by reform of the mechanisms of multinational governance, in particular the United Nations, to tackle war and underdevelopment at their source.*

*29th January 2004, Brussels*

'Liberals in this house have often echoed your words on immigration. We recognise the value that immigrants bring to Europe and we understand that closing Europe's front door will only drive the desperate to seek access through the back. We have consistently argued that a Europe of security and justice for all is a Europe that extends those rights to those who justly seek a new life here.

Your words today remind us of the power of the United Nations to transcend the parochial in all of us. The United Nations has a precious power to speak for us all.

That is why my group wishes to see the return of the United Nations to Iraq as soon as the security situation allows. The introduction of credible and legitimate democratic government in Iraq is not possible without the presence of the United Nations. We want a political settlement in Iraq that guarantees the highest standards of civil and political rights for all Iraqis.

The United Nations was founded by the same generation who founded this European Union - "to save succeeding generations from the scourge of war, which twice in our lifetime has brought untold sorrow to mankind". Like this Union it believes that the closer we sit at the table of peace and prosperity, the slower we will be to reach for tools of war. It is a sorry testament to a stubborn world that the UN still seems such an unlikely experiment in international governance.

Winston Churchill once said that the UN is not designed to take us to heaven but to save us from hell. Although there is no place in the UN's future for misplaced idealism, that is not in itself an argument against reform. As its largest contributors, the EU and its Member States have not only the weight to insist on reform but the responsibility to do so.

A mature Europe would find the political will to put behind it an institutional settlement at the UN that leaves power where it lay in 1945. A mature Europe would insist on a permanent membership that reflected the new realities of the twenty first century. It would accept that the current veto is a tool of obstruction, a political privilege that can no longer be justified.

Finally, on behalf of the Liberal Group allow me to pay tribute to the members of your organisation who will not see you take this prize in their name today. While no life lost in Iraq counts more than any other, the death of Sergio Vierra de Mello was a tragic loss. The UN staff that lost their lives with him - including Fiona Watson who was known to me - died defending a vision of national renewal in Iraq that is now our duty.'

## Is Big Brother Watching Us?

*Speech to a Biometrics Seminar in Brussels in March 2004, seven months before the US introduced visa requirements on all European citizens not in possession of biometric passports containing an electronic storage chip and digital photograph. Graham uses this forum to insist that such technology should not be allowed to proliferate in Europe without appropriate safeguards to ensure data security and personal privacy. All EU Member States were to introduce biometric passports by October 2006, following US pressure on air travellers. However, high-profile parliamentary debate on data protection has ensured that this deadline has been extended and additional pressure put on the Bush administration to modify its demands.*

*2nd March 2004, Brussels*

'I am particularly glad that the ELDR is able to host this public hearing, because its subject is both important and topical. After October 26 this year, every one of us who wishes to travel to the United States will need to have a visa if they do not have a passport that contains biometric data. These proposals raise serious questions of cost, reliability and privacy, and it is far from clear that these are outweighed by the potential security benefits. We are fortunate to have with us today Commissioner Vitorino, who has overseen the Commission's proposed response to these new requirements, and Ole Sorensen, the ELDR's rapporteur on the European Parliament's report on the proposals.

To be an advocate of data protection and privacy in March 2004 is to be confronted with two challenges. The first technological, the second political. Computerised data storage, and now digital data storage and recall, have dramatically increased the ease with which information on individuals can be stored, transferred and recalled. Predictably, governments have seen this technology as a way of monitoring the movement of people and controlling information about them. As anyone who has seen his or her old cardboard file from the Stasi or MI6 knows, our governments have not suddenly become more interested in doing this: the technology has simply put it within their reach for the first time.

The temper of political debate on privacy in the US and Europe has been badly affected by the events of September 11 and the problem of international terrorism. The frantic attempts to fix the mistakes of September 11 seem almost to have run ahead of a proper analysis of what those mistakes actually were. In particular, the belief that the increased danger of terrorism justifies a more intrusive policy with regard to personal information has taken powerful hold.

Anyone who thinks that biometric technology is likely to make us safer from terrorism should remember that all nineteen of the September 11 hijackers entered the United States in their own names, under their own passports. No amount of biometric identification could have anticipated the threat they represented. The weapon the September 11 hijackers carried was in their heads, and was not listed in their passports.

It is also worth remembering that many of the world's borders and coastlines, like the EU's Mediterranean coast or new Eastern border, remain porous simply by virtue of their great length. Focusing security measures on heavily policed points of international transit like airports may catch tourists or students on overstayed visas, and it will improve the odds of catching internationally mobile criminals, but it will not block less scrutinised routes.

If Europeans are going to need biometric passports in future, we need to be absolutely sure that there are safeguards in place to ensure data security. We use passports to prove our identity and status when moving within the European Union and abroad, and we depend on their reliability and are vulnerable when the information linked to them is recalled and stored and - probably - shared. We need to know who will access to this data and what for.

So it should worry us that there are still many doubts about the effectiveness of this technology and its high cost. Although it is not possible to falsify biometric data, the machinery for assessing it is prone to error. Even for the best technologies a false match or non-match rate of 0.5 or 1% is still routine. This may not sound like a lot but when you remember that Heathrow airport in England handles 1.2 million passengers every seven days that is a potential 10,000 mismatches a week. Given that relatively few private companies are investing heavily in the current technology - when it is all too easy to imagine the potential commercial benefits - it is fair to ask why our governments are not equally circumspect.

So we need to be clear what the debate about biometrics is and is not. It is a debate about privacy; about the extent to which information about ourselves is available to others, and how easily it is available. It is a debate about the extent to which we are willing to put freedom of movement or our rights as citizens in the hands of database technologies and the agencies that interpret the data they store. It is a debate about the high public costs of this technology weighed against the value and greater security that it delivers. It is not simply a debate about intrusive government in the Orwellian sense: if this technology develops as predicted over the coming decades it will be as invasive in the private sector as in the public.

Benjamin Franklin once said that the man or woman who was willing to trade liberty for a little safety deserved neither. We might be willing to concede that we face dangers that Ben Franklin could not have conceived of, but the primacy of personal liberty has not changed. Striking the right balance with biometrics means making sure that we do not purchase a little bit of safety at what we later learn was an unacceptable price in freedom.'

## Eurocop

*Speech to the European Confederation of Police detailing the Liberal Perspective on Justice and Home Affairs. Far from the ironic characterisation of a Liberal as 'a Conservative who hasn't been mugged yet', Graham sets out a tough, Liberal approach to winning the war on crime and terrorism - without resorting to totalitarian tendencies. Cross-border police co-operation, he says, is true to the spirit of the European Treaties and the demands of the modern world. Since this was written, international co-operation has become commonplace with proposals for a Common Asylum Policy set to be taken forward by the end of 2006.*

*12th March 2004, Brussels*

'In the old caricature, a Liberal has no business in a room full of police officers. It is true Liberals have always been suspicious of the power of the state - but no more I am sure than many of you have been in the course of your work. Liberalism has always questioned the reach of the state into our lives. But modern Liberalism has come to understand that both security and justice are to some extent dependent on the state and its instruments. In fact a liberal society is a society based on law: and without effective policing there can be no law. A society built on law needs public, accountable law enforcement. I am sure that as senior police officers you have all had to consider the balance our societies try to strike between individual freedom and collective safety. As EUROCOP's own mandate puts it: keeping the police efficient and effective under democratic control.

EUROCOP's motto is 'security without frontiers requires staff organisations without frontiers', but of course genuine security without frontiers is increasingly demanding that we also build judicial and police tools capable of reaching across national borders. There is an expression in English about 'making a run for the border' that expresses an important truth. If you can outrun the reach of the state, then you can outrun the reach of justice. The modern state has strong borders not just to keep people out, but also to keep them in, keep them where the state's instruments of law can reach them. Law may sometimes seem only an approximation to what we regard as justice, but it is an inescapable truth that the law is the justice we get, for better or for worse. If we want better justice, it is the law and the instruments of the law that we have to change.

Liberals have supported attempts to construct what was called at Maastricht the European Area of Freedom, Security and Justice. We have been firm supporters of EUROPOL and EUROJUST; we backed the enhanced co-operation measures devised after Tampere, including the European Police College. We have argued again and again in the European Parliament that Europe's national political prerogatives too often prevent effective policing in Europe. We see it as the unique strength of the Liberal agenda on justice and legal affairs that it combines a strong understanding of the value of robust law enforcement tools with the highest standards of due process and procedural safeguarding.

Last week's horrific events in Madrid are emblematic of the new challenges of policing in Europe. The explosives used at Atocha station could have originated in Berlin or Sicily, and have been driven to Madrid without ever being submitted to a border check. Those responsible could have fled the jurisdiction of Spanish police without ever showing a passport or even stopping at a border. Enlargement will create a new long Eastern border which will be one of the most porous in the world. Europe's Mediterranean seaboard is already easy to slip across. Freedom of movement in the European Union has dramatically changed the game of law enforcement. Overnight, the opening of Europe's borders handed European criminals an advantage that the State had spent centuries denying them. Europe's jurisdictions may still recognise internal borders, but European citizens and European criminals increasingly do not. The result, as we all know, has been to turn the Spanish costa into a retirement village for European criminals and to hand Europe's most dangerous and mobile criminals -the drug traffickers, the people smugglers and the terrorists - a permanent advantage over the police. How do we police a continent that looks like this? That is a question for which you know the answers as well as I. My job, and the job of the

European Parliament, is making sure that practitioners like yourselves have an influence on the debate at the highest level.

I would like to say a few words about just one Liberal-led initiative in the field of Justice and Home Affairs that I believe is directly relevant to your work. The European Arrest Warrant entered into force on January 1 this year. It is probably the most important innovation in the European criminal justice system since the creation of the area of freedom, security and justice at Maastricht. The Warrant enables a judge in one European state to request the extradition of a suspect in another European State. Rather than dealing with a political extradition process, the requests will pass between European judiciaries. I am proud to have piloted the measure through the European Parliament.

For Liberals the unlimited movement of people throughout continental Europe represents an important and vital freedom. It goes to the heart of the notion of a true single market and a common European home. But it also raises a huge new security and justice challenge. Without legal instruments that can match the new freedom of movement of European criminals we cannot bring them to justice.

So Liberals find themselves on the side of the state. Although we want the power to be handled with care, we believe the European Arrest Warrant is a crucial addition to the criminal justice toolkit in Europe. Although there is still a need for the Commission to clarify in law the procedural safeguards attached to the Warrant, I believe the European Arrest Warrant represents a mature and distinctively Liberal ability to reconcile the competing needs of security and fairness. We handed new powers to European judges - and through them to European police officers like you - but we tried to ensure that those powers were carefully weighted with the highest standards of procedural safeguarding. In fact, the Warrant will actually raise the standards of legal protection required in many European States. I should add, of course, that the seven states that have not yet done so should ratify the warrant immediately.

So Liberals are committed to the state and to working to make the state work better. We want to see European police given the ability to do the job we expect of them. We are constantly asked to weigh the reach of the machinery of government against our personal freedom, against our desire to see justice done, and against our insecurity in the face of an increasingly dangerous world. In your own work I am sure that you all know these dilemmas very well.'

## A Deal Too Far

*Speech made to the European Parliament in Strasbourg on a proposal to store records of air travellers between the EU and the US. Here Graham rejects the plan as 'a deal too far' and calls on Member States to protect the fundamental freedoms of their citizens. Two months later Parliament, under the guidance of ALDE MEP Johanna Boogerd-Quaak, rejected the Passenger Name Record for compromising personal privacy and lacking a sound legal basis. The European Court of Justice ruled in Graham and Parliament's favour in May 2006 and the deal is due to be renegotiated, taking into account MEPs concerns, by the end of 2007.*

*29th March 2004, Strasbourg*

'The Commission is in an unenviable position. Airlines are almost certainly breaking the law on data protection by giving the US authorities confidential information about their passengers. To take action would harm our airlines and may lead to disruption in travel to the US; not to act rides roughshod over individual privacy in the European Union.

The Commission has sought to reach an agreement with the United States. The concerns about this agreement are widespread. They are shared by the Article 29 Committee, and quite possibly by the heads of state and government meeting last weekend, who amended the draft presidency conclusions on this issue. They are very much borne out from this House in this report. In the United States widespread criticism of methods adopted by the government in the fight against terrorism is evident, whether it is to do with the policy of detention without trial or the way in which the heavy hand of the state is being imposed in areas like this.

The Commission's proposed deal on the transfer of data is a deal too far: more information is sought than is strictly necessary; that information can be held too long with no right for the individual to correct it; there is no right to compensation for people denied boarding of aircraft and no legal redress against abuse of personal data by the state. Liberal Democrats believe that it is possible to be tough on terrorism and true to the treaties we have signed on civil liberties. We bow to nobody in our determination to fight terrorism. We urge our Member States to act more effectively. We recognise the need to work with democracies across the Atlantic; but let us do so intelligently, with a response that is measured and proportionate, and not sacrifice our freedoms in our determination to fight those who threaten them.'

## Tough On Terrorism Yet True To The Treaties

*Speech made to the European Parliament in Strasbourg on a proposal to store and share the personal information of travellers flying between Europe and the USA. Here Graham deplores the fact that Parliamentary consent has not been sought on the PNR proposal and criticises the democratic deficit at the heart of the European Union. Parliament referred the case to the European Court of Justice which ruled in its favour in May 2006. Revised legislation is due to be negotiated by the end of 2007 by which time it is hoped that the legislation will fall under the remit of Parliament. The ALDE group is currently campaigning for the implementation of the passerelle or 'bridging clause' to make all security and justice issues a matter for co-decision between Parliament and Council.*

*20th April 2004, Strasbourg*

'I congratulate Mrs Boogerd-Quaak on an excellent report. It is perfectly possible to be both tough on terrorism and true to the Treaties that we have signed on individual freedoms such as privacy. This matter has taken a sorry course. Commission Bolkestein told us on 9 September that progress on the issues had been disappointing. Commissioner Patten has told us tonight that data transfers remain a matter of concern for the Commission. The fact is that there is no real agreement between the European Union and the United States on the scope of data required, on purpose limitation, on data storage periods or on the transfer of data to third countries.

In proposing this amendment, the College of Commissioners should be ashamed of itself. Its proposals would do justice to the authors of the United Kingdom's Official Secrets Act of 1911.

Commissioner Patten, you normally address this House in an open style, almost ad-lib. That is something we welcome. Tonight you read carefully from your script; dare I say with your lips moving faster than those of a policeman giving corrupt evidence. You constructed a quasi-legal case that is no more stable than a house of cards. You can hardly be surprised that you face criticism from all sides of this House.

The Commissioner told us there is no reason for Parliament to reject the entire agreement. The fact is that we are not even being offered the chance to do so. Despite Commissioner Bolkestein's assurance on 9 September that the procedure would involve the European Parliament's assent, as required by Article 300 of the Treaty, neither this Parliament nor national parliaments are being given the chance to comment on this.

This is a disgraceful demonstration of Europe's democratic deficit. We therefore call on the Commission to withdraw this agreement and to replace it with a proper international agreement. Failing that we will have to refer the matter to the European Court of Justice.'

## Civilisation And Its Discontents

*Speech given to the European Parliament in Strasbourg in the wake of July 7th's bombing of the London public transport network. Here Graham warns the UK's Europe Minister, Douglas Alexander, and Commission President Barroso that the EU risks winning the battle on security but losing the war on terror. Measures taken by the British Presidency to undermine civil liberties, he cautions, threaten the very foundations of our society embedded in democracy, human rights, and the rule of law. The recent outcry over illegal CIA renditions and detention without trial - which have provoked further terrorist outrages - would seem to prove this point.*

*7th September 2005, Strasbourg*

'No civilised person could excuse the indiscriminate barbarity which claimed the lives of 52 innocent civilians in London on the morning of 7 July, a city which had only the previous day celebrated the plurality, diversity and tolerance which had won the admiration of the International Olympic Committee and helped award it the 2012 Olympic Games.

Following the terror attacks in Istanbul and Madrid, nobody can deny that terrorism today is a serious challenge for Europe. My Group welcomes the commitment of the UK Presidency and of the Commission to improve policies to strengthen security across the European Union. We are concerned, however, that these policies should be measured, proportionate and value-driven. We do not agree with the President-in-Office when he said in London that the human rights of the victims were more important than the human rights of the terrorists. Human rights are indivisible; freedom and security are not alternatives: they go hand in hand, one enabling the other. As Thomas Paine warned: 'He who would make his own liberty secure must guard even his enemy from oppression; for if he violates this duty, he establishes a precedent that will reach to himself'.

Much as the public may dislike it, suspected terrorists have rights. They have the right to a fair trial. They have the right to be interrogated, not tortured, by the police. They have the right to legal counsel and to representation in a court of law. And, if convicted, they have the right to be imprisoned in a European jail.

There should be no exception for third-country nationals. There is a worrying tendency in Member States to deport people considered to be threatening public order, national security or the rule of law, to countries where they may face torture or worse. It is deeply troubling when the tools of justice and public order themselves violate the European Charter of Human Rights and well-defined international standards. To suspend those values and invoke a form of summary justice would, in the words of the lawyer Cherie Booth 'cheapen our right to call ourselves a civilised society'.

The language of the war on terror leads too easily to the justice of Wyatt Earp and 'High Noon', a point illustrated by the tragic death of Brazilian Jean Charles de Menezes at the hands of the UK authorities on 22 July.

Governments have been all too eager to exploit the fear factor in this matter. In Italy, stop-and-search powers have been given to the armed forces. In Germany, police surveillance in public places has been stepped up. In France, CCTV cameras cover the public transport system. Any of these measures in themselves may be justifiable but, in a climate of fear without proper democratic oversight and control, they foster insecurity. No wonder that faith-hate crime has risen across the European Union and many Muslims feel they are being criminalised.

It would be particularly ill fitting for those of us who were teenagers in democracies in the 1960s - sometimes called the 'freedom generation' - to deny our children the standards of justice for which our colleagues from central, eastern and parts of southern Europe fought so bravely.

Liberals and Democrats agree with the UK Presidency that anti-terrorism measures need to be implemented fully and rapidly. Why are

7 of 24 instruments considered by Justice and Home Affairs ministers on 24 May still not implemented in all Member States? Why are six un-ratified EU conventions still occupying ministerial time, when framework decisions could be more easily implemented and enforced? Why have Europol and Eurojust not been given the capacity to operate? Why has the EU's anti-terrorism coordinator not been allowed the cooperation he deserves from national capitals?

The Council sometimes laments Parliament's objections to security measures that it wants to introduce. But the European Parliament would feel far more comfortable in agreeing to urgent measures if it was satisfied that the Council was operating in the normal framework of democracy. A framework decision on data protection to accompany data retention measures, for example, would overcome the understandable fears of many colleagues that rights are being eroded. A commitment to legislation in the first pillar, with transparent policy-making and guaranteed rights, would enhance the moral standing of Europe's response to terror. A serious commitment to sharing criminal intelligence information - perhaps the biggest challenge - would be welcomed and supported by this House.

The nub of our dilemma is that the State is the main protector of both our security and our liberty. If the European Union is to provide security against supranational threats, it must guarantee liberty supranationally too.

President-in-Office, Commissioner, if you are prepared to work with Parliament in that kind of dialogue, you will have the full support of Liberals and Democrats in this serious challenge of tackling terror.'

## Criminals Can No Longer Outrun The Law

*Speech made to a European Parliament conference involving MEPs and MPs from national parliaments to study how well the European Arrest Warrant was working. When Graham was chairman of the Committee on Citizens' Freedoms and Rights, Justice and Home Affairs he steered the EAW, which allows the arrest and extradition of suspects between Member States, through parliament but expressed reservations at the time about a lack of sufficient safeguards. Here he reiterates his call for the European Council to ratify the Minimal Procedural Guarantees necessary to protect human rights - but insists that the measure has proved Europe's first line of defence against terrorism and cross-border crime in the post-9/11 world. The legality of the European Arrest Warrant was upheld by the European Court of Justice in September 2006 against criticism from a Belgian NGO that it violated prisoner rights. However the work is not yet done. A Framework Directive on Minimal Guarantees in Criminal Proceedings is still sitting in Council, after having been drafted by the Commission and examined by the European Parliament in the form of the Buitenweg Report, 2004.*

*18th October 2005, Brussels*

'In 2001 as Chairman of the European Parliament's Justice and Home Affairs committee and its rapporteur for terrorism, I had the honour of piloting the EAW through this House. I believed then, as I do now, that the European Arrest Warrant offers practical solutions to issues of the greatest concern to Europe's citizens - issues like terrorism and international crime.

Experience has shown that the EAW is Europe's chief asset in the fight against cross-border crime, allowing judicial authorities to reduce the extradition process to an average of 13 days in over half of all cases. 13 days! As opposed to the months that went before. With a maximum wait of 60 days, the arrest warrant is a big improvement. And Member States are using it. With almost 3000 warrants issued, 653 people arrested and 104 surrendered up to September 2004, it's already surpassed extradition in volume terms.

That's not to say there've not been teething problems. In addition to delays in implementation, controversial court decisions cited by Mr Lapinskas have raised concerns that the EAW violates fundamental rights. As a Liberal Democrat I bow to nobody in my concern for Human Rights. Human Right issues were debated when we took this measure through. I can say with confidence however that problems with the EAW are quantitative and not qualitative.

Court decisions in Poland and Germany did not attack the EAW itself but the national laws which failed to use the full reach and flexibility of the EU measure to render the EAW in conformity to their constitutions. The fact that the Poles are considering amendment of Article 55(1) of their constitution as their "highest priority" strongly backs this view. And one look at Austria reveals how it used this leeway to the last millimetre to protect its citizens from extradition - almost to the point where the EAW may never be used there at all. In any case, all Member States are bound by the ECHR and its case-law.

The issue lies not with the EAW, but in a lack of trust and harmonisation which stretches back to my time as Chairman of the Justice and Home Affairs Committee when I insisted on Minimal Procedural Guarantees to avert precisely such problems.

Those have been held up in Council since 2001 and remain un-ratified today, with a Framework Directive sitting at the bottom of the Council's in tray.

That is unacceptable to this House, unacceptable to national parliaments, and unacceptable to Europe's citizens, who are looking to the Council to deliver. I hope we may work with John Denham MP and his colleagues to see progress on Minimal Procedural Guarantees during the UK Presidency. I hope too that tomorrow's launch of a European Civil Liberties Network will help increase public pressure for civil liberties safeguards at EU level."

## Tackling Crisis On A Wing And A Prayer

*Speech given to the European Parliament in Strasbourg on the Israel-Lebanon conflict which claimed over 1000 lives in the summer of 2006. As EU Member States prepared to send up to 7000 troops to join the United Nations force in Southern Lebanon Graham applauds their efforts - but reminds Javier Solana that, without proper institutional backing, Europe's foreign and security policy is based on a wing and a prayer. Long term peace, he argues, can only come with long term strategies linking Europe to Israel and the Arab World and encouraging mutual interdependence. Mr Tuomioja, referred to below, was Finland's Foreign Affairs Minister who had introduced the debate during Finland's EU Presidency 2006.*

*6th September 2006, Strasbourg*

"This summer's conflict has claimed the lives of over 1000 people, the vast majority of whom were innocent civilians. It has reduced much of Lebanon to rubble. If the situation teaches us nothing else, it must teach us to look forward, rather than back.

We should waste no time in deploying the 7000 troops that the Union has pledged to UNIFIL to stabilise the situation in southern Lebanon, to cut off the flow of arms and to support the humanitarian effort. We must, however, clarify UNIFIL's mandate to turn the UN resolutions into reality on the ground.

And of course we must go further. We must speak with one voice. We must, in the short term, demand the immediate lifting of Israel's air and sea blockade of Lebanon. We must demand the lifting of the blockade of Gaza and we must help to establish an effective Palestinian Government.

In the medium term, while condemning terrorist acts we must bring Hizbollah and Hamas in from the cold and engage them in a dialogue for the establishment of a democratic framework. We must set up an independent inquiry into the civilian deaths caused by all sides in the recent conflict. As Kofi Annan has pointed out, it will not be through the barrel of a gun, but thanks to dialogue and compromise that Hizbollah will put down their weapons and negotiate a long-term solution.

We have long-term tasks too. If we are to raise a new generation that is not steeped in fear and intolerance, we must build institutions that will ensure peace in the long term. When he was President of the European Commission, Romano Prodi talked about setting up a Euro-Arab development bank, jointly financed and managed by both sides. We must look, too, at a security organisation along the lines of Mr Fogh Rasmussen's proposed conference on security and cooperation in the Mediterranean, which Mr Schulz has quoted. We must look at how we can tie in, with a proper immigration policy, all of the countries of the Mediterranean basin. And we must oversee all of this through the Euro-Mediterranean Parliamentary Assembly in which you, Mr President, have invested so much political - and no little financial - capital. Let us learn from Einstein when he told us that peace cannot be kept by force, only achieved through understanding.

Mr Tuomioja, you spoke about the European Union's remarkable achievement and its major success. I commend the work you have done, but let us not exaggerate. It is a crisis that has driven the European Union to the position it is in, though something that Michel Barnier has called the reflexe Européen. The Union does not have the European constitution that it needs and which would have equipped it far better to deal with this situation. We are deploying European forces but this is not an EU force, even if - thank heavens - it is a coalition of the coherent.

In terms of democratic decision-making we are running on a wing and a prayer. After your meeting in Lappeenranta on 25 August, Mr Solana said that this was the most important decision taken by the EU for many years. If that is so, then why is Mr Solana not here, telling us about it and telling us about the conditions surrounding this conflict? He has a mandate, but of what kind?

When we asked we were told that the rules of engagement for the forces were: 'a matter strictly between the United Nations and the troop contributors'. We were told, therefore, that this was not a European matter. It is absurd that Mr Solana is not here to talk to us about the rules of engagement for this conflict!

The danger is this: the European public at large believe that Europe has responded to the crisis. If things go wrong and we have large numbers of young men coming back home in body bags, people will want to know who in Europe is responsible. Somebody will have to take the political responsibility.

Please, President-in-Office of the Council, get Europe's common foreign and security policy together so that we are not faced with that kind of situation.

In conclusion, we should give two cheers for Europe: one for Louis Michel's rapid action and one for Romano Prodi's courage in co-ordinating our efforts to deal with this problem. We should thank the Commission, the Finnish Presidency and Cyprus - a new Member State - for the tremendous help it has given. We should also thank Turkey for having the courage to help us in committing troops.

However, we still run the risk of insistence on national sovereignty resulting in global anarchy.'

# The Future Of Europe In The World

*Whether you view globalisation as a threat or an opportunity, there is no denying it is a phenomenon that is here to stay. This chapter places the European Union's future development firmly in the context of responding to global developments and challenges, like climate change, terrorism, or migration management, that demand enhanced cooperation between EU Member States and the international community as a whole. In the speeches that follow Graham makes the case for a package of reforms that will enable Europe to compete with emerging economies like India or China - and guarantee the prosperity and quality of life of its citizens in the decades to come. Instability of energy supply, brought into relief by Russian threats and conflict in the Middle East, lead him to reflect on the need for a common European energy policy; economic crisis in the developing world and population decline within the EU form the backdrop of debate on legal migration and world trade; while a Europe without borders brings with it the need to develop effective cross-border police and judicial co-operation. Little consensus on such issues yet exists at European level. This selection of speeches gives a flavour of the debate and presents the Liberal Democrat perspective on the way forward.*

\*\*\*\*\*\*\*\*\*\*\*\*\*\*\*\*\*\*\*\*\*\*\*\*\*\*\*\*\*\*\*\*\*\*\*\*\*\*\*\*\*\*\*\*\*\*\*\*\*\*\*\*\*\*\*\*\*\*\*\*

## All Roads Lead To Lisbon

*Speech made to a Social Affairs Seminar where Graham criticises Europe's leaders for paying lip-service to economic and structural reforms while neglecting their implementation. A month after the European Parliament voted to scrap the opt-out for the working time directive he puts forward the Liberal case for a flexible, competitive internal market and questions reactionary claims that reforming labour markets means abandoning a long European tradition of solidarity in the workplace. Two years on, the reformists seem to have the upper-hand and the EU is on track to complete the internal market in goods, services, capital and people envisaged by its founding document, the Treaty of Rome, back in 1957.*

*Monday 1st March 2004, Brussels*

'One of the strengths of yesterday's discussions was to illustrate the depth and width of the Lisbon Agenda in policy terms. In contemporary Europe all roads lead to Lisbon, or at least they should.

The Lisbon Agenda is a very good idea in danger of becoming another piece of EU jargon, but it is the context for everything we discussed yesterday and everything we will discuss today. We often talk about Lisbon in terms of wealth, or competitiveness, or dynamism, but at the end of the day, Lisbon is about work. Work for those who can do it, work when and how people wish it. Work because it is the key to prosperity. Work, because fair, safe work gives people independence and satisfaction. Sigmund Freud said that "all that matters in life is love and work". The first is outside the remit of the second pillar: but work we can do something about.

Two weeks ago Belgian Prime Minister Guy Verhoftstadt suggested in his Paul Henri Spaak lecture that there was a need to refine the terms of Lisbon, to move beyond the system of peer review to something much more focused and focusing. Your discussions yesterday were about soft law and the open method of co-ordination, which is very much what Lisbon is about. For that reason the Lisbon Agenda was never properly equipped to be truly focused. It is long on aspiration and - at least in terms of Member States - short on real obligation. As Netherlands liberal democrat Commissioner Frits Bolkestein has pointed out many times: the Lisbon Agenda tends more towards bark than bite.

At the end of the next Parliament we will have exhausted the timeframe we set ourselves to achieve the goals of Lisbon. There is far too little sense of urgency among the governments of the European Council. I do not doubt that Odile Quintin and her colleagues in the Commission must sometimes feel the same sense of frustration at the slow progress being made. Liberals believe we have to renew our commitment to the Lisbon agenda because the growth it aspires to deliver is the only key to better jobs, greater prosperity and greater social cohesion. For practitioners in the area of Employment and Social Affairs Lisbon is about more, and better, work, for more people.

Liberals believe a more flexible labour market - and those words are rapidly being stripped of clear meaning - is good insofar as it creates new possibilities for work where they have not previously existed. European society needs to remove many of the disincentives to work. It needs to make work pay properly. It needs to enable and encourage people to work longer and retire later. The European Liberal Democrat and Reform Group has consistently argued that Europe needs to provide more avenues to work for women; it needs to provide more possibilities for effectively combining work and parenting; it needs to make it easier to retrain effectively, or return to the workforce. It also needs to make it easier for the thousands of hardworking immigrants who come to Europe wanting work to find that work.

Liberals have also taken a strong line on education's relationship to better work. Almost one in five Europeans still leaves school without a qualification, and this has to change. Today's unskilled teenager is tomorrow's jobless adult. In a global economy, education is Europe's comparative advantage, but we are not adding enough value for learners the first time around and we are still not encouraging enough life-long learning. So we need to produce better workers and give them more freedom to work.

But we also need to change the way we manage that work. The weight of regulation surrounding employment protection often discourages small employers from expanding and prevents companies from the kind of adaptability that lets them respond to changing demand in the market. If the costs of expanding a payroll in paperwork and protections outweighs the benefits of new staff then Europe's companies will not grow. This adds up to a staggering loss of potential.

This is overwhelmingly a continent of small businesses; overwhelmingly a continent of companies that need flexibility to prosper and grow. Of course it is crucial that we provide strong protections for workers, and that we guarantee protection for the unemployed, but to protect these things at the cost of actually generating new jobs and making it easier to work in every respect is self-defeating. In a rapidly ageing Europe it will also ultimately deprive us of the economic and fiscal resources to sustain those protections in the future.

Liberals believe that what really matters is fairness at work. The future European employment market will have to be built on a dialogue between workers and employers that is fully aware of their mutual dependence and the fact that they are all in the same European boat. I believe that too many Europeans have been wrongly sold the line that reforming our labour markets means abandoning a long European tradition of solidarity in the workplace. But I also believe that European employers need to guard against a tendency to see flexibility as a one-sided deal. Employers who look covetously at the conditions at the bottom of the American labour market are quite simply fooling themselves. Nobody wants a Europe that looks like Wal Mart. Employment is a power relationship and that means we have to handle it with care.

A flexible labour market doesn't mean junk labour. It doesn't mean weak protection for workers against unfair treatment or unacceptable standards. It means businesses and workers that are an order of magnitude more responsive to each other's needs and to their shared reality, which is that Europe now competes in a global marketplace. That its labour is comparatively expensive in global terms. That its population is ageing fast and nursing a pensions and social welfare timebomb. I am glad to welcome today Anne-Sophie Parent, President of the Platform of Social NGOs, Thérése de Liedekerke, director of Social affairs at the Union of Industrial and Employers Confederations of Europe and Reiner Hoffmann, deputy secretary general of the European Trade Union Confederation. These three know as well as any the balance that has to be struck and I look forward to hearing their perspectives.

So Liberal priorities in the legislative field are clear. We regretted last month's European Parliament request to scrap the opt-out for the working time directive. We have supported measures designed to ensure the mutual recognition of professional qualifications so that Europeans can move and work more freely within Europe. In the same spirit, we have backed attempts to help ensure that social support is also available to mobile European workers. We have called for stronger anti-discrimination measures to properly open our workplaces to all who want to work. Perhaps most importantly, we have repeatedly called for the most open possible approach to internal labour migration in Europe, especially with European enlargement. We have been deeply dismayed at the illiberal responses of too many European governments to entirely unfounded fears of benefit tourism and job-stealing by immigrant labour. In the rural part of Britain that I come from, the agricultural economy is basically kept on its feet by hardworking migrants from continental Europe: not that you would know that from much of the British press. Europe needs more worker mobility, not less.

The reason why a meeting like today's is so important is that it is you, as representatives of national parliaments who will actually be responsible for so many of these changes on the ground. One of the strategic goals I set for my Group presidency was the extension of political co-operation and co-ordination between the ELDR group in the European Parliament and our Liberal colleagues in National and Regional Parliaments. The intention of yesterday and today is to allow us to consider our common objectives and better understand each other's work. I believe that this link with national legislators and parliamentarians makes us better European legislators, but also helps us demonstrate some of the European Parliament's added value to all of you. Particularly in this field, it is crucially important that the work we do in the European Parliament is highly sensitive to the local and cultural perspectives that national parliamentarians represent. Without effective working relationships with you that is impossible. The goal for the next legislature is to get much, much further down the road to Lisbon. European Parliament, national parliaments, something we must do together.'

## A New Deal For Europe

*Speech to an EUpolitix forum, where Graham takes on Europe's anti-integrationists to argue a new institutional framework for the EU is essential to guarantee its domestic prosperity and international clout. This debate took place at a time when politicians were heavily split over the Constitutional Treaty, whose text was due to be agreed five weeks later. In the event, the Irish Presidency clinched a deal on the draft Constitution barely a year before the French and Dutch rejected it in their national referendums - sending the EU into an extended 'Period of Reflection' on its future that has lasted up to now. Designed to maintain fiscal discipline and underpin Monetary Union in the Eurozone, the Growth and Stability Pact discussed below has earned a reputation for promoting neither. Repeat violations by larger Member States like France and Germany were never penalised by the Council, while Lithuania, which failed to meet the inflation criteria by 0.1% in 2006, was denied entry to the Eurozone.*

*20th March 2004, Brussels*

'Among other things, the American President Franklin Delano Roosevelt was a poker player who knew a bad hand when he saw one. In the America of the 1930s, he saw a bad one. The New Deal - and Roosevelt used the card-playing metaphor deliberately - meant a chance for America to exchange its cards for a better hand.

I don't want to suggest for a moment that Europe today looks like Depression America. Nor are FDR's solutions our solutions. But Europe has arrived at a moment when its institutional settlement and its economic fitness are both under severe strain. If Europe seems to be picking up speed on the back of a global upturn it has more to do with the slope of the road than the state of our engine. The slow return to growth in Europe might hide the structural weaknesses of the European economy but it will not remove them. An export-led recovery could well deliver a US-style jobless recovery. We need a more durable solution.

Likewise, for all the hopeful talk of successful enlargement, the institutional settlement designed to make that enlargement possible still languishes unfinished, some five weeks before the big day. There are good signs this week that a new mood in Warsaw and a new government in Madrid might help the Irish Presidency to clinch a deal on a European Constitution, although I suspect that tomorrow's summit will be overshadowed by terrorism. But what is striking was that in the absence of any such deal there seemed to be a general feeling among most Europeans that life would - and will - somehow go on if a Constitution is not agreed. I believe the issue is much more serious than most people realise. The reality is that without some form of institutional settlement the effective management of the business of the European Union will become impossible. Europe will simply run aground on its own inability to act. It will not disappear, but the European Union will become unmanageable to the point where it will cease to be effective.

And yet there is little sense of urgency, and surprisingly little sense of what is at stake. European enlargement is an act of considerable bravura. It expresses our belief in the European model and its sustainability for the future. And yet it is taking place at a time when Europe's self confidence - and Europe's credibility in many respects - have never been lower. The collapse of the Growth and Stability pact was symptomatic of a reluctance on the part of European governments to commit to reform and the discipline it requires. It has reverberated throughout the Union. If you are sensitive to the world outside Brussels then you know that public scepticism about the value of European Union has never been greater. The European economy has been barely dented by five years of reluctant economic reform and it urgently needs a new institutional settlement to cope with enlargement.

That is why I think Europe needs a New Deal, and I don't apologise for the historical allusion. The European cards dealt out over fifty years of post-war social democracy and three centuries of statist nationalism are a losing hand and many of us have come to understand this. We may not be confronted with an economic depression on the scale of the 1930s but in the same way that the crash of 1929 revealed deep flaws in America's late nineteenth century settlement - particularly its lack of social solidarity and its vulnerability to unregulated markets - so globalisation and enlargement are threatening to reveal the deep weaknesses in Europe's status quo. Our growing world population and the rapid change in global working patterns have made some of our economic and social settlements seem very fragile when projected anything beyond the medium term. If we want to preserve them - in spirit if not in current form - then we need to act now. Likewise nobody in his or her right mind actually wants to see the EU rendered ineffective by a badly managed enlargement.

So Europe needs a new constitution. The Constitution produced by the Convention on the Future of Europe is by far the best prospect, and the failure of European governments to respect its text - a text that they mandated - has cast them in a very poor light indeed. The Convention text is not perfect, but it is miles ahead of any alternative.

The British Foreign Secretary Jack Straw likes to suggest that the Constitution is about 'tightening up the screws'. This is right but disingenuous. Where Straw is too coy is in pretending that making the enlarged European Union work better does not mean removing many of the blocks to effective decision making in the European Council and that means getting rid of some of the existing national prerogatives and vetoes. While states retain the power to unilaterally block measures in Council they can cripple the Union. With 25 states this is too great a risk. So yes, the Constitution is an integrationist document, but it demands integration as co-operation, simply because there is no other way of making the Union work.

But it is definitely an 'intergovernmental' solution and we need to be clear about that. Nobody is going to lose power to 'Brussels'. The way the European Union works European governments pool their sovereignty in the European Council. It is not 'Brussels' that will have a greater say over our lives, it is our peer societies in the European Council and - if the Constitution increases the power of the European Parliament - our elected European representatives in Strasbourg and Brussels. Either we can express our confidence in a collective future this way or we cannot - but don't pretend this is a debate about sovereignty versus bureaucracy or the end of proud nations. Sovereignty is too often a quaint notion in a globalised world and too much European nationalism more a consolation than a conviction.

The logic behind the Constitution is blindingly simple: Europe is more effective when it acts in union. Two weeks ago in Madrid we were confronted with an explicit reminder of our shared vulnerability. Terrorism is only one example of the many areas in which Europe needs a common solution to a shared problem. On the environment, on security, on immigration and asylum, on the single market, our collective response is stronger than anything we can do alone. We see this on trade. When the European Commissioner for Trade sits down at the WTO the chair creaks with the weight of 450 million Europeans. The European trading relationship with the US alone is worth about 1.5 billion euros a day, and we get the kind of leverage that that money can buy. We got it on steel tariffs for example, where bilaterals could never have shifted the Bush administration.

If we want a Europe that can act effectively abroad - which can get the kind of leverage in foreign affairs that it gets in trade - then we need a European foreign policy and a European foreign minister, backed by all Member States, all of the time.

Europe signed up to Kyoto because it was the right thing to do, but collective commitment was the only thing that kept our nerve.

Europe's common market is the key to our prosperity but in a time of recession it is only our collective commitment that guards against the political temptations of protectionism.

And Europe does not run itself. It needs political will from Member States and it needs effective, transparent institutions capable of making collective decisions. The European Constitution tries to deliver these things. If you haven't already read it, read it. And watch the progress of this Council closely. And if your government doesn't have much to say about a deal, ask why.

But the Constitution is only half our problems. Europe's economic reform agenda - what EU jargonists call the Lisbon agenda - is badly off track. Most of all Europe needs its single market, which will become the largest on the planet on May 1. Growth in intra-state trade in Europe has slowed to a crawl. There are still too many regulatory barriers to European businesses doing business with each other.

There is far too little sense of urgency among the governments of the European Council in this respect. The implementation rate of Single Market Directives is bad enough to make you cringe. Implementation time is measured in years. There are some 130 Single market Directives that have not been implemented by at least one Member State: 8% of all single market directives.

This generation of Europe's leaders has an unprecedented responsibility to get Europe's economic house in order. They really are gambling with the prosperity of the next generation of Europeans. The deadlock in the Council on key pieces of legislation such as the Community patent, investment services and professional qualifications must be broken. We need single market watchdogs that bite as well as bark. Just as they will have to learn to live by a revived Growth and Stability pact, European governments have a duty to work harder for the Lisbon Agenda. Hopefully we will see some more concerted action tomorrow and Friday. If we don't, we should worry.

The American New Deal is inevitably mocked from the right these days as a dark age of big government, but Rooseve. It's simple assumption was that smart government had the power to reshape a society for the better. That it can literally deal again the terms on which a modern capitalist culture goes about its business. Many of his changes endured, and may yet survive a savaging by the American right. As a society, Europe is faced with a similar moment and needs an equally committed leadership.

I hope I can now expand on many of these points in questions. What I have tried to do in these few minutes is to sketch what I think a European New Deal might look like.

I think Europe needs a new constitution that enables it to be effective at home and abroad. Faced with the continental policies of our major international partners I think Europe needs a continental policy of its own. Faced with global problems we need concerted solutions. Without institutional reform we will have neither.

I think Europe needs a smarter economy that delivers the flexibility, openness and innovation Europe needs to compete in a global market. Not at the price of the social model or whatever you choose to call our long traditions of solidarity, but because we cannot protect these things without reform. The only social model that matters is the one that preserves our shared prosperity for the future.

I think time is running out for both. I think it is time our governments started acting as if they knew it. As I said: watch tomorrow's summit carefully and see if you can detect any sense of urgency. If you can't - ask why.'

## Unity Through Diversity

*The integration of legal immigrants and their families in the EU has not been an out-and-out success. Under-achievement; high unemployment; and social exclusion are among the difficulties facing such communities - not to mention the specific difficulties faced by Europe's Muslims in the fallout from terrorist bombings in London and Madrid. In a speech given to an ALDE seminar on European Integration Policy in the Parliament in Brussels, Graham argues that Member States must do much more to break down the barriers to integration and encourage a culture of citizenship, compromise and pluralism. The notion of 'Leitkultur' can be translated as 'core culture' and has featured strongly in Germany's increasingly xenophobic immigration debate where it has become associated with western supremacy and policies of cultural assimilation.*

*5th January 2005, Brussels*

'Welcome to the ALDE seminar "Unity through Diversity". We have chosen this subject for today's conference because we believe that Liberalism and multiculturalism can be reconciled, however seemingly great the current difficulties right across the European Union. Immigration and integration have become major issues on the political agenda in all of our member states. Though hitherto integration has been essentially a competence for member states, the new draft Constitution gives EU law a role in promoting integration.

Integration is a subject of particular concern for Liberals and Democrats. It is no coincidence that we have twice in recent years bid for the chair of Parliament's justice and home affairs committee, nor that our commitment to and understanding of the issues have ensured our bids were successful. The role of Liberals and Democrats in promoting successful multicultural societies is widely recognised. Indeed, the world's best integrated multicultural industrial country - Canada - has enjoyed a Liberal government for most of the past 100 years.

If there is one aspect of 'Old Europe' that puts the EU to shame it is our failure to eradicate the prejudice and persecution which contributed to more than 300 years of net emigration from our continent. Now that economic imperatives require us to encourage immigration we find our citizens too often ill-prepared, ill educated and deeply reluctant to embrace new arrivals. According to the Eurobarometer, just one in five of our citizens is 'actively tolerant' towards immigrants, encouraging their social integration: twice that number is intolerant or ambivalent towards new arrivals. We cannot and must not allow Europe to become a "cold house" for immigrants.

Nor need we. The creation of societies which are liberal and multicultural, where common institutions are shared by those of different origin, ranks among the greatest achievements of human civilisation. Recent events in all our countries may serve to remind us how fragile is this achievement. Nor can any Liberal or Democrat deny that there are problems to address and work to be done to persuade those of all backgrounds to embrace the core values which form the foundation of liberal society. Some of these values relate to political and legal process. Others are moral values such as tolerance, free speech and belief in the equal value of each person.

We are right to demand from all comers an acceptance of Liberal values democratically enshrined in law. For Liberals, rights belong first and foremost to individuals. No group right can justify disregard for the rights of women, for example. For newcomers to learn a country's common language is essential. Active participation in society, in the institutions of democracy and civil society is the right way to provide a forum for debate. This is not the "Leitkultur" sought by Angela Merkel's Christian democrats in Germany, but a recognition of overarching, timeless, universal values.

Yet all persons - as individuals or in groups - have the right to live free from fear of attack, harassment or discrimination. Abuse of free speech to advocate any of these must be actively opposed. Indeed, even as we defend freedom of expression and encourage all sections of society to recognise its importance, we must act against those who would use such freedom to destroy it.

I expect that today our conference speakers will address three dimensions of integration: political representation, participation in the labour market or in the education of children and the cultural meeting of minds. To me these are interlinked and inseparable elements of integration. I am grateful to all our speakers for coming here today to share with us their expertise and insight into these matters.

The south-east Asian tsunami and our reaction to it serve to remind us of the global village nature of the planet we share. Nowhere in that debate do we hear distinctions between Muslim, Christian, Buddhist or Jew. Indeed, the sense of solidarity engendered by shared grief and shock is testimony to humankind's capacity to rise above such distinctions. So allow me to share with you today two areas of concern.

The first is that when memories fade as the newspapers and television turn their attentions elsewhere, western foreign policies will once again be reviled in the developing world for the self interest and the double standards they too often betray. Support for tyrannies as a trade-off for cheap oil or military bases or co-operation in the 'war against terror' is not a strategy but a short term and unsustainable use of force majeure by the powerful against the dispossessed. Unless we grasp the opportunity provided by the tsunami to change our approach to aid, to debt and to trade in weapons, many even in our own societies will feel alienated, insulted and the victims of cultural condescension.

The second is that the secular state which Liberals and Democrats fought so long and hard to achieve is in danger of falling prey to the expression of an intolerant secularism. I believe a profound and wide-ranging debate is required on the role and rights of religions in a secular liberal democracy. We were right to keep a reference to 'Christian heritage' out of the EU's new Constitution. But open, transparent dialogue by our institutions of government with churches and religious communities should be welcomed. In a Liberal and democratic society, such activity is as valid as antennae of business, trades unions or civil society making representations.

I fear that a new secularism is in the ascendant which is far from a dispassionate, unprejudiced intellectual exercise. Those deemed not to hold the politically-correct views of the moment are too often vilified and expected to remain silent or stay out of public life. True Liberal notions such as tolerance and diversity are cast aside. Such secularism, masquerading as pluralism, is no liberal value.

Nor will it assist us in the integration of Turkey into the European Union. The debate over Turkey's EU destiny has led some to question the EU's sense of identity. Yet although Prime Minister Erdogan's Justice and Development Party has a genealogy which can be traced to Islam, since coming to power it has pressed hard for liberal and democratic reforms. The AKP shows us that a party with an Islamic religious heritage can take the lead in boosting economic, social and political freedom, just as Christian democrats were sometimes advocates of similar reform in Christian societies. In the words of Mr Erdogan "A political party cannot have a religion, only individuals can... religion is so supreme that it cannot be politically exploited."

The banning of headscarves in Turkish universities and in government buildings causes tension, just as the banning of headscarves and other religious symbols in French schools is an emotive topic. Yet tension between the secular state and the religions of its citizens can also be creative. In any case, it keeps all parties on their toes.

Different EU member states have sought different formulae for managing such tensions. None has worked entirely well, though all have their advantages. For Liberals and Democrats, an acceptance of a multicultural society must lie at the heart of a policy of unity in diversity, of shared values beyond different individual beliefs. And underlying this must be active promotion of tolerance. A racist taxi driver is a minor social irritant. A racist policeman or other public official is a major social hazard.

I hope today's conference will explore these different approaches and identify a Liberal and Democratic approach to current challenges. And I hope it will do so in the spirit of solidarity which we see in the response to Asia's natural disaster.

Indeed, if I ask you to forgive me now for departing from this conference for a short while it is because I must attend the formal ceremony of the Union's citizens to show solidarity towards the victims of the disaster, whatever their race, colour or creed. I hope to re-join your discussions before long. I am convinced that today's conference will be of value to Liberals and Democrats.

# The Future Of Europe Sixty Years After The Second World War

*Speech to the European Parliament in commemoration of the 60th Anniversary of the Second World War armistice. For most of its history, the European Union has been legitimised on the basis of maintaining a lasting peace between countries that had fought two costly, bloody, wars within the space of 21 years. However, public opinion suggests this argument has now reached its sell-by date, with EU citizens more worried by the lack of jobs and security than such historical considerations. This in turn has led to resurgent nationalism and protectionism, particularly amongst the larger Member States who perceive the free movement of workers, capital, and services from the Eastern EU to be a threat to their prosperity. Here Graham explains how Europe can only succeed if it works together and that the challenges of globalisation will provide a new purpose for the EU, as compelling as the imperative of peace was fifty years ago.*

*11th May 2005, Strasbourg*

'The British poet John Donne observed: 'No man is an island, entire of itself, but a piece of the continent, a part of the main. If a clod be washed away by the sea, Europe is the less'.

That was in 1624, yet for over 300 years peoples and states continued to wage war across our continent. Tribalism and hatred are Europe's ugly legacy. If we had not learned it earlier, the 'war to end all wars' should have shown us the futility and the trauma of organised warfare. Our awakening from that nightmare led to the League of Nations, yet we continued to distil the fruits of scientific advance into the firewater of the weapons of mass destruction. By the time World War II ended in Europe, on 8 May 1945, more than 40 million people had lost their lives.

A cynic might say that 20th century Europeans were slow learners. It took two bloody wars and a continent in ruins to teach us that a united Europe is worth more than the sum of its parts.

Not all of us were able even then to realise our aspirations for peace and freedom. While for most Europeans May 1945 marked the liberation of their countries from Nazi tyranny and the beginning of a new path to freedom and reconstruction, for those who found themselves on the wrong side of the Iron Curtain, one tyranny was quickly replaced by another. A further two generations were denied the liberty we now enjoy. As a student at the Karl Marx University in Leipzig in 1976, I saw this at first hand.

Our historical perspectives are inevitably different. But this must be a debate about the future, not the past. Let us rejoice that Europe is united in peace and that we can sit together in the same debating chamber with a set of common supranational institutions of government deciding on matters of mutual concern.

It was the imperative of interdependence that brought the European Union into being and saw the Soviet bloc finally crumble. We started with coal and steel, the building blocks of post-war Europe; we built the common market, the basis of prosperity undreamt of by my parents; we made the single currency a reality for 300 million Europeans at the dawn of this new century.

As we mark the 60th anniversary of a lasting peace, we see that Europe has come a long way, through gradual steps to build solidarity between our peoples. There is no doubt that the European Union has been a success: liberté, egalité, fraternité have become part of our common legislative and social fabric. But there is no guarantee it will always be that way, and we stand now at a watershed, represented by the constitutional treaty. Can we move forward and consolidate this unprecedented era of peace, stability and prosperity, or will it melt before our eyes and be replaced by a new national rivalry and brinkmanship?

A Financial Times columnist reminded us last week how thin is the veneer of civilisation, how weak the voice of human conscience when tempted away from the rule of law and respect for our fellow human beings. This is the challenge before our Member States as they are called upon to ratify the Constitution.

A peaceful and prosperous Europe was always based on the premise that strength lay in convergence and shared mandates. Cooperation has grown from trade to encompass social policy, employment, immigration, justice, policing and foreign policy. The revolutions in central and eastern Europe have lifted from our shoulders the yoke of Yalta, but we are confronted with new challenges. The challenge, for example, of feeding, clothing and housing a growing world population, while more and more are pushed into migration by war or hunger or sheer desperation. The challenge of dealing with a hole in the ozone layer, melting ice caps, rising sea levels and climate change. Or the threat of internationally organised crime, where some criminal gangs are now more powerful than some national governments, bringing misery to many though the trade in drugs and small arms and the trafficking of people, and working hand-in-hand with terrorists. None of these challenges can be faced by our countries acting alone. To provide the security, prosperity and opportunity which our fellow citizens expect government to deliver, we have to work together. And work together, too, with the United States and Canada, to whose people we owe so much and whose values by and large we share, not only to confront with them common challenges but to make them feel more comfortable with a new and more powerful Europe.

Europe has the potential to be a beacon of hope, a model of tolerance, diversity and stability, in a world where these attributes are still rare.

We can insist on a bill of rights, or we can see our rights eroded. We can ratify the European Constitution and put our faith in democracy and accountable government, or we can continue to leave too much power in unelected hands. We can hold out the hand of friendship to the dispossessed, or cocoon ourselves in an illusory haven of prosperity. We can welcome Romania, Bulgaria, Turkey and the western Balkans and accept that Europe should be plural and diverse, or continue to treat each other with hostility and suspicion.

Convergence is not just an ideal, it is an economic and political necessity. It is time to move beyond national self-interest towards greater convergence. Cooperation is the way forward, enabling us to face global challenges together.

strains on our societies. The three biggest challenges we face - Third World misery and the migration it generates, climate change, internationally organised crime - all require supranational responses. You are right to direct EU priorities to meeting new global demands, complementing the work of the G8. But we look forward to seeing how you will do all that on 1% of GNI.

You are correct, too, that there is a cognitive dissonance between reality and political debate, that we need to get the politics right and give Europe a compelling narrative. So let me give you three suggestions.

First, Council transparency. Europe can no longer be built on secrecy and spin. If people do not understand what is happening, you cannot reproach them for rejecting it. Change the rules of the Council of Ministers. The public has a right to know what is being decided in their name and by whom, even if they disagree. That is the nature of democracy.

Second, parliamentary scrutiny. National parliaments do not need a European Constitution to scrutinise the European work of their ministers more closely, but they need to be engaged in a process of monitoring and holding ministers to account. The European Parliament must also be listened to if we reject draft laws for infringing citizens' rights or exceeding EU competences.

Third, public debate. This debate cannot wait for the need to underwrite a treaty that governments have already signed. Did you go out and meet your trumpet-blowing people in your recent general election? As President Borrell pointed out last week, the rejection of the Constitution was less about the text than the context. Last week Le Monde called you 'le nouvel homme fort de l'Europe'. Show it. The EU will be leaderless for as long as its national leaders play to their public galleries. You will not secure support for supranational solutions if you claim the credit for common successes and blame Brussels for every ill. Stop referring to 'Europe' as if it were a thing apart.

Liberals and Democrats will back your presidency and your drive for better regulation. We will help you forge a Financial Services Action Plan to make money move more easily. We will support a single market in services if you protect proper public provision and if you heed our concerns for personal freedom we will tackle terrorism together with the Council.

We also welcome a debate on the structure of a budget inconsistent with the competitiveness and innovation foreseen in Lisbon. Rapid and radical reform of rural spending cannot credibly be contemplated, however, without co-financing the CAP to redress French and British budget imbalances.

Prime Minister, I welcome your speech today. It offers the promise to our continental colleagues of a less perfidious Albion. Heed the words of St Francis of Assisi, quoted on a similar occasion by one of your predecessors: bring pardon where there is injury and harmony where there is discord. That is the road to new respect for Britain and the European Union.'

## Migrations Are Necessary

*Speech to the European Parliament in Brussels on the issue of migration management in Europe. This had been put on the agenda at the last minute following the deaths of several would-be migrants when they were attempting to climb the fences that separate Morocco from the Spanish enclaves of Ceuta and Melilla in a bid to start a new life in the EU. Here Graham asks why, in the face of population decline and a looming pensions crisis, European states have not yet worked together to create a common migration policy that serves the best interests of the economy, Europe's citizens and the migrants themselves.*

*12th October 2005, Brussels*

'Barely 15 kilometres south of my Gibraltar constituency, thousands of sub-Saharan migrants are massed near the border of Fortress Europe. Many are hungry and weak after their journey through the deserts and mountains of Africa. They struggle against disease, violence and the exploitation of criminal gangs. Now we learn that they are dying at the fences which separate poverty from prosperity, or that they are left in the desert without food and water. Many of us remember such scenes from Bible study. The difference is that this Exodus will not be solved by divine intervention - only by political action.

Africa is Europe's backyard: our near neighbourhood. We cannot fence ourselves off from it, closing our doors and our eyes to its social and economic problems. In the words of the poet Thomas Gray, we must not 'shut the gates of mercy on mankind'.

The flood tide of migrants along our southern borders is upsetting our cosy calculation that inequality can be sustained without cost. With developing countries, remember this: the hungry vote with their feet. So either we accept their produce and allow their economies to prosper or we accept their migrants.

Our futures are interdependent. Sustainable economic, social and political development in Africa is a common concern, essential to Europe's future. We recognised this in 1995, when the Barcelona Process enshrined multilateral relations across the Mediterranean as the new strategic reality. Ten years on, Spain is negotiating a plan with Morocco to tackle immigration and promote cooperation with the countries of origin.

Partnership is certainly the way forward. However, until Morocco's border guards stop shooting unarmed refugees; until Morocco stops dumping them near its borders unable to fend for themselves, the European Union cannot, and should not, offer support for these proposals. Most of those affected today are not Moroccan nationals: they are third-country nationals who entered the Union via Morocco and who deserve the protection of our laws.

Up to now, plans for a European consensus on migration policy have been buried at the bottom of the political inbox. Why? Member States cannot agree on any one approach the European Union suggests. But that does not stop them demanding European action when they face specific immigration problems of their own.

The problems facing Melilla and Ceuta are not just Spain's problem: they are Europe's problem. The challenge in Lampedusa is also Europe's problem, however much Italy seeks to hide it from visiting MEPs. No wonder the southern countries of the Barcelona Process have run out of patience.

We need to think bigger and to recognise, as Kofi Annan said, that 'migrations are necessary'. We need a consensus on economic policy. We need Doha and Hong Kong to bring results to help Africa.

When Commissioner Louis Michel outlines his strategy for Africa later today, I hope the Member States will heed his message that it is time for a European consensus on development and immigration that respects the values of democracy, human rights and the rule of law. '

## Redefining The Purpose Of Europe

*Lecture given to staff and students at the College of Europe in Bruges - a specialist centre for advanced European Union Studies which trains many future EU leaders like Jo Leinen and David O'Sullivan, mentioned below. In 2005 the European Commission announced the beginning of an extended 'Period of Reflection' to examine the European Union's future role, structure and mandate. Here Graham examines how the major challenges of the modern world - international terrorism, a global economy, or climate change, to take but examples - can be met only through strengthened co-operation between Europe's Member States and supranational governance on a global scale. The European Court of Justice decision discussed below concerns the Passenger Name Record agreement on air travel negotiated between the EU and US authorities, which Parliament successfully challenged. Jean Monnet, quoted in the introduction, is widely regarded as the architect of European Unity, despite never having held public office.*

*22nd November 2005, Bruges*

'Jean Monnet once observed: "Each man begins the world afresh. Only institutions grow wiser". That's a claim I'd like to ponder. No-one can deny we've come a long way fast. Within my lifetime we built the single market, bringing prosperity undreamt of by my parents. We've established a world reserve currency to rival the dollar. And we've laid the basis for peaceful co-operation in so many areas. In a Union now embracing 460 million people.

Centuries of tribalism and hatred had been Europe's ugly legacy. Now, war on a continental scale in Europe is almost unthinkable. The architects of European integration knew that the key to peace and progress lay in interdependence. They built institutions on a foundation of coal and steel. Their successors took on the torches and deepened co-operation. Their work in turn has been augmented by many - some of them graduates of the College of Europe. Your unparalleled institution distils and infuses the values of our Union, giving us men of the calibre of Manuel Marin, David O'Sullivan and Jo Leinen.

But new threats and challenges are now upon us. New responses are needed. New countries are queuing up to join. Our institutions, the building blocks of the Union, must be developed and adapted. That is patently not happening at present. Monnet, Schuman, Adenauer and others rose to the challenges of their time. Europe's present Leaders must rise to the challenges of ours. Leadership is needed. By statesmen who define a vision and prepare the path towards it. Not by politicians who pore over opinion polls and preach popular prejudice back to their citizens. Where there is no vision there is no commitment. No looking forward. No sharing of responsibility. As WB Yeats wrote in The Second Coming: "The best lack all conviction and the worst are full of passionate intensity".

So what challenges do we face and how should the Union respond? First, rapid population growth beyond our borders but decline within. Second, a climate changing faster than at any point in recorded history. Third, an unprecedented threat from terrorism and organised crime, plaguing this new century just as war did the last. Finally, a sluggish economy at risk from newly emerging economies like China and India. I will argue today that Europe is failing in its historic responsibility. Because our institutions are failing. And Member States are failing to put long term strengths and common concerns above short term interests and individual gain. And the Commission is lacking the courage to act.

Fear, fatalism and fanaticism are spreading in Europe. They threaten our social cohesion and the institutions of our economic and political success. Add to this equation the way today's leaders seek to unite Europe without uniting Europeans. And you see why we came off the rails at referendum junction. But as Mark Twain said of Wagner's music, "It's not as bad as it sounds". Help is at hand. But that's for later in this speech.

In June the European Council declared a year's pause for reflection on a Constitution which was a reasonable attempt to make Europe more effective, more responsive and more relevant. It's principal failings were its length, its title and its marketing. But the principal cause of its downfall was the lack of courage and conviction of national leaders. The subsequent silence from Member States has been deafening. And the institutional response uncertain. The pause for reflection is already more pause than reflection. The Commission has given us a "Plan D" for dialogue. But we need a "Plan V for vision" and a "Plan L for Leadership".

Much must be done to show how the European Union adds value to our daily lives. If we fail to communicate what Europe does, how it works and where it is heading we will lose the battle for people's hearts and minds. It will not do to wait for better circumstances before engineering a re-vote in France and the Netherlands. We did it in Denmark with the Maastricht Treaty, it's true. We did it in Ireland with Nice. But a nascent Constitution needs broader backing and further thought, not just a quick fix.

When the time is ripe to re-consult citizens there should be a Europe-wide, simultaneous debate and vote. I argued this in a letter to Europe's newspapers, co-signed by an MEP from each of the fourteen member states - over three years ago. The problem is less the text than the context. Before we take the matter further we have to get the politics right. National governments cannot "attack Europe from Monday to Saturday, then expect citizens to vote for it on Sunday", as Mr Barroso so perceptively pointed out.

The word 'crisis' is widely over-used. But not always. John F. Kennedy once observed that, when written in Chinese, the word "crisis" is composed of two characters - one representing danger and the other opportunity. That is how I see the EU at present. Becalmed between threatening storms and the winds of opportunity.

## 2. POPULATION GROWTH AND MIGRATION

Today's big challenges are supranational. Take world population growth. If you're poor, you need kids. To provide for your old age. And with five billion poor, population is rising dangerously. So we need to pull people out of poverty. Pronto. How? Education, especially for women. Micro-credit for business. Investment in good governance. Development policy must do these. But market access too. Because the hungry vote with their feet. So either we accept their produce or their migrants. That's what's at stake in Hong Kong.

Of course, Europe needs some migrants. Our population is in free fall. By 2050, on current trends, Italy will lose a quarter of its people. By 2050 - unless your generation is particularly prolific ! - people over 65 will account for nearly half the EU population. Putting an intolerable strain on pensions and social services. So Europe needs workers. To pick our crops, drive our trucks and staff our care homes. To help create the wealth which pays for social policy. Developing countries need emigrants too, remitting valuable earnings back home.

"Migrations are necessary", as Kofi Annan said recently. The time has come for national governments to put in place an immigration policy which serves our needs and those of others. Not just the current sticking plaster solutions. To shut the gates of Fortress Europe is not just, in the words of poet Thomas Gray, "to shut the gates of mercy on mankind". It is to shut the gates of opportunity on ourselves.

But migrants, and the children of migrants, must feel welcome in Europe. Burning cars, looting and rioting do not emerge from nowhere. And they are not found from Glasgow to Marseille unless something, somewhere, is seriously wrong. For 300 years, Europe was a continent of net emigration. In the last 30 years we've seen net immigration. Have our perceptions kept pace with this process? All EU communities are of immigrant descent. Many have successfully settled and integrated. By and large, the longer they've been here, the better.

However religion is the old bugbear. And where once we ghettoised the Jews, now it is the Muslims. An ever-increasing number of young people is out of work and out of luck. Tolerated until the war on terror and subjugated since, they are turning on society, looting the stores and burning the banlieue. If these people had been treated with dignity from the start, would we be facing such phenomena today? Why has it gone wrong for Europe? Because for all the fine words at the Tampere

Council, there's no policy run by institutions. Every Member State is lost in the fog, feeling its way gradually from tolerance to inclusion. Addressing the socio-economic problems is half the answer. The other half has to do with citizenship, identity and the attitudes of their fellow Europeans.

Europe cannot be a white Christian club which reserves no place for others. That approach is both intolerant and illiberal. But it can expect immigrants to abide by universal values of respect, tolerance and the Rule of Law which are the fundament of our political system. Only then can we enjoy the "Unity in Diversity" promised by the Constitutional Treaty. These values, and not the traditions of individual Member States, are the values which define what it means to be European in a Union of 25 different countries. They apply as much to Europeans moving around as to those joining us from elsewhere. And it is these values which will create a European civic identity to which those of immigrant descent can adhere- whether or not they identify with the culture and norms of their host nation.

## 3. CLIMATE CHANGE AND THE ENVIRONMENT - PRESENT AND FUTURE CHALLENGES

Another key challenge for Europe is to address climate change. In the last fifty years the Earth experienced its fastest period of warming in two millennia. Almost certainly linked to greater use of fossil fuels, particularly oil. If we'd all heeded the warnings a quarter century ago we might have prevented it. If America acts in concert with us now, we might yet control it. A hole in the ozone layer, severe weather patterns, increasing desertification. Problems affecting our capacity to grow crops to sustain life.

That's why tackling Climate Change has been at the heart of the EU agenda since Kyoto. Led by our institutions: Council, Commission and Parliament. We've not only cut emissions from cars and other greenhouse gases. European Emissions Trading came into force this year. And from 2008, aviation will be included. To offset a forecast 83% rise in aircraft emissions by 2020. Our Renewables Obligation has forced governments to invest in sustainable energy sources.

The EU's collective response to environmental challenges has been an undisputed success. Some see "greening Europe" as more burdens for business. But it can bring economic reward. In green technologies, opportunities for the future abound. Already, investment in cleaner energy has brought new jobs and new technology and driven down energy prices. Think of 'Smart' energy meters, soon to be in every home, allowing consumers to save money and monitor the impact of their energy use. Can we do more of the same? Look at the REACH proposals! Registering, Evaluating and Authorising up to 30,000 chemicals. Essential to protect human, animal and plant life. But it will also boost the market for greener goods. A market which exists already and will continue to grow - giving Europe's industry competitive edge.

Are we on the threshold of a Third Industrial Revolution, as predicted by Jeremy Rifkin? Able to resurrect the European Economy on the back of sustainable new technologies? Perhaps, if our institutions prevail. But we'll not achieve it on a budget of 1% of GNI. Doubling the budget for the 7th Framework Research Programme, offers huge opportunities. Within ten years, for example, we could have a hydrogen economy. That makes not only environmental sense. It makes political and business sense too. Remember 1973? Looking around, maybe not! Read about it? Reliance on fossil fuels could hold Europe's governments to ransom and knock our economy for six. It is imperative to reduce our dependence on oil. Hybrid cars have already been successfully trialled. And if the home of the motor car, California, plans to cut emissions by 30% in ten years, why can't we?

Nor do the possibilities stop there. Think of things we can do with pooled R & D money. Things no country could do alone. Fund research into bio-mimicry. That's inventing processes which mimic life. The Americans have found a butterfly in the desert. Which strains water from the air through its wings. They have copied its technique for the walls of tents. Providing water for refugees. We use enormous energy to heat kilns to fire porcelain. But the abalone grows a shell both stronger and finer. And it's made from? Pure sea water. Could we do that? We think we could. But not if Europe cuts its research budget.

The Commission proposes a European Research Council to encourage our scientists to come up with the unexpected. Geared towards groundbreaking discoveries, taking a creative approach, exploring new directions. It is in these new discoveries that sustainability and prosperity - our environmental and economic futures - will merge.

## 4. OPEN BORDERS AND SECURITY IN THE TWENTY FIRST CENTURY

But to build a successful economy Europe must also confront political challenges. Our borders now stretch as far as the Ukraine. They may go further yet. Bulgaria and Romania will take us to the Black Sea. Turkey would take us to the Middle East.

Robert Schuman said that a country's European vocation is determined by the European spirit of its people. Perhaps the limits of enlargement lie not between the Atlantic and the Urals but wherever people share, and live by, European values. That is a debate for the future. In the meantime, abolishing internal borders is not only a boon to tourists and legitimate business people. It makes life easier for criminals too.

Criminal gangs are sometimes more powerful than national governments. Producing and selling drugs on the rich world's markets. Trafficking people for the sex trade. Trading in arms and sometimes in nuclear materials. Counterfeiting luxury goods. And increasingly linked to terrorism. Experts say that up to 8% of the money passing through our financial systems is the proceeds of crime. Running into trillions of dollars. Combating crime needs more multilateral cooperation than has ever existed before. And it needs effective institutions. Not bickering over who will lead Europol.

The tragedy of 9-11 gave some much needed impetus. Actually, I've never seen the Commission move so fast. Five days before that fateful day, Parliament adopted an own-initiative report on where Europe was failing in the fight against crime and terrorism. It would have lain on a shelf for months. But, as its author, I'd put in it some practical proposals.

Like the European Arrest Warrant - turned into law in less than four months and now Europe's chief asset in the fight against cross-border crime.

But a lack of powers for the European Parliament and absence of unanimity in Council have led to impasse on several matters of importance like plans to share criminal intelligence information that would make it easier to track down and convict people threatening the security of our citizens. Or plans for data retention and other forms of intelligence-led policing; powerful tools in combating crime.

For three years I had the honour to chair Parliament's committee on citizens' rights and freedoms, justice and home affairs. I saw what member states mean when they talk of freedom, security and justice. At the time I backed Minimum Procedural Guarantees in criminal proceedings, intended to avert potential human rights pitfalls. Blocked by the Council in 2001, they remain unratified. With a Framework Directive sitting at the bottom of the Council's in tray as I speak. The same fate befell a Framework Decision on Data Protection which would counteract concerns over data privacy which lie at the heart of the debate on Data Retention legislation.

Parliament has fought the Council tooth and nail for the right of co-decision. Too many rights are being eroded without proper parliamentary scrutiny. Whereas legislation in the first pillar, with transparent policy-making and guaranteed rights, would enhance the moral standing of Europe's response to terror. Just as harmonisation of foreign policy in security and defence - too often gridlocked by the third pillar need for unanimity - is essential to preserving Europe's security. Of course, there is a trade-off between liberty and security. But we risk making Europeans both less free and less safe. Pressures for deportation of third-country nationals to places where they may face torture or worse, or the threat of arrest for "speech crimes" like glorifying terrorism, are more likely to fuel than to douse the fires of fanaticism.

A civil society must treat everyone - even suspected terrorists - according to the Rule of Law. Everyone has the right to a fair trial and to non-violent questioning by the police. Even suspected terrorists have the right to legal counsel and to representation in a court of law. And, if convicted, to be imprisoned in a European jail. Failure to uphold these rights 'cheapens our right to call ourselves a civilised society'. Who said that? The British barrister Cherie Blair, Tony Blair's lady wife. Failure to uphold these rights destroys the essential value of what it means to be a European. And then the terrorists will have beaten us.

## 5. BOOM OR BUST? THE FUTURE DIRECTION OF EUROPE'S ECONOMY

The final challenge confronting Europeans is the state of our economy. To compete we must reform expensive social models. And build a dynamic marketplace for goods, services, capital and labour. But member states are shirking economic reform. As Jean-Claude Juncker said in March, "We all know what we have to do. We just don't know how to win elections afterwards". Europe's growth rates are less than half those of America or Japan. We are losing ground every year. And losing our best brains to their companies. Can we double our rate of growth? Yes, and Frits Bolkestein told us how. The trouble is how he did it. In typical Bolkestein style. If you're going to explode a firework the instructions say "Light the blue touch paper and retire". And that's exactly what Frits did.

If we could create a single market in services to rival our single market in goods, we could double growth rates easily. All that is missing is the political will. I hope Parliament's shows the way forward this afternoon with agreement in committee on the Bolkestein directive. It is not by turning inwards that we will overcome our sluggish economic growth and compete with emerging economic giants like China or India. Certainly there will be hard decisions to take on whether we can maintain our competitiveness in some sectors. But the world is on the move and so must we. Jobs may have to go in one sector to be created afresh in another.

Look at this summer's so-called "bra-wars" with China. How can we exhort China to open up its economy to our businesses when we re-impose quotas on Chinese exports? After years of quotas there was bound to be a surge in in-bound trade when they were lifted. Just as with footwear. Southern European shoemakers have had the Commission open an investigation. Into alleged dumping from China and Vietnam. Why? They're being priced out of the market. By whom? By the northern European shoemakers who've re-located production. All EU countries knew quotas would be lifted. Some manufacturers planned ahead. They've brought cheaper shoes to shoppers. Others are now crying foul. The Commission would be fools to heed them.

Agriculture, Europe's bastion of protectionism, is starting to show the way forward. Until recently producing more quantity than quality - with more concern for EU cash back than for the demands of the market place. Now much improved, as the 2003 reforms which replaced price support mechanisms with direct farm payments have changed the equation. Now farmers can direct their efforts towards high-quality products and environmentally sound production methods. Which is just as well since Europe's agriculture is under the spotlight in the Doha Development Round of World Trade negotiations.

The Lisbon Agenda offers the chance for Europe's economy to pull itself up by its bootstraps through a virtuous circle of action at EU and national levels. But let me end here with a warning. Strategies are all very well. But Member States have demonstrably failed to live up to their fine declarations and commitments made under the Portuguese Presidency in the spring of 2000. Its headline goal of creating the world's most dynamic and knowledge-led economy by 2010 has become a standing joke. If Europe is to succeed, Member States must do much, much better. Don't just take it from me. Concluding the High Level Group's Report on the Lisbon Strategy in November last year, Wim Kok wrote: "much of the Lisbon Strategy depends on the progress made in national capitals: no European procedure or method can change this simple truth. Governments and especially their leaders must not duck their crucial responsibilities. Nothing less than the future prosperity of the European model is at stake"

I couldn't have put it better myself.

## Eastern Promise Versus Western Wisdom

*Speech to a European Parliament Seminar on the EU's 7th Research and Development Framework, which will act as the blueprint for our future knowledge economy by specifying Europe's technological priorities. Here Graham argues that the EU is falling behind other leading nations, like the USA, China, and India, when it comes to investing in ideas and risks losing its competitive edge in the field of high-value technologies. The debate was timely since it coincided with final negotiations on the Union's long-term funding priorities to determine the importance and investment assigned to each policy area. In the event, Liberal lobbying, backed by the Commissioner for Science and Research, Janez Potocnik, paid off and research funding increased by 75%. Jack Straw was British Foreign Secretary during the British Presidency while Janez Potocnik has been the European Commissioner for Science and Research since 2004.*

*7th December 2005, Brussels*

'From the Renaissance to the Enlightenment people demanded that science be given the academic freedom to reveal the truth. Then, during the Industrial Revolution, they demanded that governments support research required to bring about technological progress. This potent combination of support and innovation ushered in a period of economic growth that turned early-modern Europe into one of the world's great powerhouses.

But - as this seminar has shown - the same ideological and financial commitment is required of today's leaders if Europe is to maintain its competitive edge in an increasingly globalised world. As I speak, Jack Straw is meeting a conclave of EU foreign ministers to discuss Europe's Financial Perspectives from 2007-2013. I hope that their deliberations will do more than pay mere lip service to the Research and Development agenda.

That's not just me being a cynical Liberal. Up to now the Council has blocked the spending required for Europe to raise its game. The 130 million euro package ALDE originally proposed for this, the final year of the 6th Framework Programme, got progressively cut to a paltry 21 million euros by the time negotiations were completed.

It is imperative that - this time round - the British Presidency understands what is at stake and negotiates a substantial increase in funding for the 7th Framework Programme - as called for today by Commissioner Potocnik. It must not allow the Council to carry out its threats to cut the Research and Development budget while China and the USA are spending ever greater amounts to keep ahead of the competition.

Liberals know that such a move would be disastrous for Europe. Just look at the moribund state of the Lisbon Agenda, at this half way point to the 2010 target date of creating a dynamic and competitive knowledge-based society. Look at the 20 million unemployed Europeans who rightly hold their governments responsible for not creating the climate for growth and job creation. Look at the state of much of Europe's manufacturing base and the enormous growth of the Chinese and Indian economies that make it ever more difficult to compete on price.

We need our scientists to be able to take the lead in all areas which pursue truth and progress. This cannot be done by tossing aside our values - for these are the foundation of our European Community - but by making sure that there are no barriers to their work which are not scientifically thought out, and reasonable in themselves. With that approach, just think of what we could do with the kind of increase to pooled R+D money envisaged by Commissioner Potocnik - things no country could do alone.

A beefed-up 7th Framework Programme has the potential to resurrect the European economy on the back of new technologies. Within ten years, for example, Europe could be a Hydrogen economy. We already have the means to reduce our dependence on oil. Hybrid cars, such as those developed by Audi and Toyota, have been successfully piloted. Canadian enzyme technology allows food and plant waste to be converted into fuel. Even the home of the motor car, California, has forged ahead with proposals to cut emissions from cars by 30% within a decade, through increased use of alternative fuels.

If they can do it, why can't Europe do it? With oil prices high it makes economic sense. And with climate change threatening it makes environmental sense. Equally, the European Research Council proposed by the Commission is a direct attempt to encourage our scientists to come up with the unexpected. As a body, it will be specifically geared towards making groundbreaking discoveries, taking a creative approach and exploring new directions. We must give it - and the 7th Framework Programme in general - the freedom and the funding required to do so.

## Don't Turn Back The Clock

*Speech to Parliament where Graham decries the fact that certain Member States attempted to protect their 'national champions' in key industries from foreign takeover bids in violation of European competition law and internal market principles. Revelations that mergers involving banks and energy companies in a number of EU Member States had been blocked by their own governments caused the European Commission to take unprecedented action and instigate legal proceedings against the offending parties. What followed was an unholy row on implementing the Take-Over Directive and completing the single market. Commissioners McCreevy and Kroes are responsible, respectively, for the Internal Market, Services, and Competition policy. Ursula Plassnik is Austria's Foreign Minister and the Austrian Presidency's representative in this debate.*

*15th March 2006, Strasbourg*

'More than at any time in the Union's history there is a disjunction between those who seek to move forward and those who wish to turn back; between those who defend the single market and the Lisbon Agenda as the best means to guarantee long-term efficiency, competitiveness and growth, and those who reject free trade in favour of economic patriotism akin - as Giulio Tremonti said - to that immediately before the 1914-18 war.

The irony is that this so-called patriotism - thinly disguised economic nationalism - will bring as few benefits to the citizens of France, Spain or Poland as it does to the rest of Europe, for it is fair competition that drives the global market, raises quality and lowers prices, and it is fair competition that protectionism undermines. If any company can see commercial logic in merging with another, what business is it of ours to put roadblocks in its path? The great success of the euro, as the President of the Commission has pointed out, is that mergers and takeovers are proceeding apace. European industry is gearing up for the challenges of competing in a global economy.

These are issues for the Spring Council. They are issues for the Commission because the Commission is going to be tested in this climate as a defender and guarantor of the Treaties. Faced with an unprecedented assault on the internal market, the Commission must hold firm to the Treaties, hold firm to the basic freedoms and speak out when necessary - as you have, President Barroso, and as Commissioners McCreevy and Kroes have too - and act to defend the Union. But defence of the single market falls not only to the Commission; the Council has a role, as we stress in the motion we debate today. That means the Spring Council expediting transposition and implementation of the Union's directives to deliver a single market with free movement of goods, services and capital. We want to see the European Council deal seriously with free movement of services, free movement of workers and free movement of capital. As they discuss the future financing of our Union, let the Heads of State and Government find the funds necessary for the training of our workforce, for the trans-European networks and for research and development through the European Institute for Technology, which will secure future economic dynamism.

It is time for our Heads of State and Government to formalise the Council meetings that take place in March and October. These need not be billed purely as economic policy summits; the demands of energy security, of peace in the Middle-East and of fighting internationally organised crime are equally urgent and should be on next week's agenda. There should be public discussion too of the Union's burgeoning defence policy, currently being planned behind closed doors. The Austrian Presidency opened to public scrutiny a recent Environment Council meeting; why not make this openness universal practice in the Council?

My group welcomes the Commission's proposal to bring forward a concept paper so that we can discuss defence policy here in Parliament and involve our citizens in the discussion of what our continent can become.

President-in-Office, a century ago your country had a foreign minister who studied in Strasbourg, restored the old regime and dominated continental politics for 30 years. If Mrs Plassnik can emulate Metternich's achievements, Europe will prosper. If she fails, she can always follow his example and flee to Britain.'

## Nuclear Peril And Potential

*Speech to the European Parliament in Brussels on the 20th anniversary of the Chernobyl disaster. Following a winter of discontent that featured massive hikes in the price of crude oil from the Middle East and an energy standoff between Russia and her ex-Soviet neighbours Europe's leaders agreed to pursue a Common Energy Policy that would provide more security and stability of supply. Here Graham argues that for Europe to avoid dependence on unstable sources of fuel it must radically rethink its energy mix and invest in technologies for the future, including - despite anti-nuclear protests in his youth - research into safe forms of nuclear fission.*

*26th April 2006, Brussels*

'At 1.23 a.m. on 26 April 1986 an alarm sounded that signalled the world's worst ever civil nuclear accident.

The explosion at the Chernobyl power plant spewed radioactive waste over vast swathes of the former USSR and Western Europe, and rendered an area with a radius of 30 km uninhabitable to humankind. It is fitting that we express today our solidarity with the victims of that accident and that we recognise the serious impact that it had on so many lives.

Official UN figures predicted up to 9000 cancer-related deaths as a result of that accident. However, a Greenpeace report released last week estimated 93000, which could rise to around 200000 if we include other related illnesses.

I want to speak, however, of the future, not of the past. Chernobyl remains a symbol of the perils of nuclear fuel and the reason why we must work with the countries of Central and Eastern Europe that have nuclear reactors based on the same design, to render those as safe as possible while they must function, and take them out of commission as soon as we can.

I particularly welcome the Commissioner's commitment to the development of renewable technologies. The Commissioner will shortly be visiting my constituency, where we are closing nuclear power plants and developing renewable fuels. With finite resources fast depleting, Europe will have to radically re-examine its patterns of energy supply and consumption.

This is especially true at a time of chronic instability in the Middle East, of alarming hikes in the price of crude oil, and increased competition for resources. If we are to avoid being 90% dependent on Russian oil by 2020, we have to achieve greater autonomy in energy supply and develop a common energy policy with an intelligent, balanced energy mix. Money invested in clean green technology is not money wasted and if Europe can lead the world in researching green technologies it will create more jobs, revive manufacturing, and generate greater export potential for our products.

That is why my Group applauds the Council and the Austrian Presidency for backing plans to double the use of biomass, including organic waste, for energy purposes, allowing us to cut energy imports by over 6% and bring up to 300 000 jobs to rural areas.

With overall consumption rising, greater energy efficiency combined with the renewables could generate around 25% of our needs. We have got to increase that figure, we have got to make a genuine commitment to investment in technologies for the future. Investing in projects such as hydrogen fuel might have the potential to achieve oil savings equivalent to 13% of global oil demand.

Given the substantial contribution that nuclear power already makes to our energy autonomy, there must be renewed momentum to invest in safety, both to ensure that nuclear power stations produce less waste and present less risk and to develop Europe's research into fusion energy through the Euratom framework and the experiment in Cadarache in France.

Lenin believed that progress could be achieved only through socialism and electricity. History has judged him wrong on the first count but perhaps not on the second. Nobody denies that we need a sustainable and secure energy supply; they disagree only on the mix.

The anniversary of the Chernobyl disaster is a reminder of the challenges we face in delivering our energy requirements while minimising the risks. We owe it to the victims of Chernobyl to develop safe, reliable and sustainable sources of energy.'

## 'Finlandia' Is Music To Liberal Ears

*Speech to the Parliament on the day Finland assumed its Presidency of the European Union and Matti Vanhanen, its Liberal Prime Minister, launched his Presidency Priorities for 2006. The Finnish Programme was seen as a boost for key Liberal strategies, particularly completing the single market in goods and services and boosting innovation. Over the past years, stalemate in Council and Parliament over both the need for and speed of reform had held up such developments, which ALDE considered necessary for Europe to maintain growth and prosperity in a highly competitive world. Article 42 is the clause in the Treaties which would allow legislation on justice and security policy to fall under Parliamentary co-decision, thus increasing democratic scrutiny on issues of major European importance like fighting terrorism and organised crime.*

*5th July 2006, Strasbourg*

'With the Finnish Presidency's emphasis on productivity, accountability and transparency, 'Finlandia' is music to Liberal ears.

The programme you have presented today, President-in-Office, reflects both the strong reforming tendencies of your government and the egalitarian and innovative impulses of a nation which repeatedly tops the league tables for education, innovation and development. Liberal values will be on the march with your Presidency.

I would like to refer to just a few areas which my group feels to be important. First, the market-driven programme. Priorities like completing the internal market, particularly in services and the energy sector, are key goals for us in the months ahead, as are efforts to deliver a directive on the portability of supplementary pensions and promoting market openings for new technologies. The latter will pay more long-term dividends than any government-funded initiatives on research and development', and provide the growth and jobs and prosperity that our Union desperately needs.

October 2005 - Graham and ELDR Party President Annemie Neyts MEP
await Europe's Lib Dem leaders.

October 2005 - Graham opens the Rainbow Centre for Hope, a new
community centre in Buia, Romania.

January 2006 - With UK Lib Dem Leadership candidate Sir Menzies
Campbell QC MP and colleague Chris Davies MEP at his hustings
in Brussels.

February 2006 - Graham shares a joke with the former Commission President,
now Italian Prime Minister, Romano Prodi.

March 2006 - European Commission President José Manuel Barroso and Graham celebrate their 50th birthdays together (Graham is precisely four hours older). At the microphone is EP President Josep Borrell Fontelles.

May 2006 - Graham Watson MEP and the Dalai Lama hold a joint press conference in the European Parliament.

May 2006 - On the local election campaign trail in Dorset with Annette Brooke MP.

June 2006 - Graham directs Finnish Prime Minister Matti Vanhanen to his seat at a meeting of the ALDE Group in the Åland Islands just before the start of Finland's EU Presidency.

# Strengthening A Liberal World Order

*Despite the rapid growth of democratic movements; the emergence of global governance in areas like trade and environmental policy; and predictions from some quarters about the 'End of History', Liberal Democracy has yet to establish a firm foothold in many parts of the world. Rather, increasing insecurity and inter-religious tensions - much of it stoked by the conduct of the US-led war on terror - is actually threatening to undermine many of the hard won Liberal achievements of the last fifty years. In this series of speeches Graham Watson reflects on the potential of the European Union's Neighbourhood and Foreign strategy to promote human rights, democracy and the rule of law at global level and respond to the common challenges facing humankind through a policy of constructive multilateralism.*

\*\*\*\*\*\*\*\*\*\*\*\*\*\*\*\*\*\*\*\*\*\*\*\*\*\*\*\*\*\*\*\*\*\*\*\*\*\*\*\*\*\*\*\*\*\*\*\*\*\*\*\*\*\*\*\*\*\*\*\*

## Religion Doesn't Have To Be A Political Conversation Stopper

*Speech to the 52nd Congress of the Liberal International in Dakar, Senegal. The Congress was debating a resolution on 'Islam and the West' in response to those claiming a Clash of Civilisations was being played out in the 'War on Terror'. Deconstructing the myth that Islam and democracy don't mix Graham argues that the real fault-lines lie within not between civilisations and explains why Liberals everywhere should be working towards an 'a-confessional politics'.*

*25th October 2003, Dakar*

"Un homme politique n'aime rien de plus que le soulagemant d'être parmi des amis. Mme la Presidente, chers frères et soeurs de la famille Libérale, c'est avec un grand plaisir que je me retrouve ici à Dakar, de nouveau dans votre compagnie. Chers collègues, je vais parler du theme et, bien que j'apprécie la langue de Molière, je continuerai en Anglais, ma langue maternelle.

The subject of our theme resolution this week is one that we have returned to again and again in the last decade and with increasing urgency over the last two years. It was given a vivid and terrible quality by the events of September 11 2001. As the tectonic plates of religion and politics on this planet grind together, throwing sparks which make our world less stable, and the chance to speak across the divides of culture and belief more difficult, we must unite the people of independent mind.

Around the world religious extremism provides a rationale for intolerance, for hatred and for violence. Like any form of absolutism, religion of this kind is a political conversation-stopper. It cannot grasp the value of dialogue and hates the possibility of compromise and coexistence. Yet for Liberals these things are what makes politics possible and gives politics purpose.

Earlier this year the European Liberal Democrats held a seminar in Brussels that was designed to help us focus on the questions that Christianity and Islam posed for Liberalism. Again and again speakers on that day came back to this problem: the issue is not the divide between Islam and the West, but between secular government and it enemies.

The Real Faultlines

So rather than simply invoking once again some imagined faultline between Islam and the West our task as Liberals is to criticise those who would exploit religious belief for social control or political gain. The faultline that concerns us runs not between Islam and the enlightened West but down the middle of every one of the Abrahamic religions, through every major church, and through the political lives of every one of us. The good news is that we - Liberals from the West and Islamic cultures alike - stand together on one side of this line.

Because although the link between confession and political creed is sometimes invoked, the reality is that liberal democracies can survive and prosper alongside almost any religious belief when it is practised with tolerance and dignity. In my own position as leader of the ELDR in the European Parliament I have worked hard to turn European Liberal politics outward, to forge links with a growing international Liberal family that contains believers of every creed, and believers in none. Christians are not natural democrats. Muslims are not inherent authoritarians. Atheists are not inevitable communists. All can be Liberal Democrats.

There is no one Islamic political reality, anymore than there is a single Western way of practising politics. Here in 'Islamic' Senegal, where the majority of the population are Muslim, there is a liberal government led by one of the most impressive spokesmen for international Liberalism alive today. In many parts of the supposedly 'Western' United States, the influence of religion in political life continues to affect a woman's right to choose whether or not to bear a child. Anyone who continues to believe that the West can somehow lean on its spade and offer advice to the Islamic world about the separation of church and state or freedom of conscience is in need of an urgent corrective.

If a Liberal society is distinguished by the belief that it falls to the religious to justify the place of their beliefs in our public lives by showing that they respect the freedom of conscience and action that is the right of every human being, then by God the West has work to do. There are some politicians and churches in the West who continue to deny this Liberal principle outright. Some Western churches continue to be instruments of terrible ignorance in the developing world, and America.

Our Liberal Work

Whatever the temptation to divide ourselves into tribes or cultures, as Liberals our eye must be on the line between what Diderot called 'the altar and the throne'. We have inherited the political liberalism of Locke and Milton, who understood that to guarantee the individual's freedom of conscience, religion must be kept out of the marketplace and the rooms of government.

I have already criticised the Old Testament sensibilities of the current US administration, and of many of the voices in American politics. Yet even in Europe, secularists continue to struggle against attempts to define Europe in Christian terms and as a Christian culture. The ELDR party has vigorously opposed and will continue to oppose the attempts of the Christian Democrats to insert a reference to a Judaeo-Christian God into our new European Constitution.

Of course Europe retains many of the ethical values associated with Christianity, but these are not necessarily Christian values, any more than Europe is necessarily a Christian Civilisation. Europe is home to, among others, 15 million Muslims and 55 million Atheists and both of these populations are growing as Europe's Christian population shrinks. Fencing off our transforming culture and values in this way simply makes no sense. There is no denying Christianity's legacy for Europe. Yet Liberalism finds it impossible to talk about culture the way that conservatives and some religious people do, as something unmoving and unchanging. We are uncomfortable with the language of 'civilisations' when it is used to define abstract chunks of human geography. For Liberals culture is something that is always in flux. A civilisation is something never greater than the individual people whose common life expresses it.

Moreover, the European Union can and must be ready to welcome Turkey and predominantly Muslim states like Bosnia Herzegovenia when they meet the criteria for membership. In Turkey, as here in Senegal, secular Islam is making important advances in the face of fundamentalism. I anticipate that the European Commission's next report will send another strong signal to Turkey that valuable progress towards accession is still being made. There are many problems, not least a troubling human rights record, but we owe it to Turkey's reformers to share their ambitions for secular Islam. It is vitally important that this Congress sends a powerful message of support to Turkey, especially as many in Europe continue to question its European vocation. Why do they? For no other reason than because they believe that Turkey lies on the far side of some cultural divide. How short is their historical perspective!

Everywhere else where secular Islam is doing its important work we must offer our support. This Congress should express its admiration for Shirin Ebadi, who was recently awarded the Nobel Peace Prize for her struggle for Women's Rights in Iran.

At the same time we must be unflinching in our criticism of those who would use religious fundamentalism as justification for exploitation or repression.

Everywhere where religious extremism legitimises terrorism we have a duty to undo its work. In the wider Middle East we will only achieve a settlement when the rule of law succeeds the rule of violence and the religious rationale that too often underpins it.

Until Jewish hopes are defined by the practicalities of coexistence and not biblical prophecy there will be no peace for Israel.

Until we replace the delusions of martyrdom with the prosaic promise of peace and normality there will be no peace for Palestine, or end to the suicide bombers of Al Qaida.

Until we finally understand that no religion that continues to hate the realities of human sexuality, to claim rights over the bodies of women or the minds of children, can properly play a part in our public lives, then we will not have achieved our Liberal work.

Closing Remarks

Rather than starting with a claim about power, Liberalism begins in a claim about freedom. The freedom of each and every one of us. Respecting the freedom of individuals to practice and preach their religious values is a liberal duty. But so is questioning religious values when they demand a place in our public lives.

For the profoundly religious, accepting that a religious conviction is an opinion like any other can be counter-intuitive. Last year, Britain's on steel imports. The sanctions approved by the WTO last week will be the biggest such measures in the history of the organisation.

Again, the question is, how did we get here? The Bush administration came to office promising to outdo Clinton as a free-trade Presidency. Instead we got the 2002 Farm Bill, then this three-year protection program for the US steel industry that the WTO describes as 'inconsistent' with the US's free trade commitments. The Bush administration's free trade credentials are starting to look a little doubtful.

The WTO does of course allow limited protection for an industry undergoing reconstruction. This has been the defence that Zoellick and the current administration have provided for their steel tariffs. Whether you buy that really depends on whether you think the US steel industry has a sustainable future in a global free market. If you don't, then you have to conclude that the Bush tariffs are not a shield for restructuring but a political quid-pro-quo for an industry with more lobbyists than longevity. The United Steelworkers of America was quick to call the proposed EU sanctions 'blackmail', but I am inclined to say that political blackmail is exactly what the American steel industry has paid so handsomely for in Washington.

Hypocrisy and Free Trade

That's not to say that all American politicians shouldn't take what is happening in the American Rust Belt extremely seriously. Industrial change creates huge social problems in advanced societies. European politicians have a similar duty to their coalmining communities, and to their farmers and fishermen. But to give false hope to these communities through these distortive measures is dishonest and counter-productive.

It's dishonest because it creates the illusion that these industries somehow exist outside a rapidly changing world. It's counter-productive because it aggravates other American industries like car makers, who have to pay higher prices for raw materials, and it alienates America's international partners. It also leaves a US administration with no small taste for the moral high ground looking opportunistic and hugely compromised.

Nobody should have to suffer through watching Bush's officials shamelessly scolding China for non-compliance with its WTO obligations. Bush's government is making a fool of the United States and they must know it, however brazenly they try to spin the current line.

However, Europe shouldn't be too self-righteous. We might briefly savour the idea that we can deliver a kick directly to the seat of the Bush administration's electoral pants by raising tariffs on Florida orange juice. But a trade war - however justly waged - is in nobody's interests, whatever their feelings on the Bush administration.

If we are honest with ourselves, Europe's free trade credentials are hardly what they should be. We went to Cancun with grand words about the benefits of free trade, but we practice an indefensible Common Agricultural Policy that all but denies those benefits to the developing world. For Liberals like myself, it turns my stomach to hear the EU preach about free trade when it continues to subsidise every European cow at the rate of two euros a day. And this when one billion people on this planet live on one euro a day. If we really believe in the power of free trade to break the shackle of poverty, it is time for Europe to practice what it preaches.

The Temptations of Protectionism

Of course, we come down to the same old conflict between politics and principle. Free trade or French farmers? Subsidise or sink-or-swim? The political value of protectionism is obvious. We are elected by men and women with mortgages to pay and jobs they are afraid of losing. People who are not afraid to make protectionism the price of their vote. I have yet to meet a voter sufficiently disinterested to allow me to legislate them out of a job - or fail to legislate to keep them in a job - without consequence. In a system where politics is essentially funded by vested interests, a similar problem will arise. These industries don't spend a fortune in campaign finance and lobbyist fees for nothing.

The trouble is that experience shows that protection is a short term solution at best. Successful modern economies need to be flexible things, and protectionism is the enemy of adaptability. Rather than creating a sustainable culture of competitiveness it just perpetuates the problems of industrial change by delaying them. The Bush administration might think it's made a pragmatic political alliance with protectionism, but there is no such thing. They will wake up to discover they have sold their soul along with their free trade credentials. Bush is now in the unenviable position of having to take the bottle away from the baby of mid-west farming and the US steel industry. And this in an election year.

We already see that the need to keep the subsidy-hungry steel industry sweet probably means that if Bush does remove these tariffs he will simply replace them with others. In the end it will probably just land them back in a WTO courtroom where they started.

Moving On

We have to move on from this. However rocky the last year has been, America and Europe are still a community of common values. Free trade is at the heart of this. The GATT regime, and the WTO that it became, expressed the belief that open markets brought peace and prosperity. Europe and the United States have both profited hugely from global free trade. That's what makes so much of our current policy so indefensible.

The idea that this long-standing commitment to open markets might be reduced to just another 'coalition of the willing', strung together bilaterally by Bob Zoellick when the US feels like it, is a non-starter. You can't preach the moral value of free trade one day and close your own markets the next. And however powerful the US becomes, its politicians cannot allow its international relations to become just another side-effect of the campaign trail and the pursuit of American votes. The same goes for Europe. To paraphrase Nixon's Treasury Secretary John Connolly, the current US and EU policy towards the developing world seems to be 'well, it may be our economy, but it's your problem.'

Our size and economic strength should make us conscientious, not careless. We have the ability to lead, to shape the forces of globalisation so that they work for everyone. We do this chiefly by example. Once the moral authority is gone, it is hard to reclaim. Unless we show that we are genuinely committed to free trade for manufactures and farm goods, then we will never get the agreements we want from the developing world on trade in services or intellectual property. It's no wonder Cancun failed.

And there is another problem. A trade war creates just the kind of background noise that we just don't need at this crucial time in EU-US relations. It has never been more important that the EU and the US find common ground and rebuild what they lost over Iraq. There is no making light of our differences. Much of Europe remains surly over Iraq, although it now knows it must assist the US and Britain. It will push ahead with structured co-operation on defence in spite of the criticisms of the Bush government. It looks as if the transatlantic relationship will have a new dimension of candidness for the foreseeable future. But anything is better than talking past each other, or pretending that we don't have common responsibilities and common concerns. Given time, I trust, the strength of the EU-US connection will reassert itself.

This kind of friction over trade is bad news. It erodes trust between the officials who actually provide the substance of the special relationship. One of the things that kept the transatlantic relationship in any sort of business during the public rift over Iraq is that these men and women kept talking in private. It's crucial that political posturing does not sour the atmosphere in which they have to work.

I can't pretend that President Bush will receive anything other than a public cold shoulder in London tomorrow. What matters is that we don't turn the European reaction to his presidency into a symbol of the transatlantic relationship as a whole. While the US and Europe are directing their energies into quarrelling with each other, we are distracted from a world full of quarrels that need our joint attention. The sooner our collective minds are focussed on these, the better.'

## The Emperor's New Clothes

*Speech to the European Parliament in Strasbourg one week after the 12th EU-Russia summit took place in Italy where leaders agreed to "strengthen strategic partnership" in preparation for 2004's EU enlargement. However questions over human rights abuses and the Yukos affair, soured the event and Russia's image. In this speech Graham warns Putin that he should not dress in European clothes without adopting European values - and lambasts the EU President, Silvio Berlusconi, for his ill-considered comments on Chechnya and the detention of Mikhail Khodorkovsky.*

*19th November 2003, Strasbourg*

'Mr President, when Peter the Great wanted to make Russia more Western, he dressed up the Russian aristocracy in Western European clothes and moved the capital of Russia westwards from Moscow to St Petersburg. President Putin's westward-looking government has described the European Union as its 'natural political partner', and until recently Russia has appeared to dress in the clothes of Europe: the clothes of free trade, the clothes of political and civil rights, the clothes of infant democracy.

The ELDR Group welcomed this EU-Russia summit. We are right to look for political and economic spaces where our two societies can work together. Under the right circumstances, we welcome closer economic relations between the European Union and Russia. Easier travel is a necessary and important part of making this work.

Russia and the Union share a common security environment and a high degree of mutual interdependence, so we are right to seek to make our joint borders more secure and our shared hemisphere more safe. We welcome Russia's ambitions to join the WTO and this may be possible, even if it is made more difficult by recent events.

However, Europe is right to rail against Russian repression and governmental meddling in the lives of its neighbours. The issue of Chechnya will not go away, nor will Russia's refusal to ratify Kyoto. It is not enough to wear the clothes of Europe. Closer relations should carry the price of full subscription to modern European values, and at the very least we must continue to be critical and frank.

At this summit, Mr President-in-Office, our position was badly compromised by those charged with representing us. The presidency's ill-considered comments on Chechnya and on the arrest and detention of Mikhail Khodorkovsky were out of line. Mr Berlusconi speaks for Europe and he should choose his words with care. His own presidency drafted a declaration last month that was strongly critical of Russian conduct in Chechnya. However, not only was there no reference to Chechnya in the summit communiqué, but the President of the Council even thought it appropriate to contradict Europe's affirmed position with an improvised display of bluster worthy of a cheap lawyer. In any case, why should we deny the difficulties of the Russian minorities in the Baltic states? They are nothing compared to the persecution of the Chechens.

Internal security may be complementary to justice and human rights, as the President-in-Office said, but as practiced in Chechnya it is not. We have condemned Russian action in Chechnya and the attempt to intimidate sources of political opposition in Russia for good reason. Despite their European clothes, it is not clear that Mr Putin's government shares our values of democracy, human rights, the rule of law and freedom of expression. If it does, why is Mr Khodorkovsky in gaol?'

## Life In The Global City

*In 2002 Bulgaria and Romania agreed a roadmap of reforms to set them on course for EU Membership in 2007. In this speech, to staff and students at St Kliment Ohridski University in Sofia, Graham expands on ideas outlined in his collection of essays entitled 'Liberalism and Globalisation', which had recently been translated into Bulgarian. He shows how the Liberal Democratic model of governance adopted by the EU can provide an effective framework to overcome global hurdles like climate change, migration and economic development. The more globalised we become, he says, the more Liberal we need to be.*

*19th February 2004, Sofia, Bulgaria*

'Before I begin, let me extend my thanks to the St Kliment Ohridski Univeristy for the chance to address you today. A professional politician does not often get the opportunity to speak at length to an academic audience. I work in the world of practical action - but my work is shaped by my political beliefs. I want to use my time today to look at the political fact of globalisation through the prism of Liberal ideas. I will speak for twenty minutes or so, and then I would like to take your questions.

I am the President of the Liberal Democrat and Reform group in the European Parliament. With 53 MEPs out of the total of 626, we are the third largest group behind the European People's Party (EPP) and the Party of European Socialists (PES), but we hold the balance of power in the Parliament. I myself am Scottish, but our group is made up of MEPs from across the EU and observers from the new Member States that will join the EU in May. If Bulgaria joins the EU in 2007, we will be joined by Bulgarian Liberals too. Although the members bring different nationalities, cultures and languages to the group, they share a liberal democratic political tradition and work together as one political family in the European Parliament.

The European Parliament is an historic experiment in international democracy. It brings together elected representatives from across Europe to participate in the process of European government. Like the European Union itself, it was founded by the same generation who built the United Nations: liberal thinkers and internationalists who had come to doubt the ability of the nation state to confront the challenges of international governance. The great depression, the Second World War and the arrival of the nuclear age had globalised war and poverty. They aspired to globalise prosperity and peace.

What is Globalisation?

What is Globalisation? What does it mean? The word globalisation has come to represent many things: the expanding culture of multi-national business; the increasingly visible fate of the global poor; the streets full of protestors in Seattle or Genoa; the common landscape we increasingly share in our high-streets and cities, or when we log on to the internet. Globalisation is all of these things.

One way of understanding globalisation is as a measure of speed. Imagine a circle drawn around Sofia, measuring the distance a person could travel from the city in twelve hours. A hundred and fifty years ago that circle might have stretched to Pernik or Samakov, down tracks and muddy roads. By the turn of the last century it would have stretched, by rail, to the coast of the Black Sea and Bucharest. With the invention of the car, the circle would have expanded as far as Hungary and Modern Greece. Now, in 2004, the circle would stretch out in an enormous arc as far as Singapore and the Pacific coast of the United States. In half a day a person can travel half way around the world. Electronic and satellite communication means that information races even faster. News, intelligence and money can now move around the world in an instant.

All of the phenomena that we associate with globalisation have to do with acceleration. Markets in Europe four hundred years ago were filled with products from the other side of the world, just like today. People, given the economic freedom or time or motivation travelled huge distances, just like today. But Asian spices used to take seven months to travel from India to London. Now global produce markets fill and empty in weeks. Where a Victorian tourist in the nineteenth century might take two years to see Europe, a modern European backpacker can do it in a month or two. A rising tide of technology and prosperity has made travel easier and more accessible to almost all Europeans. Every single person in this room will travel and perhaps work outside of Bulgaria in their lifetime, if they have not already. The huge majority of you will travel beyond Europe. Yet your grandparents, and perhaps even your parents, probably live not too far from the place they were born. This new flood of experience demands new tools of communication. You are listening to me speak in English, a language your great-grandparents probably never heard spoken in their lives.

Faster movement and instant information have transformed the way we see ourselves and the world. Our sense of what is foreign has been challenged by the constant presence of the world on our TV and computer screens. As we have become more aware of each other we have become much more interconnected and interdependent. We understand more clearly than ever that we share responsibility for the planet and for the wellbeing of those on it. The American writer Marshall McLuhan described the new world as a global village but that is not really true. Villages are usually distinguished by their neighbourliness and sense of solidarity, and no one could look at the inequities of our world and be reminded of those things. But we do live in a global city, in which the spaces between places and the spaces between people are being crushed by travel and technology. Where extraordinary wealth and terrible poverty exist side by side. We are being pushed together, at once anonymous and deeply intimate. Intimate, because our problems are increasingly collective problems: the environment, international security, international crime. Anonymous, because in a crowd of six billion we rely every day on the trust and the good will of strangers.

In a world of strangers we quickly realise that we rely on shared values. Law, for example, is what enables us to live in a world where we do not know the huge majority of people we live among. The mutual respect for the individual rights of others is what makes it possible to live this way.

That is what Liberalism argues. A liberal society is a society built on the protection of the rights of individuals by the law. Liberalism developed as a response to our growing realisation that we have to live alongside and trust, people we do not know. The more globalised we become, the more Liberal we need to be.

The American political theorist Francis Fukuyama wrote at the end of the Cold War that we had arrived at the end of history. He argued that the long ideological debate about how human beings should live had been decisively won by capitalist democracy, and that it was left to the next generation - your generation - simply to figure out the details. There is of course no end to history, and more than just details to debate. But for Liberals the dramatic spread of free market social democracy is the key to enabling people to live better and more peacefully. Karl Popper once said that the meaning of democracy was a state where the governors can be changed without violence. That we live in a world where this is very often true is a testament to how far we have come. But we have not come far enough, if only because the world is changing fast and we have to run to keep up. What I want to do today is to discuss four challenges raised by globalisation - there are of course many others. I will say a little about how liberalism addresses each of them. These are: migration, the environment, international crime and global poverty.

Migration

A month ago, the secretary general of the United Nations addressed the European Parliament on the subject of migration. He warned us that Europe's shrinking population made it more important than ever that Europe open its doors to immigrants. Europe has traditionally been a society that people emigrated from rather than to. Although Early Modern Europe had its migrants - the Jews, the Huguenots in Britain and Ireland, the Roma - and these minorities often received a welcome much like that the one Europe too often gives to modern migrants. Which is to say no welcome.

Yet economic migrancy is an irrefutable good. Economic migrants are ambitious and enterprising. They bring skills and a willingness to work hard, and they do jobs that need filling in most developed societies. However, although they want to assimilate with their new society they often value their difference and it can be hard for host societies to adapt. Liberals believe that we can ask of migrants that they make certain minimum attempts to adapt - learning the language and complying with the laws of their new home - but we should not ask them to give up what we would not give up ourselves.

Liberalism argues that societies are not hermetically sealed. That there are no nations worth protecting at the cost of the freedom of individuals. Liberals believe strongly in self-determination, but we have come to see over the last century and a half that the language of self-determination can be abused by national groups to remove the freedom of individuals and to justify aggression towards our neighbours or towards minorities in our own societies. Our cultures are always changing, and migration is just another part of that. While pride in where you come from is important, our senses of national identity too often defy reasonable understanding. We have a lot in common with our neighbours because they are our neighbours, not because of the colour of their skin or their religion or where they were born.

Liberals believe that Europe must open the door for migrants because Europe needs migrants. If we close the front door, we will only drive the desperate to seek access through the back, where they fall victim to smugglers and criminals. Liberals believe that we must learn to tolerate cultural difference in our societies, so long as we are respected in turn. Accepting the values of those we disagree with is the mark of a Liberal intellect. In historical terms this a radically new approach to human relations, but in the global city it is the only way we will ever succeed in living together.

Global Development

I have already said that the globalised world is more of a global city than a global village. If the world really were a village rather more of its wealthier citizens would be shocked by the misery of the poor and motivated to greater self-sacrifice. Of the six billion human beings on our planet, half live on less than two euros a day and almost a billion go to sleep hungry every night. Figures provided by the World Bank show that 80% of the world's population lives on just 20% of its GDP. Although populations in Europe and the developed world are stalled or shrinking, population growth in the developing world is adding tens of thousands to the ranks of the hungry and hopeless every single day. The world is beginning to look like a mediaeval city, with the wealthy blinded to the anger and resentment of the poor. Even if the demands of equity did not require that we act, self-interest should. As the President of the World Bank James Wolfensohn has said: development assistance is not charity, it is investment in global peace and security. The developed world fails year after year to meet the United Nations spending targets of 0.7% of GDP on development aid. Without that aid, the poor are also deprived of the private investment that would follow it. It is a sickening realisation that the inhabitants of wealthy countries still seem to prefer the death of those in the developing world to their own inconvenience.

Liberalism is a political philosophy of equality of opportunity. When we know that the poor starve, or that our own selfishness limits opportunities in the developing world then it is no longer possible for us to believe that we live in a world where all are free to achieve their potential. That is why Liberals believe not only in development assistance but that Europe and the rest of the developed world have a duty to open their markets to trade with the developing world. In fields such as agriculture where European farmers already have significant advantages the developing world would have to work hard to compete. While Europe subsidises its farmers and hides behind export tariffs they find it impossible.

The argument for modern Liberalism began in the demand for free trade. The power of free enterprise to unlock individual potential and reward human innovation and hard work is the centrepiece of the Liberal vision of a free society. Over two centuries it has transformed European society, delivering a level of prosperity that has no historical precedent. Yet it is an opportunity that we in the first world continue to deny to the developing world.

International Crime

If globalisation has revolutionised the way that we trade and move around the world: it has also presented new opportunities for criminals. The extraordinary power of international criminal gangs means that states struggle to stop the smuggling of drugs, guns and even people. The long shadow of terrorism means that these networks are also increasingly suspected of trading in nuclear technology or chemical and biological weapons. The traders in human beings, the men who sell women and children into what amounts to sexual slavery, have preyed upon thousands of women from the former Soviet Union and Eastern Europe.

Internationally the drugs trade is believed to be worth about eight percent of global GDP, the international trafficking of humans somewhere between 12 and 20 billion euros a year. While our governments fail to agree on effective ways to stop the laundering of this money criminals are simply laughing at us. In Europe, where open borders leave criminals free to outrun the reach of domestic law enforcement, we are similarly helpless .The United Nations has constantly tried to persuade governments to co-ordinate their responses by improving co-operation between police forces and national judiciaries. A lack of political will and arguments about national sovereignty still prevent co-operation between national police forces, just as the absence of internationally recognised warrants for arrest, the calling of witnesses or production of evidence prevent closer judicial co-operation.

Again Liberalism asks that we transcend our borders. What use are our national law enforcement agencies if they cannot catch criminals who simply run to the neighbouring jurisdiction? Is national sovereignty so important that we cannot trade a little of it for a better and more effective justice system? International criminals can be halfway around the world before we have even got our boots on. While extradition remains a political process it will be slow and clumsy. The European Arrest Warrant, which came into force on the first of January this year, is a limited answer to this problem. It makes it much easier for one European state to act on behalf of another in criminal justice matters. And yet, almost half of the current Member States have not yet ratified it.

## The Environment

And finally, the environment. If you want an image for the globalised world then the environment is it. Rivers do not stop at borders. The polluted ocean is shared by all of us - as is the polluted sky. We can no longer escape responsibility for what we do to the natural world. Shrinking ice sheets, rising sea levels, changing weather patterns, migration of plants and animals and the increasing carbon content of air tells us that climate change is making our planet warmer than at any time in the past 10,000 years. The growing evidence that people are doing irreversible damage to the natural environment demands urgent action.

Liberals believe that the environment is our collective inheritance, and the right of our children. Liberals in Europe have worked hard to make sure that we are the first major contributor on the planet to ratify the Kyoto protocol. Liberals believe that we have to start now: investing in sustainable technologies, raising the financial costs of pollution and helping businesses get cleaner and greener. Europe has some of the strictest environmental legislation on the planet, and it is a good thing. Because the problem is huge and there is no time to waste.

Limiting and reducing the growing volume of gases which human beings and nature emit into the atmosphere will require a concerted effort by government at all levels in all countries. Yet the United States with four percent of the world's population and 25% of global emissions is living in denial and refuses to co-operate. Russia and China are also unwilling to help. Unless we can convince these countries that their interests are not served by ignoring environmental damage we will all pay the price.

The Capability Gap

Let me conclude with some more general thoughts on Liberalism, governance and globalisation.

We live in political times that are defined by what we might call a 'capability gap'. We are struggling to find the political tools to do the work we need done. In a world of international problems, our solutions are still national solutions. Where instruments of international government do exist, like the United Nations, they are captive to the political will of nation states; effective only in rare moments of consensus. For all of the good work that the UN does, it works only at the indulgence of the powerful.

Liberalism argues that the demands of common action must outweigh the claims of national sovereignty where our common interests are at stake. Liberals believe in local government and direct democracy wherever it is practical, but they are committed to international solutions because they believe that what the American James Madison called our "great and aggregate interests" can no longer be addressed at the local or national level.

Questions of security, the environment, development and European economic prosperity are questions we have to answer together. In his famous defence of Federal government for the huge young American republic in the The Federalist Papers Madison argued that good government meant deciding what should rest with the American states and what "aggregate interests" should be passed up to the new Federal government. His description could be lifted from a modern Liberal manifesto for Europe, and indeed for the world.

At the beginning of my speech I called the EU and the European Parliament an unprecedented experiment in international government and democracy. The European Union has enabled European states to overcome the problems that do not stop at their national borders. Because it is rooted in internationalist principles the European Union is in many respects a Liberal idea, and it has unfolded along Liberal lines. It is built on the legal protection of individual political and civil rights, the legal guarantee of free and fair trade and the principle of international common action. To be sure, the EU needs to be more democratic. It is also constantly undermined by the failure of national politicians to transcend their national politics and think as Europeans. But it has achieved a remarkable stability in Europe and the single market of which it is the guarantor has delivered astounding prosperity. Given the capability to act in fields such as Justice and Home Affairs the EU can deliver greater security and a stronger guarantee of justice. It is turning Europeans into cosmopolitans and cosmopolitans make better and more tolerant neighbours.

The word cosmopolitan in English is derived from the Greek word cosmos, meaning universe, and the Greek word polites meaning citizen. It is no coincidence that it was the European Enlightenment that first brought the word into wide usage. For the enlightenment the cosmopolis was the ordered world that human reason revealed: a world of inherent human equality, checked and balanced political power and fundamental human community. A cosmopolitan was a person who felt at home in that world.

These cosmopolitans believed, much as modern Liberals do, that human beings can design systems of government that reflect a reasoned view of the world. What globalisation has done is to dramatically change the terms on which politics takes place. Liberalism argues that there is new power to be checked and balanced; new problems to be solved, new challenges to overcome, and that many of our old political solutions are no longer adequate. I would contend today that Liberalism's focus on legal protections, individual rights, free, open and co-operative international relations are the only firm foundation for a politics capable of addressing this new globalised world.

Life in the Marketplace

In such a short speech I have perhaps raised more questions that I have answered. Let me finish with another metaphor. If you have ever looked closely at a market when it is busy you might have been struck that it is much more than a place for buying and selling. In markets we meet and discuss, we haggle and argue, we confront difference and we are reconciled with it. There is a good reason why every single European town is built around its marketplace: because the marketplace is our public space. The market is where we live out our public lives. The Athenian philosophers of ancient Greece used to meet in the agora in Athens. They often complained about the traders, but *they knew that that was where life was lived.* The life of the marketplace is much more than a life of commerce and it forces us to deal with others openly and fairly - and peacefully. Societies that trade are less likely to go to war, it really is that simple.

The American liberal philosopher Richard Rorty has written that the great virtue of Liberal democracy is that it creates a political market, where citizens can shop for the politics they choose, without violence or fear. For Liberalism the market is a powerful metaphor because it symbolises all these things: choice, openness, diversity, collaboration and creativity. It is in the marketplace that we recognise our collective problems and solve our public disputes. It is where we realise our public potential. What globalisation has done is to create a world in which our marketplace is often the world itself. It is time to get used to living in it.

## Applied Liberalism

*Speech delivered in Malaysia to a meeting of the Council of Asian Liberals and Democrats (CALD) which was founded in 1993 as a pan-Asian forum to support democratic movements. The ELDR Group, with Graham as its leader, teamed up with CALD in 2002 to promote stronger ties between Asian and European Liberal parties. Here Graham outlines the factors that make Liberalism a formula adaptable to the world's different cultures - rather than a blueprint into which they must be squeezed - and examines how this can be adapted to meet the challenges of the new world order.*

*27th August 2004, Penang*

'I have been asked to say a little about political challenges for liberalism at the national, regional and international level in this new century. This is a fairly challenging brief for a fifteen-minute speech but I thought that I could introduce our discussion by making a few remarks about what I see as the key battlegrounds for liberalism in the twenty-first century. Inevitably, as a European politician I am strongest offering a European perspective, but I have deliberately chosen to speak about the challenges that I think liberals face everywhere they are in government or aspire to be.

I see the political challenge for liberalism everywhere as being one of what we might call 'applied liberalism'. More has been written about the political theory of liberalism than any other political philosophy. This morning we did some work on defining what we think liberalism is and is not and we returned to a set of broad ideas which would be echoed by liberals in most times and most places: the freedom of the individual, civil and political rights protected by law, open markets, tolerance of diversity, secular government, protection of the weak and the dispossessed. But these are abstractions, not political actions. And politics is about political action. Applied liberalism means transforming these ideals into workable politics.

Towards the end of the nineteenth century and the beginning of the twentieth century, Liberalism became a concrete political program in Europe and elsewhere. People began electing liberal politicians rather than just reading liberal philosophers. Liberalism was forced to become applied liberalism. Its ideals of human freedom were reshaped by the real world. For the first time it dealt with the poor, and the freedom of the poor. It dealt with the rights and the freedom of women. It looked at the people of the European colonies and had to answer for their freedom, or lack of it. Liberalism came to understand that where human potential is denied, through poverty, or poor education, or fear, there is only a caricature of freedom. Applied liberalism quickly came to see freedom - as Amartya Sen would put it - as development. As the freeing of human potential.

One of the lessons I have learnt from working alongside liberal colleagues in Europe and meeting liberal colleagues throughout Asia and North America is that liberalism is a formula, not a blueprint. Liberals are always trying to balance freedom and fairness, emancipation and empowerment, to achieve the greatest measure of freedom and opportunity for each individual and this can mean different things in different places. Scandinavian liberals, with their lumbering social democratic states, are likely to be tax-cutters, whereas British or Canadian liberals are just as likely to be defending greater investment in public services.

Liberals everywhere are trying to work out the best way to make government tolerant of social or religious diversity, but there is no one single way of achieving that.

Free markets are important tools when they work well, but they can fail in any one of a thousand ways, and effective liberal government means recognising and adapting to those failures, many of which are often due to local differences or preferences that must be respected. Again, there is no blueprint. Just the formula of freedom and fairness. That is the challenge of applied liberalism.

I think we can strip applied liberalism down to a few basics. The first has to do with the need to make political power accountable, the second has to do with breaking a long habit in modern politics and learning to see people rather than states.

Liberalism began in the defence of the individual from the power of the state, or the majority, or simply other powerful individuals. Liberalism has always tried to make power accountable, first by ensuring that power rests in laws and constitutions and institutions, not individual people. Then, in the twentieth century, by making those institutions subject to democratic control.

A world of law and common values and multilateral institutions is the only effective way of ensuring that power respects the weak. It is easy to mock the failures of the United Nations - until you consider the alternative. Whatever you think of current US policy in the Middle East, the snub dealt to the United Nations by two of the world's most powerful democracies undermined not just the UN but the idea that we live in a world of rules at all.

Another example: last year in Europe, the credibility of the eurozone suffered a heavy blow when France and Germany decided they would break the eurozone's rules on fiscal discipline and maintain steep public deficits. These were rules they had made themselves - in fact Germany was their chief architect. As large states and political heavyweights there was nothing to stop them, just as there was nothing to stop the United States invading Iraq. But the broken rules are not easily mended, and the precedent has been set.

This applies also in areas like free trade. Rich states often speak as if free trade were a deeply held principle. But they do so in one breath and defend their agricultural subsidies and tariff barriers in the next, and we are left with the same sense that the rules are for the weak, but not for the strong. The fact that the Doha round has now been re-launched on the back of serious European and US commitments to end this hypocrisy is to be welcomed. But the poor need action not words.

In a world of strangers we rely on common values. Even the strongest states must ultimately fear a world without rules. The US neo-conservatives believed that American power was its own justification and its own sustenance. They were wrong. Whoever wakes up as President of the United States on November 3, we have to hope that the lessons of unilateralism have been learnt. We can't reshape the world with power alone. Even if we believe we are using power for the right reasons, the smaller our coalition of the willing, the greater by definition the coalition of the aggrieved we leave behind us.

Containing and influencing the large and the powerful is a challenge for liberals everywhere. While strategies may not be the same in every case, liberals know that vigilance, courage and peer pressure are essential. In Canada former Liberal Prime Minister Pierre Trudeau once described living alongside the United States as being like "sleeping with an elephant". In Western Europe, Liberals were long divided over how to deal with the Moscow-based Soviet Communism which dominated the Eastern half of our continent. It was the skill and courage - and the patience - of former German Liberal Foreign Minister Hans-Dietrich Genscher which created the conditions for peaceful regime change. Here in Asia, Liberals in Taiwan or Hong Kong may not always see eye to eye with Liberals elsewhere on how to sow and nurture democracy in the People's Republic of China, but firm principles, courage and peer pressure will no doubt be elements in any successful strategy.

On the global level, maintaining these networks of common values and common expectations is a crucial challenge for liberals. We should be leading attempts to reform the United Nations so that it can respond better to the developing principle of humanitarian intervention. Some people are already suggesting that the crisis in Darfur in the Sudan may require a Kosovo-style intervention outside of UN auspices. It is hard to see how the UN can remain relevant if its political structure ensures that it cannot act in situations such as this. Strong and coherent regional voices from Europe and Asia are also needed to balance a wilful friend like the United States.

Liberals should also be pressing for democratic reform of the WTO and pressuring the governments of Europe and the United States to take the promise of free trade seriously.

We should be building a strong moral consensus around the ambitions of the Kyoto Protocol and pushing beyond them to stricter limits on carbon emissions.

We must give credibility and strength to the International Criminal Court so that national sovereignty can no longer guard the breakers of international humanitarian law.

Everywhere where power is exercised there need to be clear limits to its reach, and it is liberals who should be defining them. The war against terror has given governments a new and dangerous rationale for encroaching on civil liberties and limiting personal privacy - often in the name of our own safety. This year the European Parliament was forced to take European governments to the European Court of Justice when they authorised an agreement with the United States to share confidential data on European airline passengers travelling across the Atlantic. As in the US, many European governments have used the war on terror to fast-track untested biometric technology. If these things make us marginally safer - and there is not a lot of evidence that they do - they do so at a real cost in reduced privacy and liberty.

The war against terror leaves us afraid, and fearful people will listen to governments who tell them they can only be safer when government is more powerful. Benjamin Franklin said that the man who would surrender liberty for a little safety deserves neither. As liberals we need to be on our guard against claims that we can be more secure by being less free.

Even in our daily political lives, liberals should always be asking if institutions could be more open, and more accountable. I am a firm believer in the European Union, but I have spent my entire European political career working to make the institutions of the European Union more open and more democratic. The developing powers of the European Parliament mean that Europe now has a functioning and strong supranational democracy, but that Parliament could still connect to citizens better, as could the other institutions of the EU. Freedom of information is crucial in this regard. From the IMF and the World Bank down to our local village councils people should see and understand the decisions that influence their lives, and the people who make those decisions should be accountable for them.

The second insight of applied liberalism relates to people and states. Liberals do not accept that individuals in one country are fundamentally different from individuals in another. One of the consequences of seeing the world as a planet of individuals and families and local political communities is that nation states begin to look very different. Our national identities seem a lot more arbitrary.

This is why liberals are both committed localists and instinctive internationalists. I serve in the world's first supranational democratic parliament, which is part of the world's most ambitious experiment in supranational government. I would argue that where the European Union is succeeding is where it sees people, not states. Pollution doesn't stop at national borders. Fundamental human rights cannot be different in France and Belgium. Spain cannot be secure against international terrorism if Portugal is not. A genuine free market in Europe means the rules we make for business cannot be different in Poland and Germany.

The state is still the key administrative unit in human affairs, but the time has come to detach it once and for all from the politics of identity. Liberals are right to be deeply suspicious of the conservative language of 'civilisations' or 'cultures'. Liberals believe strongly in self-determination but they know enough history to know that the language of nationalism and self-determination can be abused by national groups to remove the freedom of individuals and to justify aggression towards neighbours. We know that open and pluralistic societies are historically richer and more pacific. We know that economic nationalism is a gamble that can have terrible consequences for prosperity and peace.

The challenge for liberal politics is to see - as much as possible - people rather than states. We need a mature attitude to international migration, that recognises the value that economic migrants bring rather than flattering the fears and prejudices of those who will not welcome them.

We need to accept and shoulder our responsibilities to the global poor by investing in aid and development.

We need to build regional, and ultimately, international partnerships in the war against terror, because there is no more safety in national sovereignty. We cannot offer a state's defence against a stateless enemy like Al Qaeda.

Every bit as important, we need to build similar alliances in the desperate struggle to reduce and reverse the damage we are doing to our shared natural environment.

States can be a tool in this work, but they can also be an obstacle to it. National governments still tend to look inward rather than outwards. The success of the European Union can be attributed to the simple fact that it allows European states to reclaim some of their power over the forces of global change. It enables them to do together what they could not do alone. When the EU leaves local government to local people and concentrates on serving their 'aggregate interests' at the European level it is probably the most practical vision of effective international government in the world. It can and should be a model for liberals everywhere.

Colleagues, testing our liberal principles in the world of practical politics shows us that there are many ways to a liberal society: as many as there are free people in charge of their own political futures. This applied liberalism may not have the abstract simplicity of a treatise by Locke or a pamphlet by Mill but it is a programme for a practical and truly democratic politics.

What I have tried to suggest this afternoon is that there are a number of threads that should run through our work. The first is a consistent and unwavering defence of the irreducible liberty of the individual in the face of power of all kinds. Liberals have always believed that power is dangerous, and must be contained by rules and systems of shared values. Liberals designed and built the United Nations and European Union to do just that. When power invokes the war against terror to remove our freedoms, it will be liberals who will stand in its way.

The second thread is the need to see people and the political challenges that bring them together, rather than the states that keep them apart. I have named global warming, international terrorism and the global gap between the rich and the poor, but there are many others.

Liberals in Asia face challenges of their own: societies and communities in which liberal solutions must be built for local problems. Here in Malaysia the challenges of a pluralistic and racially diverse society and a rapidly developing open economy call for liberal and secular government, but the liberal formula will produce a Malaysian liberalism subtly shaped to this unique culture and society.

This is a time of renewal for the Council of Asian Liberals and Democrats. By setting objectives here you will be giving impetus and direction to the work of liberal democrats throughout the region. As a colleague and friend, and on behalf of the European liberal family, I am privileged to be able to share with you some of my humble ideas.'

## Understanding The East Is A Career In Itself

*Cooperation between Asian and European Liberals and Democrats sometimes takes the form of joint parliamentary conferences, like that which Graham organised and hosted in the European Parliament in November 2004. In his introductory speech, he highlights how Europe's Atlantic focus has prevented it from keep pace with change and growth in Asia, the powerhouse of the future. However he also outlines how broader European engagement should be founded not on the potential commercial value of these connections but on a deep and durable mutual respect for human rights and democracy.*

*10th November 2004, Brussels*

'The British Prime Minister Benjamin Disraeli once said that understanding the East is a career in itself. And I have no doubt that our politics are sometimes fairly strange to you. For all of the ways in which the modern world has made our lives the same, politics remains, much as it always has been, a local practice.

However similar the challenges we face - and my expectation is that we will come away from these two days of talks with a strengthened sense that as Liberals and Democrats we face the same challenges and we share the same ambitions - but however similar those challenges are, we remain the representatives of local people and local priorities and local politics. We need to bridge that space in whatever ways we can.

In an era of unprecedented globalisation, we often struggle to globalise the voice of the people we represent. Too often, in a world where the voices of government or finance can be heard in seconds and around the world, the voices of the men and women who elect us remain local, much as people have always been. But local or not, the reality of globalisation is that we are all neighbours now. And strangers make bad neighbours. If we cannot find a way to bridge the local and the global, our politics will not be ready for a century of global challenges.

This Parliament is an unique attempt to bring the local and the global together. It represents 450 million Europeans and it is the only directly elected international Parliament in the world. In the EU the nation state is far from dead, but it is forced to share the stage with a practical and powerful prototype of international democracy. It can and should be a model for liberals everywhere.

That is why forums like this matter. Bringing Parliamentarians together - be it in the WTO Parliamentary forum or the Asia Europe Parliamentary Forum or any one of the growing number of interparliamentary assemblies - bringing Parliamentarians together is an important way of creating an alternative political network to that offered by national diplomacy. That we can speak openly with each other, even to the discomfort of our nation states, is a vital part of a healthy international civil society.

This week will also help us strengthen our network as Liberals and Democrats. We are a growing international family, and need to build the links that will sustain that growth. For ALDE, this is also a chance to deepen our strong engagement with Asia and Asian Liberal Democracy.

In general, Europeans live in a very Atlantic world. The palpable hope that existed in Europe for a Kerry Presidency only underlines the extent to which Europeans still look to the United States as a cousin civilisation - if one we sometimes do not completely understand. Yet globally this century will belong to Asia.

Given the extraordinary changes in the Asia-Pacific region it is important for Europeans to build stronger links with your region and to understand better the changes that are transforming it. Until Europeans know as much of the geopolitics of the South China Sea as they do of their own Atlantic, they will be seeing the world with one eye closed. Unless they grasp what is at stake on the Korean Peninsula or across the Taiwan Strait they will fail to understand the mood of this new Asian century.

Europe must continue to strive for a broad policy of engagement in the Asia-Pacific region. It has aspired to be a leading provider of development assistance and a friend in East Timor, Cambodia, and on the Korean Peninsula. Increasingly it seeks to build similar mutual links with the region's new and maturing democracies. The European Commission has worked to build a deeper trading and investing relationship between the EU and the Asia Pacific Region. New EU delegations in the region will be established in Malaysia, Singapore, Cambodia, Laos and Nepal.

The European Parliament plays its own role in the development of these policies and works hard to ensure they are shaped by our voices as elected representatives. The European Parliament's Foreign Affair's Committee has consistently insisted that Europe's relationship with the Asia-Pacific Region be founded not on the potential commercial value of these connections but on a deep and durable mutual respect for human rights and democracy. In the last Parliament ALDE Rapporteur Jules Maaten produced an influential blueprint for a new European engagement with Asia based on shared political values and mutual respect for human rights. Our group continues to be deeply involved with EU-Asia relations. Your job over these two days is to show us how we could be better engaged, or how we could do more.

Nowhere is this more important than in the Peoples Republic of China. Simply by virtue of its size, China remains key to Asia's future. The Canadian Premier Pierre Trudeau once said that living next to America is like sharing a bed with an elephant. Even its smallest movements were likely to keep you awake at night. Well, China is your elephant. From Europe the scale of this change is sometimes poorly understood, but in Asia it must both impress and unnerve you. We need to hear your perspectives and strategies.

You are also fighting your own war against terrorism; in Indonesia and the Philippines, in Thailand and elsewhere. Like Europe you are working to find a peaceful road to religious and ideological diversity. In a region where Buddhist lives alongside Christian and Muslim and atheist you will have your own experience with the Liberal mission to teach and to demand tolerance.

One of the intentions of this meeting is to allow us to have parallel discussions on the challenges that Liberals and Democrats face in Asia and Europe. My expectation is that we will leave this meeting with a sense of common challenges and common goals.

Liberals and Democrats in Asia and Europe are united by their shared belief in democracy and the rule of law; human rights and tolerance of diversity. Asia and Europe are both societies of astounding diversity, jostled by political change.

Three months ago I had the privilege of addressing the Council of Asian Liberals and Democrats in Penang. At the time, I spoke about applied liberalism. I argued that if the nineteenth century had marked liberalism's move from political philosophy to political practice, then the twenty first century should mark liberalism's coming of age as an international political movement.

One of the lessons we learn from working alongside liberal democrat colleagues in Europe and meeting liberal colleagues throughout Asia and North America is that liberalism is a formula, not a blueprint. Liberals are always trying to balance freedom and fairness to achieve the greatest measure of freedom and opportunity for each individual, and this can mean different things in different places. That is the challenge of applied liberalism.

Colleagues, testing our liberal principles in the world of practical politics shows us that there are many ways to a liberal society: as many as there are free people in charge of their own political futures.

What I know we will be reminded of this afternoon is that there are many common threads to our beliefs that run through our work. The first is a consistent and unwavering defence of the irreducible liberty of the individual in the face of power of all kinds. Liberals have always believed that power is dangerous, and must be contained by rules and systems of shared values. Liberals designed and built the United Nations and European Union to do just that.

The second thread is the need to see people and the political challenges that bring us together, rather than the states that keep us apart. I could name global warming, international terrorism and the global gap between the rich and the poor, but there are many others.

The best work we can do this week is to get to know each other better, and learn a little more about the people we each represent. In a time of unprecedented international uncertainty, a better understanding of each other - a better awareness of our common goals - is perhaps the greatest guarantee of our security. That is the real purpose of our work today and tomorrow: to close the gap between us and recognise the challenges that unite us not as Asians and Europeans but as fellow citizens of a small planet.

## The Semblance Of Reform Must Not Be Allowed To Mislead Us

*Speech given to a hearing in the European Parliament that debated whether the Chinese arms embargo, which has been in place since the 1987 massacre of pro-democracy campaigners in Tiananmen Square, should be lifted. Some EU Member States had been lobbying to replace the ban with a voluntary code of conduct to improve their trading relationship with Hu Jintao, the Chinese President. Yet as Graham points out, such codes tend to be honoured more in the breach than the observance and that, according to human rights experts, the human rights situation in China is actually deteriorating. The EU, he argues, must not make a Faustian pact in pursuit of short-term economic gain.*

*9th March 2005, Brussels*

'The recent willingness of the People's Republic of China to engage with the rest of the world is a major geopolitical development which we should all welcome. The Chinese have traditionally been generous and peace-seeking in such periods of opening. Indeed, the export nearly 600 years ago of Chinese technology and knowledge gave a major boost to the development of European civilisation, even though Europe was the one continent they failed to reach in their travels of the early fifteenth century.

The participation now of the People's Republic in global efforts to tackle the challenges of population growth, climate change and internationally-organised crime is essential to their solution. China must be encouraged to assume her role as a full member of the global community.

I believe the time has come for China to put into practice what it has long stated in principle: Gai Genh, Kai Fang - Change the System and Open the Door. Deng Xiaoping's rallying cry transformed China into an economic powerhouse. In my view 'Reform and Opening' should now evolve to embrace the ideals of human rights, democracy, and freedom that those words can, and should, entail. Only then should the EU consider lifting the arms embargo and fully welcome China into the community of nations.

Consider why this embargo was first put in place. It was no cynical political ploy but a humane response to an inhumane act. The Tiananmen Square massacre was witnessed by the global community and universally damned by it. Although China has changed beyond recognition in the last decade, no human rights group today would claim that it meets the standards of political and civil freedom that Europe expects of its allies. Indeed, many of the students who demonstrated are still in prison 16 years on.

Jacques Chirac would have Europe "remove the last obstacles to its relations with this important country." But these are not the last obstacles. Even the normally conservative UK Foreign and Commonwealth Office has observed that the human rights situation in China continues to be a matter of serious concern for European states.

China may have amended its Constitution to include the clause, "the State respects and protects human rights". It may have a reforming, outward-looking president. Yet it continues to persecute religious minorities and pro-democracy activists. It continues to torture and to execute dissidents. It continues to deny freedom of religion, association, and movement. It uses 09/11 and the "war on terrorism" as an excuse to crack down on unrest in Tibet and Xinjiang. The internet revolution, often viewed by the global community as a sign of a new, progressive China, has been used systematically by the state to entrap and prosecute dissidents.

Let us not forget that China terms itself a democratic republic. Actions, not words, are required. The semblance of reform must not be allowed to mislead us. It is high time the EU took the Convention of Human Rights in both hands and approached the Chinese Government with a series of specific conditions before it even considers lifting the ban.

I join with Amnesty International, China Human Rights Watch and other concerned bodies in calling on the Beijing Government to ratify the International Covenant on Civil and Political Rights which it signed six years ago. There should be an end to the use of military power against peaceful democratic action and acceptance of democracy in Hong Kong. No more slave labour camps, where people are sent without trial. And reconsideration of a justice system that carries out 70% of the world's capital penalties.

As President Clinton famously said "China is on the wrong side of history". Just last Friday China announced an increase of more than 12% in its defence budget on top of 11 _% hike last year. Yesterday they published an anti-secession bill which would allow the State Council to take military action against Taiwan without reference to wider bodies. Under such circumstances, pressure from within the EU to lift the ban reflects not political change in China, but a new willingness by some in Europe to ignore the lack of it.

Liberals and Democrats do not argue for maintenance of the embargo sine die. But nor do we wish to lift it with nothing to show in return. Ratification by China of the ICCPR, recognition that the events of Tiananmen Square were wrong, progress towards the freedom of speech and assembly which are in any case essential to sustainable economic success - all these would be signs of a meeting of minds long overdue.

Until then, the embargo should stay. Javier Solana's code of conduct will have zero credibility while the distinguishing feature of codes of conduct everywhere is that they are honoured in the breach. A common position of the Council would at least be politically binding. But let us not be deflected by half-measures from the main issues. The Council's ambitions are dangerous in three respects.

First, Council's determination to ignore the clear and repeated opposition of the European Parliament and some national parliaments is a danger to democracy and the principle of parliamentary consent. Second, the U.S reaction in denying technology to Europe will endanger our economic prosperity. Why should the Americans give us weapons technology for use against their seventh fleet in the Taiwan straits? We underestimate congressional retaliation at our peril. Third, proliferation of weapons technology is a threat to world peace. The ballistic missile arsenals in Pakistan, Iran and North Korea are all China-provided. China has offered Saudi Arabia ICBMs with a range of five and a half thousand kilometres. And this is to say nothing of the fragile military balance in Asia where democracies such as Japan or Taiwan could be under threat. We risk arming to the teeth a series of unsympathetic and unpredictable autocrats. No wonder so many urge caution.

What surprises me most about the current debate is the way the Luxembourg Presidency is allowing itself to be used.

Italy wanted to lift the embargo eighteen months ago but did not have the courage. The Irish Presidency would not offend the Americans. The Netherlands deftly passed the exploding parcel on, unwrapping it a little bit but not enough to have it explode. And the British Presidency is hugely keen for the Council to take the decision now which it would lack the boldness to do later this year for fear of offending Blair's friend George W. Jean-Claude Juncker should look to whose tune he is dancing and recognise that Balkenende was nobody's fool.

We are pleased to bring here today Sharon Hom and Meg Davis of Human Rights Watch to be with us, and Dick Oostling of Amnesty International. And I welcome Helen Flautre, the highly esteemed President of Parliament's committee on human rights. I welcome you all.'

## Gender Equality Is A Liberal Challenge

*Speech given to the Arab International Women's Forum in Cairo a month after Egypt's constitution was amended to allow contested presidential elections for the first time - and supporters of the governing party, the NDP, attacked women demonstrators in the street. Here Graham encourages participants to make their voices heard in Egypt's changing political landscape and points to democratic and social advances sweeping the Muslim world, from the election of women in Gulf States to reform of the Family Code in Morocco.*

*12th June 2005, Cairo*

'Thank you very much for inviting me to this conference. The Alliance of Liberals and Democrats for Europe is pleased to work together with the other sponsors at this conference hosted by the Arab International Women's Forum, a follow-up to the Brussels conference which was held in the European Parliament in April.

We are confident that this conference can make a valuable contribution to the Barcelona process at the Euro-Mediterranean Partnership Conference in November.

Our interest in this dialogue is not new. As Liberals and Democrats we are eager to promote peace. We know that war is the most destructive obstacle to human development, which is why we harbour deep reservations about the invasion of Iraq. Here, where the tectonic plates of Islam, Judaism and Christianity grind against each other, intercultural understanding, mutual tolerance and exchange of ideas is crucial. That is why we held a conference on Liberalism under Christianity and Islam in January of last year and we were keen to host your conference in Brussels earlier this year.

May I say I am delighted to see so many faces, arms and legs. Attractive as they are, I do not regard them as an incitement to immorality or promiscuity. Nor as a danger to society or family or home.

235

Standing before you today I am humbled in the presence of participants who are truly role models for their societies. Participation in politics in Western Europe is an easy choice for a man and not impossible for a woman: women struggle against greater odds but normally succeed. 40% of the MEPs in the Group I lead are women. This would have been unthinkable twenty years ago. It is the product of a struggle over four generations. It is a continuing challenge, with many obstacles, as today Italy's referendum demonstrates.

Here in North Africa the difficulties are far greater; but it is through conferences and networks like this that we learn about our mutual support. Today I look forward to thought-provoking exchanges, which will ensure that this community of bright people and bright ideas continues to grow.

The topic of the discussion - the situation of women in the Arab region - tugs the heart of a Liberal. Liberalism is not just a political philosophy. It is also a programme of action. It expresses and encapsulates the ideals of human freedom from oppression, from poverty, from social pressure to conform. Liberalism lends each citizen the maximum scope for self-development, encouraged but not obliged to participate in society, guided but not shepherded by the State, open to new ideas but rejecting extremism in all its forms. In that sense, Liberals Democrats are feminists; we are committed to defend the social and political rights of women to allow them to make their own choices as citizens, and enjoy equal opportunities regardless of race, religion or residence.

To a Liberal Democrat, gender equality is not a "woman's problem". Indeed, it is a man's problem when opposition to equality betrays the fears and insecurities of male supremacists. A freer society is one in which all its members are free. And the converse of tyranny is not only justice but also freedom and opportunity. As the Ottoman writer Narik Kemal wrote 140 years ago "women are not inferior to men in their intellectual and physical capacities. In ancient times they shared in all men's activities, including even war. In the countryside they still share in the work of agriculture and trade. Many evil consequences result from their social position, the first being that it leads to a bad upbringing for their children". As he and others in Arab and Muslim cultures have recognized, you cannot catch up with the modern world if you modernize only half of the population. From the writings of the Egyptian lawyer Qasim Amin one hundred years ago to the writings of Nawal Al Sadawi today, the fundamental problem in modern Arabic civilization in changing the status of women is to recognize that this is not westernization but modernization. So spend less time rocking the cradle and more time rocking the boat!

I know you are already mobilising women. Ten years ago, the Barcelona process opened up a debate on citizenship, democracy and human rights in the region; it also opened up a debate on economics. The process still has to prove itself as an engine for further integrating women in the economic sphere, which is why I am planning a conference on micro-credit in the autumn. But already in politics we are living new and refreshing times.

The 2002 UNDP report by Arab scholars produced a tsunami of new ideas. The region is thirsty for democratic change. And many a leader in the Middle East needs to take ever quicker steps in order to follow the demands of his - and it invariably is a male leader - people. The UNDP report saw women's empowerment not simply as a problem of justice and social equity but also as a major cause of economic weakness.

What has changed since then? The political train is moving through a new landscape of reforms. Last year, women were elected to the Afghan parliament in free elections. Bahrain appointed a woman to head a government post. This year women have played an important part in the first ever democratic elections organised in Palestine and in Iraq. Saudi Arabia has banned forced marriages and called for local elections, though still only men can vote. Women played a crucial role in the recent events in Lebanon and are actively engaged in the forthcoming elections. Legislative elections were held with women as candidates and voters in Oman. Kuwait has recently granted women the right to vote and run in elections, after street protesters demonstrated in favour of women's rights. Even in Iran the voices of Qurrat Al Ayn and Princess Taj es Saltana have found a new echo. I believe these changes, with other positive developments in other countries, are more than cosmetic. As Dr. Rima Khalaf Hunaidi, UN Assistant Secretary-General and head of Arab States bureau for UNDP said: "We are moving with greater confidence in a new direction now, and there is a strong awareness of the irreversibility of change - change driven by the Arab street, not change adopted from afar".

The real test of these changes will be when women occupy top positions as has happened in Indonesia, Pakistan, and Bangladesh.

I am eager to hear from your analysis of recent developments. What is clear to me is that more needs to be done. Few women stand for office - even when they are allowed to do so by law. Access to education is not equal for men and women. Female illiteracy in the region averages 42% while the average male illiteracy rate in the region is half that (21%). Women's participation in the labour force ranks among the lowest in the world. It is still very difficult for women to file for divorce. Honour killings continue and forced marriages are still arranged. All these forms of discrimination afflict women's economic, political, social, civic and cultural activities.

I am pleased you will focus also on education. Greater democracy without better education does not necessarily bring progress. Look at what happened in Iran in 1979. Or in Morocco in 1999, when many women opposed reform of the family code.

This year's Arab Human Development Report urges a rapid acceleration of democratic reform, together with economic reform, women's rights and education. The authors say that unless Arab governments move much more quickly towards reform, they could face "chaotic" social upheaval, while a balanced participation of women and men in decision-making can pave the way for equality and greater stability.

But against this optimistic tableau, allow me a few cautionary remarks:

First, the relationship between women's rights and democracy is not as simple as it appears. Democracy will not automatically improve the day to day lives of women in the Arab world. Democratic political institutions can be established without women's rights emerging. When my country started developing strong democratic institutions in the nineteenth century, it was without the benefit of women's suffrage or participation. That is why Liberals speak out specifically for women's rights. Once women are organised, mobilised and engaged in their societies, the democratic system will not be able to stop its' people from demanding equal rights. This is why democracy building is a key part of promoting gender equality. And why women's rights' are an excellent barometer of progress in the process of democratisation.

Second, the spread of religious fundamentalism - Christian, Islamic or other - poses a major challenge. Last month, when the Kuwaiti National Assembly granted women full political rights, an article by Iranian author Amir Taheri appeared in the New York Post, under the title: "Kuwaiti Women Gain, Islamists Lose". Are the challenges the Arab world faces, a "zero sum equation"? If so, then women's rights lie at the very core of such a struggle between the secular and the religious, the conservative and the progressive. So, let's open the Quran at chapter 2, verse 256.

Third, the European Union and its' institutions risk distraction from support for the reform process which the Arab world is conducting. That is why Europe's Liberals and Democrats are redoubling their efforts to support the Arab International Women's Forum and I salute especially the work of my colleague Emma Bonino. The European Commission has outlined three priorities for its' Euro-Med programme for the next five years: human rights and democracy, sustainable economic growth and reform and education. We must hold them to it, whatever the Union's constitutional and budgetary challenges.

I set much store upon the recent creation of the Euro-Mediterranean Parliamentary Assembly, composed of 240 European and Mediterranean parliamentarians, which met recently in Cairo. As a representative of the European Parliament, together with Emma Nicholson and Emma Bonino, my aim is to build on the work of that assembly to develop specific projects.

The Arab world has tried Socialism and Nationalism and both have failed. It is time to try Liberalism.'

## Turning Peace On Paper Into Peace On The Ground

*Speech to a European Parliament Hearing assessing prospects for peace in the Great Lakes region of Africa. In this speech Graham talks of the need to implement peace accords and the rule of law, strengthen democratic development, and target social inclusion across the region - particularly in the Democratic Republic of the Congo where conflict has claimed up to three million lives in the past five years. Two weeks later the DRC held a referendum to establish a new national constitution and set the timetable for a general election - with ALDE's General Morillon named Chief Observer of the electoral process.*

*7th December 2005, Brussels*

'War in the Great Lakes Region stopped - on paper at least - in 1999. But building a lasting peace will require more than just conflict resolution - it will mean healing an entire society.

There 127 million people still struggle to survive against a background of displacement, drought and disease. According to NGOs, the region is home to some one fifth of the world's 25 million internally displaced persons. Most live in camps, which are overcrowded, unhygienic and lack even the most basic of services. Where armed attacks are frequent and Human Rights abuses almost routine.

What has displaced them? A conflict which recruited thousands of children and turned them into killers. And turned thousands more into orphans. Not including more than 3 million AIDS orphans - the product of an HIV pandemic. This is humanitarian catastrophe on a biblical scale. But it won't be resolved by divine intervention - only by political action.

It's true, peace and reconciliation might seem like impossible propositions, as they must have seemed in Europe after the Second World War. But as Harry Truman - author of the Marshall Plan - once noted, *"A pessimist is one who makes difficulties of his opportunities*

*and an optimist is one who makes opportunities of his difficulties".*
Assessing Prospects for Peace in the Great Lakes Region, it seems,
depends on which side of this divide you fall.

A pessimist could point to the decades of conflict which rendered the
Great Lakes one of the world's most volatile regions. Where the
numerous accords signed between Governments of DRC, Rwanda and
Uganda have not stopped tensions flaring nor brought much in the way
of tangible benefits to local people. An optimist, by contrast, could point
to two major peace deals in the last six years. A ceasefire brokered in
DRC in 1999 which remains in place to this day. And an agreement
signed by 13 Central and Southern African countries in Dar Es Salaam
- the city of peace - which committed the region to fighting the forces
of genocide and destruction. All that was lacking, a pessimist might
have noted, was implementation.

Implementation. Democratisation. Inclusion. These are the biggest
challenges facing the Great Lakes Region today. And as Liberals and
Democrats we will do everything we can to bring prospects for peace
ever closer. To strive for the defence of human rights, to support the
reconciliation process and encourage National Parliaments to enshrine
this in law. And to bring War Criminals before the International Criminal
Court - criminals who have operated with impunity up to now.

The personal engagement of our Commissioner Louis Michel and
MEP's Emma Bonino and Johan Van Hecke in furthering this process -
to name but a few - is well known. Now, following his appointment as
Chief Observer of the electoral process in DRC Philippe Morillon faces
the task of getting a legitimate referendum result in Congo on the 18th
of December. I understand that over 21 million people have now
registered to vote - an incredible result for a country so lacking in
infrastructure and which still suffers regular incursions from illegal
armed groups.

ALDE's engagement in the DRC is a long-standing one and October's
delegation reported from its trip with some specific recommendations.
These will certainly be discussed in today's seminar and I won't go into

them in depth here. But I will say this. It is absolutely essential that the Congolese authorities respect the will of the people and maintain the electoral timetable. And that the international community - the EU in particular - uses its influence to ensure that armed rebels who continue to destabilise the Eastern regions return to their countries of origin - through sanctions if necessary. For Liberals and Democrats know that successful elections in DRC this Christmas will mark a significant step towards turning peace on paper into peace on the ground. Not just in DRC but across the entire region.

There are other hopeful signs that this is now happening. 39000 former combatants have already been repatriated and reintegrated into Rwandan society. Though many more remain in DRC, the ball is now rolling. All that is required is political will to finish the process. That is why I was pleased to note that - just one month ago - legislators from Uganda, Rwanda and DRC resolved to speed up implementation and move the troops out. Increased regionalisation of conflict management is surely welcome and will pave the way for greater future cooperation.

Most importantly, perhaps, political instability and repression is giving way to democratisation. And democratisation and development form the backbone of a peaceful and prosperous society which in turn will create a more peaceful and prosperous world order. As former US President Bill Clinton once said: "the best strategy to ensure our own security and to build a durable peace is to support the advance of democracy elsewhere." For democracies - specifically, liberal democracies - never or almost never go to war with one another. And they never, or almost never, foster the hatred that breeds genocide: a memory still so vivid and so bitter for millions of Rwandans. For them, much depends on a successful transition to a multi-party state which respects the rights of all citizens, one which doesn't institutionalise the tyranny of the majority.

They can look with hope to the progress made by neighbouring Burundi which has suffered its fair share of inter-ethnic rivalry. National Assembly elections in July this year brought hopes for sustainable peace to the region. A process reinforced by August's Presidential Elections.

The world is now turning to President Nkurunziza to bridge decades of mistrust between Hutu and Tutsi - and bring the last active Hutu rebel group into the fold. Only then can Burundi revive its shattered economy and start to forge national unity. The democratisation process is gathering speed elsewhere too. Uganda, once a by-word for dictatorship under Idi Amin, endorsed the reintroduction of multi-party politics in July. And its notorious rebel group, the Lord's Resistance Army, has made overtures for peace after 19 years of conflict.

The task now is to ensure free and fair elections in 2006. Everyone - citizens, National Parliaments, the International Community and Political Families from across the Globe - has a stake in this process. Building a sustainable future for the Great Lakes will require an iron will and a steadfast determination to turn our backs on the evils of division, domination and confrontation. Working together, I know we can succeed. And I hope that this Seminar will prove one small step on the road to reconciliation.'

## Promoting Europe's Values In The World

*In January 2005, Hamas - a group on the EU's list of terrorist organisations - won the Palestinian elections and the EU considered cutting off funding to the new regime. Here Graham takes Europe's leaders to task for promoting collective punishment of the Palestinian people and exacerbating the crisis in the region. However Graham reserves most of his criticism for their failure to agree on common foreign policy objectives without which, he argues, Europe's Member States will lack the leverage to promote democracy and stability in their near neighbourhood and beyond.*

*1st February 2006, Brussels*

'A common foreign and security policy that promotes Europe's values in the world and brings peace and security to our neighbours is what Liberals and Democrats strive for. But it is what Europe's leaders are manifestly failing to provide.

Acting together, our Union could have used its leverage to promote democracy and stability. Instead, its policies have given tacit support to tyrannies like Tunisia, Egypt and Syria. We never demanded that diplomacy depend on releasing democrats like Egypt's Ayman Nour; or, in Asia, on the right to a free return to his country for opposition leader Sam Rainsy, now in exile while we fund the dictatorship of Hun Sen.

Mrs Ferrero-Waldner, Mr Solana, why are you surprised at the Palestinian poll? The European Union has peddled promises of democracy, peace and human rights in Palestine while our development aid has fed Al-Fatah, whose members now burn images of one of our prime ministers and peace negotiations have got nowhere. Far from being a key player, Mr Solana, the consequences of Europe's failure are plain for all to see.

Israel, undeterred, builds a wall around East Jerusalem in violation of its roadmap obligations and international law. The Palestinians, tired of slow progress and shameful social services, turn to Hamas at the ballot box. And now the prognosis is worse than ever. After demanding democracy, some EU leaders talk of shunning one of the only democratically elected governments in the Arab world! Of course, Hamas must renounce violence and commit to a two-state solution. But so must Israel. As Leila Shahid, the General Delegate for the Palestinian Authority said today: 'It takes two to tango'.

The Commissioner has spoken of policies based on human rights, the rule of law and democratic principles, but where is the emphasis on those fine things when pragmatism devoid of principles is so often the order of the day?

A global drive for peaceful conflict resolution would be a major counterweight to the heavy-handed US approach; it would assure Europe's security, prosperity and global repute; and it would also give us far greater leverage over micro-states like the Maldives or the Seychelles, whose governments abuse human rights despite being almost totally dependent on our aid and trade. That is why Liberals and Democrats believe that the time has come for an accountable, properly funded and values-driven European foreign policy. According to Eurobarometer, it is a desire shared by 70% of our citizens.

Mr Solana, Liberals and Democrats object to Parliament's views being ignored or disregarded on matters of global importance. We want to see less of you on television and more of you here in this Chamber. And we are tired of Council secrecy and its disregard for Parliament's right to prior consultation on policy priorities. Those rights are enshrined in Article 21 of the Treaty and in the 1999 Inter-institutional Agreement.

We are facing many grave challenges: to democratise our Near Neighbourhood, especially former Soviet republics currently at the mercy of Russia's energy politics; to ensure that the elections in Belarus are free and fair; and to ensure that the referendums in Kosovo and Montenegro do not end in violence.

The role of foreign policy must not end there. I understand that selling arms to China is back on the Council's agenda, yet China has still not recanted the Tiananmen Square killings, nor released, after 16 years, all those jailed. So we demand an assurance from you, Mr Winkler, that the Austrian Presidency will not lift the Union's arms embargo.

Most pressing is the question of Iran. The IAEA board of governors meets tomorrow to decide whether to report Iran to the Security Council. Stopping Iran building nuclear weapons must be our aim. That is why Europe must commit to respect the IAEA's findings due in March. But making progress towards the disarmament of the current nuclear powers, in line with the commitments we have made, is the strongest and most convincing message we could possibly send. A Europe which learns to use its muscle as a force for good is truly a force to be reckoned with.'

## Viruses Don't Respect Borders

*Speech made to a Hearing in the European Parliament on ways of closing the gaps in global health security. In 2003 the SARS virus, which originated in China and spread to every corner of the globe, revealed the need for comprehensive health coverage for all, wherever they may live. Taiwan, because of its disputed status, falls outside the World Health Organisation just as it falls outside the WTO or the UN. In the wake of the 2006 Avian Flu outbreak which the Taiwanese authorities struggled to contain, Graham reflects on the need to put politics aside to protect human lives.*

*25th April 2006, Brussels*

'The WHO constitution states that enjoyment of the highest attainable standard of health is one of the fundamental rights of every human being. Under this principle, the 23 million people of Taiwan - including more than 400,000 foreign nationals residing on the island - should have the right to direct, full and immediate access to the WHO system.

Yet Taiwan falls into one of the few "uncovered regions" of this global public health network, posing a grave threat both to its own people and the rest of the world. That's because viruses don't respect borders. They become pandemics, like those which thrice decimated the globe in the twentieth century at the expense of over 50 million lives.

It was because of this gap in global health security that the Taiwanese authorities were denied access to WHO expertise and resources for the first seven weeks of the 2003 SARS epidemic and the main reason that a mild outbreak became a major tragedy. As Dr Jong-wook Lee, Director General of the WHO has emphasised, we can no longer afford any gap in our global surveillance and response network, both in terms of the human cost and its enormous potential impact on the global economy.

Yet little has changed. Three years on Taiwan's access to WHO facilities remains limited at best at a time when avian flu threatens to become the first major human flu pandemic of the 21st century. That is the challenge that brings us here today in Brussels. It is our privilege that Martin McKee, Professor of Public Health at the London School of Hygiene and Tropical Medicine, has agreed to join us discuss how to move the situation forward. I am especially pleased by how many eminent experts and opinion-formers are here today. We look forward to the exchange of views.

From a Liberal Democratic perspective it is critical that Taiwan participates in WHO technical meetings and the Global Outbreak Alert and Response Network. The EU - backed by Canada - recognised this in 2004 when it demanded that Taiwanese medical and public health officials be allowed to take part in WHO activities. Despite our strong stance, the Taiwanese authorities are still only allowed to attend WHO meetings on a case-by-case basis: of the 32 meetings it has sought to attend since May 2004, only 12 were granted.

It is my view that the WHO secretariat should now invite Taiwan to participate - as an observer - in all WHO technical meetings. This is in keeping with current practice which allows entities like the Holy See, Palestine or the International Red Cross - which do not, in terms of international law, constitute sovereign states - to hold observer status. I am sure these questions will prove a focal point for discussion today. And that many other relevant, and lateral, approaches will bring us closer to closing the gap in Global Health Security.

The EU has suffered its own public health threats, ranging from Foot and Mouth Disease to the recent discovery of birds carrying the Avian Flu virus within our own territory. It is our duty to share our knowledge, our expertise and our solidarity with countries like Taiwan to build a world in which everyone shares the same basic rights. Not least among these is the right to health.'

## Congres UDF pour le Referendum, 21 Mai 05, Sofitel St Jacques, Paris
## Speech by Graham Watson MEP on Mon 23rd May 2005

Cher Francois, Chers amis,

Parmi vous, ici, il y en a qui, comme moi, sont venus de loin pour soutenir le "Oui" à la Constitution. Parce que l'Europe regarde la France, parce que la France nous tiens à coeur et parce que, au coeur de l'Europe, nous voulons un bon gros "oui" français!

Comme toujours après la commémoration de la fin de la Deuxième Guerre Mondiale, il me paraît incroyable que le pays de Jean Monnet et de Jacques Delors puisse dire non. Personne en Grande Bretagne ou à Bruxelles ne peut imaginer une chose pareille!

Cette semaine, j'ai voulu voir de mes propres yeux. Je suis venu en France pour faire campagne avec Marielle de Sarnez, ma vice-présidente au groupe ADLE à Strasbourg et Bruxelles, François Bayrou, qui se dépense sans compter pour cette bataille européenne, et d'autres comme le Général Morillon, qui m'a même emmené pour chercher à convaincre des pêcheurs bretons! Moi! L'ennemi héréditaire!

De Senlis à Deauville, d'Amiens à Lorient, de Rennes à Compiègne, j'ai fait du tractage, j'ai serré des mains, vu des visages, argumenté .... beaucoup argumenté. Et partout la même impression, confirmée par les sondages: l'opposition est forte à la Constitution, voire parfois à l'Europe. J'ai entendu les gens râler contre la proposition de directive sur les services. Bien que la France figure parmi les premiers exportateurs des services. Bien que la Constitution soit le premier traité européen qui donne une existence juridique aux services publics et qui reconnaît que les services publics peuvent déroger au principe de concurrence. D'ailleurs, c'est bien simple, chez moi les opposants à la Constitution râlent que ce texte est trop social. Ici les opposants français font campagne contre un traité trop libéral. Trop social, trop libéral: avec de telles critiques, cette Constitution elle doit quand même être vachement bien équilibrée!

J'entends dire "Si la France vote Non, il n'y aura pas de referendum en Grande Bretagne". Mais nous aurons toujours une obligation juridique de ratifier cette Constitution. Et il sera également difficile que chez vous. Je vous invite à venir faire campagne avec nous.

Il est difficile de répondre aux approximations, aux contre vérités, aux mensonges qui marquent cette campagne.

Mais je trouve particulièrement lamentable que certains prennent l'avenir de l'Europe en otage pour des raisons de politique nationale. Lamentable parce que les partisans du "non", à force de replis nationaux et de combinaisons politiciennes, en arrivent à agiter la peur du travailleur Polonais. Le référendum du 29 mai nous concerne tous, Français, Polonais, Britanniques. C'est justement le premier grand progrès de l'Europe: nous donner à choisir de vivre ensemble dans un même cadre institutionnel après des siècles de guerre et de conquête. Personne n'a le droit de toucher à cet héritage en jouant de la peur de l'étranger, cette même haine qui nous a conduit si souvent à la guerre.

Il faut garder courage. Et continuer d'expliquer et d'expliquer encore l'Europe. Parce qu'une chose m'a vraiment surpris pendant ces quelques jours en France: c'est combien on connaît mal l'Europe. Presque aussi mal qu'en Grande-Bretagne. Si on m'a harcelé à propos du plombier polonais, je n'ai entendu aucune opposition à la directive européenne sur la qualité de l'air, qui nous a tellement réduit la pollution.

Si j'ai eu mille questions sur les délocalisations, je n'ai vu aucune plainte contre le fait que les banques françaises soient aujourd'hui obligées de rémunérer les comptes courants, grâce à une directive européenne. Personne ne se félicite des règles de l'Union européenne sur les produits sanguins, qui permettent à un touriste français d'avoir la même confiance dans le sang qu'on lui transfuse dans un hôpital d'Athènes ou de Budapest qu'en celui du Centre national de transfusion sanguine. Personne, parce que personne ne leur a dit que l'Europe l'a décidé.

Trop de gouvernements ont peur d'expliquer l'Europe, on se complaisent à dépeindre l'Europe comme le problème et non comme la solution. Et nos chefs d'Etat et de gouvernement n'ont pas voulu admettre que l'Europe a changé parce que le monde a changé. L'union n'est plus un simple marché commun, il est devenu une communauté des valeurs partagées.

Chacun sent ainsi bien, confusément, au fond de lui-même, (à part les fanatiques eurosceptiques,) que les principaux défis auxquels nous faisons face, ne peuvent être résolus que collectivement. Que ce soit la croissance, la cohésion sociale, la gouvernance économique de la zone euro à laquelle mon pays doit s'ancrer. Que ce soit la lutte contre l'effet de serre et la protection de l'environnement. Que ce soit la lutte contre la criminalité organisée et le terrorisme. Sans parler des responsabilités mondiales qui pèsent sur l'Europe et qu'il est temps qu'elle assume. Je pense notamment au développement des pays du tiers-monde que tant de personnes quittent pour échapper à la faim, la guerre et la misère.

Cette vaste tâche, la Constitution l'organise: des compétences bien définies entre Bruxelles et les capitales, un contrôle des Parlements nationaux, des Institutions européennes démocratisées avec un rôle renforcé pour le Parlement européen, des droits fondamentaux garantis par la Cour de justice.

Qui peut nier, tout ce que nous a apporté l'Europe avant même cette Constitution. Je suis né il y a presque 50 ans sur une petite île en Ecosse. Mes parents n'étaient pas riches et nous étions six enfants à la maison. Mais j'ai eu la bonne fortune d'être, avec une de mes soeurs, le premier membre de la famille, au fil des siècles, à entrer à l'université. Le Royaume-Uni venait d'adhérer à la CEE. J'ai deux enfants: je m'attends à ce qu'ils aillent tous les deux à l'Université. Ils parlent anglais, ma langue. Ils parlent italien, la langue de ma femme. Ils apprennent le français et l'allemand au lycée. Mon cas n'est pas particulier. L'Europe, de part et d'autre de la Manche, nous a doté non seulement d'un bien-être qui aurait été un rêve pour nos parents, mais aussi a permis l'émergence d'une jeune génération européenne, mieux éduqués, en meilleur santé, hors du danger d'être moissonnés par la guerre, pleine d'espoir pour l'avenir. Moi je vais lutter jusqu'à la ratification complète de cette Constitution pour qu'on ne ferme pas la porte sur tout cela.

Je sais qu'entre la France et l'Angleterre, les relations ne sont pas simples. Il y a des méchants chez moi qui disent que si la France vote Non un Oui en Grande Bretagne sera plus probable. Croyez moi, on se ressemble. Je commence à vous connaître. Et j'ose vous dire que vous êtes parfois aussi insulaires que nous, sans avoir l'excuse d'être une île. Nous étions tous deux les puissances mondiales et nous n'avons pas encore pris conscience que le monde ne tourne plus autour de nous. Mes concitoyens britanniques ne veulent pas une Grande-Bretagne européenne: ils veulent une Europe britannique. Vous voulez une Europe française. Illusion trompeuse, pensée irresponsable, chez nous comme chez vous. Il n'y aura qu'une Europe: une Europe européenne, avec le meilleur de chaque pays. Prenons garde que notre fierté nationale ne nous aveugle pas et nous éloigne de l'Europe, notre seul avenir commun.

Ceux qui clament chez moi que l'Union Jack flotte toujours sur le Commonwealth et qui chez vous entonnent l'Internationale, ceux qui chez moi ne jurent que par le grand large américain et qui chez vous montent sur leurs ergots nationalistes sont les deux faces d'une même schizophrénie.

Libérons nous de ces vieilles lunes et affrontons l'avenir: la France et le Royaume-Uni doivent réaliser leur destin européen pour continuer de peser sur une scène mondiale qu'ils ont tant contribué à forger.

Dans ces derniers jours de campagne, ne vous laissez pas décourager par vos impressions, les sondages, la peur que distillent les adversaires de la Constitution. Ce sont des baudruches. Quelle crédibilité ont-ils, que la vérité et notre conviction européenne ne puissent emporter? Monsieur Fabius était aux commandes comme ministre ou Premier ministre pour l'Acte Unique européen, pour Maastricht, pour Amsterdam, Nice, autant de traités dont il dénonce aujourd'hui les effets néfastes. Ca ne l'empêche d'ailleurs pas de vouloir les garder en faisant voter "non" à la Constitution et aux progrès qu'elle apporte! Mais alors, soit M. Fabius est incompétent d'avoir pendant 15 ans négocié des traités si horribles. Soit c'est un hypocrite et il ne dénigre l'Europe qu'il a contribué à bâtir que par calcul personnel. Mais dans les deux cas, il s'est disqualifié aux yeux de ceux avec qui il prétend renégocier.

Car voilà la pire imposture des partisans du "non", ce fameux plan B, C, ou D. Une éminente fabiusienne, Pervenche Beres, une de nos collègues à Marielle et à moi au Parlement Européen, siégeait à la Convention qui a élaboré ce traité constitutionnel. Elle en a vanté les mérites pour maintenant les dénoncer. Qu'elle explique les rapports de forces politiques et nationaux, qu'elle explique les contradictions que cette enceinte à du résoudre, qu'elle explique les compromis si favorables à la France qui ont pu pourtant se dégager, qu'elle explique enfin comment un meilleur texte pourra être renégocié. Avec qui? Avec Jan Rokita, qui devrait, au grand dam de Bronislaw Geremek, gagner les prochaines élections polonaises et qui est l'inventeur de la célèbre formule "Nice ou la mort"? M. Fabius veut lui rendre Nice et M. Fabius croit que M. Rokita va vouloir le renégocier? De qui se moque-t-on? Et quand renégocier? Qui peut croire qu'il y aura la moindre volonté de remettre l'ouvrage européen sur le métier si les Français rejettent un texte d'inspiration française que l'on a mis 3 ans à élaborer.

Alors non. Qu'on ne se trompe pas de combat. La Constitution est une opportunité unique qui ne se représentera pas avant longtemps, peut être jamais, et sûrement trop tard face au monde qui avance et qui n'attend pas l'Europe. Bien au contraire. Croyez vous que dans certains cercles de pouvoir à Washington ou à Pékin on ne serait pas ravis d'un échec de la Constitution européenne.

Pendant ce bref séjour en France, je l'ai bien senti: les Français ont envie de gueuler. Je comprends qu'un pays qui a voté Chirac à contre-coeur veuille exprimer son ras-le-bol. Mais, voilà le message que j'aimerais porter aux Français, à travers vous: ne gueuler pas sur l'Europe quand vous en voulez au gouvernement. Ne mettez pas en péril ce que nous avons construit ensemble. Le 29 Mai ce n'est pas l'heure de râler, c'est le moment de dire "oui" à l'Europe. L'heure des comptes viendra, en 2007, et c'est à ce point là que vous pourrez voter UDF et François Bayrou.

**Graham Watson, MdEP, Vorsitzender der ELDR-Fraktion im Europäischen Parlament, vor dem FDP-Bezirksverband Ostwestfalen-Lippe, Bielefeld, 22. Januar 2004**

Liebe Freidemokraten,

Meinen Glückwunsch zu Ihrem FDP-Europatag! Eine Partei, die bereit ist, einen ganzen Tag europäischer Politik zu widmen, ist schon so gut wie zurück in Brüssel und Straßburg, wieder mitten drin in Europa; eine Partei, die begriffen hat, daß Europa sich ändert; die eine andere, eine bessere Europapolitik machen möchte. "Wir können Europa besser": ein starkes Statement, das Reform und Erneuerung verspricht.

Brüssel braucht die FDP. Meine Fraktion vermißt Ihren politischen Beitrag. Der Europäischen Liberalen Fraktion fehlt das deutsche Element, das in Europa so wichtig ist. Wir rechnen fest damit, daß Sie im Juni wieder zu uns stoßen werden!

Die Liberalen spielen eine wesentliche Rolle im Europaparlament: Unsere 53 Fraktionsmitglieder sind das Zünglein an der Waage zwischen links und rechts; unsere Argumente werden ernstgenommen; unsere Stimmen sind oft die entscheidenden. Mit den FDP-Stimmen jedoch wären wir noch schlagkräftiger.

Wir sind eine Reform-Partei. Wir haben stets mehr Verantwortung der EU-Institutionen vis-à-vis dem Bürger gefordert. Wir wollen, daß der EZB und der EU-Kommission einschlägige, neue Standards auferlegt werden, die sie zur Offentheit zwingen.

Eine unserer Prioritäten ist jetzt Realität geworden: das Europaparlament kann den EU-Haushalt kontrollieren und entsprechend handeln. Im letzten Jahr wurde, unter Anleitung der ELDR-Fraktion, das rigoroseste EU-Budget seit zehn Jahren verabschiedet.

Aber unsere herausragendste Errungenschaft ist die Erweiterung der Europäischen Union. Sie ist unter einer liberalen Ratspräsidentschaft zustande gekommen. Im Europaparlament war die Liberale Fraktion die einzige, die einstimmig für diese Erweiterung gestimmt hat. Wir, und nur wir, haben konsequent von der Pflicht zur Wiedervereinigung Europas gesprochen.

Das Jahr 2004 ist für mich der Schlußakt der Revolution, die hier, in Deutschland, 1989 in Leipzig begann.

Leider nimmt die Öffentlichkeit das bisher Erreichte zur Zeit nicht wahr. Ihr Bild von der EU ist geprägt vom Zusammenbruch des Stabilitätspakts und dem glücklosen Gipfel im Dezember. Man hat das Gefühl, daß es noch nie so schwierig - und so wichtig - war, für Europa zu werben wie jetzt.

Ich kann Guido Westerwelle nur zustimmen: Er sprach am letzten Wochenende von einem "Konferenztisch-Europa", einem Europa, das sich in der Theorie verliert und nicht zum Bürger durchdringt. Als der Dezember-Gipfel zusammenbrach, war deutlich wie nie zuvor, wie viele der dort anwesenden Regierungschefs offensichtlich keine Ahnung von der Europäischen Verfassung hatten. Sie kamen mit ihren Mindestforderungen und posierten für die Kameras, aber es mangelte ihnen an Verständnis für das Grandiose, das Außerordentliche der Sache. - Man hört immer wieder, daß Europa keine Menschen mehr hervorbringt, die die nötige Vision mitbringen. Das stimmt nicht. Es waren nur zu wenige davon in Brüssel an diesem Dezember-Wochenende. Es gibt sie, die Frauen und Männer, die sich unter "Europa" etwas vorstellen können: sie sitzen beispielsweise hier, in diesem Saal, Leute wie Sie.

Wenn ich dem Jahr 2004 und der Erweiterung etwas mit auf den Weg geben dürfte, so wäre es dies: Vertrauen in Europa, Glauben an Europa. Wir müssen das Vertrauen der Bürger wiedergewinnen. Solange Europa durch seine öffentlichen Mißerfolge definiert wird, ist und bleibt es ein Mißerfolg in den Augen seiner Bürger. Die europäischen Regierungschefs haben wenig getan, sie vom Gegenteil zu überzeugen.

Man hatte politische Statements zum gemeinsamen Europa erwartet. Statt dessen kam nicht, überhaupt nichts.

Was Europas politische Maulhelden nicht verstanden haben: Wir alle sind jetzt Minderheiten. Selbst die großen Länder müssen nun in Begriffen von Koexistenz und Kooperation denken. Die deutsch-französische Allianz hat bisher sehr viel für die Gemeinschaft getan, aber unter Schröder und Chirac droht sie mehr Schaden als Gutes anzurichten.

Die EU-Kommission hatte keine Wahl; sie mußte Deutschland und Frankreich gerichtlich verklagen. Die eigentliche Herausforderung besteht darin, ein neues, funktionierendes Rahmenabkommen zu schaffen. Wir können zwar die realen Machtverhältnisse an Europas höchsten Konferenztischen nicht verändern, aber wir müssen denen, die diese Macht mißbrauchen, die Glaubwürdigkeit verweigern.

Sollte es Europa gelingen, sein gesamtes Potenzial zu mobilisieren, dann müssen sich die europäischen Regierungschefs mit einem neuen, echten politischen Willen profilieren. Wie gut, daß die irische Ratspräsidentschaft in diesem Sinne angetreten ist.

Europa braucht Reformen, genau wie Deutschland. Ihre Regierung ist immer wieder daran gescheitert zu erkennen, daß jetzt ein Wandel stattfinden muß. Der Sinn der Sozialdemokraten für Reformen ist aufgebraucht. Genau die gleiche Vorstellungskraft fehlt Europa.

Europas Wirtschaftswachstum kriecht im Schneckentempo voran. Der stetig zunehmende, grenzüberschreitende Handel wird mittlerweile gehemmt durch außertarifliche Handelsbarrieren und Infrastrukturprobleme.

Wenn wir es heute versäumen, in Forschung zu investieren, vertut Europa seine Chance, bei den Innovationen von morgen dabeizusein.

Wenn wir es heute versäumen, unsere Sozialsysteme zu modernisieren, so daß Arbeit sich bezahlt macht, dann laden wir uns öffentliche Schulden auf und sind schuld am Produktivitätsverlust.

Mit unseren Strukturfonds investieren wir in Regionen, versäumen aber dabei, Europas regionale Wirtschaften zu einem echten gemeinschaftlichen Markt zu machen.

Im Falle der Übernahmerichtlinie und der Arbeitszeitrichtlinie hat sich die politisch gefährdete Schröder-Regierung auf die Maßnahmen der Lissabon-Agenda berufen, um sich so um eine echte Reform herumzuhangeln - und die Briten haben mitgemacht. Solchen Regierungen geht es nicht wirklich um Änderungen.

Die Lissabon-Agenda ist zu einem Stillstand gekommen. Warum? Weil nationale Regierungen weder Interesse an der Einhaltung dieser Agenda haben noch Verstand genug, den eigentlichen Sinn und Wert zu erfassen. Unseren Mitgliedstaaten ist nicht klar, daß Handelsbarrieren zwischen einzelnen Ländern Wachstum und Prosperität behindern. Sie scheinen nicht zu begreifen, daß die Glaubwürdigkeit des Euro auf strengen Regeln basiert, die es zu respektieren gilt.

Zu viele Mitgliedsländer benehmen sich so, als sei Europa ein anderes Land. Aber achtzig Prozent der meisten nationalen Gesetze stammen aus Brüssel. Europapolitik ist Innenpolitik. Und es ist Zeit, daß unsere Politiker und die Presse dies anerkennen.

Wenn die Europäer verstanden haben, was sie mit gemeinsamen Kräften alles erreichen können, dann werden sie auch liberal wählen.

Unsere Mitbürger halten den Frieden und Wohlstand, den die EU ihnen beschert hat, für etwas völlig Normales. Wir müssen sie daran erinnern, daß diese Werte so selbstverständlich nicht sind.

Sie meinen auch, daß Europas Rolle bei internationalen Treffen, auf denen es mit einer Stimme spricht, selbstverständlich ist. Erinnern wir sie daran, daß dies nicht immer so war.

Die Leute meinen, es sei selbstverständlich, daß ihre Grundrechte geschützt sind. Rufen wir ihnen in Erinnerung, daß auch dies nicht immer so war.

Ob es um das Kyoto-Protokoll geht, um den Internationalen Gerichtshof, die Ottowaer Landminen-Konvention oder um die Internationale Konvention über die Rechte des Kindes - Europas Werte sind eindeutig, und sie werden nicht immer von anderen geteilt. Europas politischer Vertrag kann und soll der Welt ein Vorbild sein. Wir müssen sie daran erinnern.

Silvana Koch-Mehrin will dafür sorgen, daß Europa wieder in unseren Herzen wahrgenommen wird, nicht nur in unseren Brieftaschen. Solange wir uns nicht als Europäer empfinden, werden wir auch nicht europäisch denken und handeln. Europa muß heraus aus den Büros und Brüsseler Korridoren, zurück ins Leben der Bürger.

Es gibt Leute, die behaupten, es gebe keine Europapolitik, da es kein europäisches Volk gibt. Ich behaupte, gute Politik hat mit Erziehung und Engagement zu tun. Die beste Politik hat sich immer festgefahrenen Meinungen stellen müssen und Überzeugungen zu ändern vermocht; sie hat nie der Angst vor Wandel das Wort geredet. Europas Zukunft kann einzig und allein auf das Verstehen der Öffentlichkeit und auf Vertrauen gebaut werden. Deswegen ist es richtig, daß die FDP in Deutschland eine Volksabstimmung zur Europäischen Verfassung fordert, so wie ich es auch in Großbritannien gefordert habe. Europaabgeordnete aller Parteien und aller Mitgliedsländer haben den "Club des 13. Juni" gegründet, der jeden europäischen Staat auffordert, gleichzeitig mit den Europawahlen ein Referendum mit Beratungscharakter über die Europäische Verfassung durchzuführen. Denn die Debatte über die Zukunft Europas sollte so großflächig und offen wie möglich sein. Gerade weil die Europäische Union größer wird, ist es wichtiger denn je, die Verbindung zwischen Bürger und Union aufrechtzuerhalten. Diese Notwendigkeit zwingt uns, uns für Europa einzusetzen. Wenn uns das gelingt, werden wir unübertrefflich sein.

Sie müssen Europa verteidigen! Aber entschuldigen Sie sich nicht für Europa! Niemand gibt vor, die EU sei perfekt. Eine Regierung auf EU-Ebene ist oft nicht besser als eine Regierung auf nationaler oder kommunaler Ebene. Darum sind wir eine Reform-Partei. Weil wir an Europa glauben, hat unsere Kritik mehr Gewicht.

Ich unterschätze nicht, wie schwierig es sein kann, in diesen Zeiten ein Europa-Aktivist zu sein. Aber von heute an müssen wir sechs Monate lang auf die Straße gehen und eine Kampagne über europäische Themen führen. Wir dürfen diesen Europawahlkampf nicht zu einer weiteren Schlacht der Bundespolitik verkommen lassen. Diese Wahlen müssen ein Plus für Europa sein.

Trotz kultureller und sprachlicher Differenzen und eventueller akzentualer Unterschiede: Der Europäische Liberalismus ist eine Einheitswährung, eine europäische Marke. Unsere Parteien werden es sein, die an der Spitze des Wahlkampfs stehen, als Europäer, und sie werden siegen.

Ich glaube, daß das 21. Jahrhundert ein liberales Jahrhundert sein wird. Der Liberalismus bietet eine europapolitische Alternative - nicht nur wegen eines langen, kalten Jahrhunderts von Staatssozialismus und eines in die Jahre gekommenen Konservatismus, sondern auch, weil unsere Antwort, die liberale Antwort, die einzig glaubwürdige auf die Ansprüche einer sich ändernden Welt ist:

Denken wir an die Herausforderung einer schnell wachsenden Weltbevölkerung; immer mehr Menschen verlassen ihre Heimatländer, um Hunger und schierer Hoffnungslosigkeit zu entkommen; oder an die Folgen der Klimaänderung für Luft, Wasser und Boden; oder die Bedrohung des internationalen Terrorismus und organisierter Kriminalität; gemeinsame Bedrohungen erfordern gemeinsame Antworten; gemeinsame Antworten erfordern liberales Denken.

Sehr geehrte Damen und Herren, zur Zeit haben wir in Europa Liberale an der Spitze der Kommission (Romano Prodi) und des Parlaments (Pat

Cox); wir sind stolz auf fünf liberale Premierminister. Liberale sind in elf europäischen Staaten in der Regierung vertreten. Die liberale Familie wächst. Diese Welle kann und muß die FDP nach Brüssel zurückbringen. Sieben Prozent wären ein Anfang.

Die FDP hat sich für eine Liste junger, schwungvoller Kandidaten entschieden. Heute morgen habe ich zusammen mit Silvana Koch-Mehrin und Rainer Brüderle eine Pressekonferenz gegeben. Ich wurde gefragt, warum die ELDR die FDP braucht. Ich zeigte auf Ihre Kandidatenliste und sagte drei Worte: "Sachlich, ehrlich, kompetent."

So wahr ich hier heute stehe, sage ich Ihnen: im Juni wird die FDP wieder ins Europaparlament einziehen.

## " IL CUORE DEI LIBERALI BATTE SEMPRE PIU' A SINISTRA"

**Spunti per intervento al Congresso Federale della Margherita, Frascati 2003**

Sono molto onorato di essere il primo Presidente dei Liberal-democratici Europei a rivolgermi al Congresso Federale della Margherita. In un momento in cui l'Italia sta per assumere la Presidenza del Consiglio Europeo, è importante rafforzare i nostri legami con gli amici della Margherita.

Sono stato molto lieto di accogliere Francesco Rutelli durante il recente Congresso ELDR a Bath a novembre dell'anno scorso. Ma desidero anche rendere omaggio all'instancabile lavoro svolto da Lamberto Dini in seno alla Convenzione e in qualità di vice-presidente del Partito ELDR.

Con loro, la sintonia è completa. Del resto, i Liberal-democratici Europei sono una forza politica solida e crescente in Europa, con un cuore che batte sempre più a sinistra.

I Liberali Democratici Europei sono più forti di prima. Durante il Consiglio Europeo di Salonicco siamo stati lusingati nell'essere intorno ad un tavolo insieme a quattro Primi Ministri (Danimarca, Belgio, Finlandia e Slovenia), a Romano Prodi e Pat Cox.

Attualmente vi è soltanto un Primo Ministro Liberale in meno rispetto ai Socialisti nei 15 paesi (tre contro quattro Socialisti). Tra i paesi membri candidati presiediamo un governo di centro-sinistra in Slovenia, siamo al governo insieme ai Socialisti in Ungheria e in Lituania, e siamo anche al governo in Estonia e Slovacchia.

Siamo una forza crescente anche nell'Europa Occidentale. Con gioia abbiamo accolto la rielezione di Guy Verhofstadt, leader liberale in una coalizione con i Socialisti in Belgio lo scorso mese. Una riconferma voluta dall'elettorato che dimostra che, se basato su rispetto reciproco, il rapporto fra le due famiglie può essere la risposta giusta ai problemi della nostra Europa.

E proprio recentemente, i nostri due partiti finlandesi hanno formato con i socialdemocratici il nuovo governo di centro-sinistra guidato dal Primo Ministro ELDR Vanhanen.

Ho buone notizie anche dal mio paese: nel regno Unito, i Liberal Democrats hanno confermato un risultato elettorale mai ottenuto prima con il 30% dei voti nelle elezioni nazionali, tornando inoltre al potere con i Laburisti in Scozia.

Applaudiamo inoltre l'ottimo risultato ottenuto dalla Margherita nelle sue recenti elezioni regionali e comunali. La Margherita ed i suoi alleati sono parte integrante del nostro gruppo al Parlamento Europeo. Luciano Caveri è stato un magnifico presidente della Commissione parlamentare dei Trasporti ed un prossimo Presidente della Regione Val d'Aosta. Auguriamo a Paolo Costa, vice-presidente dell'ELDR, di proseguire il suo ottimo lavoro. Francesco Rutelli ed io abbiamo lavorato insieme su argomenti che vanno dalla concentrazione dei media, alla lotta contro la corruzione nel settore privato, al sostegno del Tribunale Criminale Internazionale. Giovanni Procacci ha assunto nella prima parte della legislatura il ruolo di portavoce del gruppo sulle questioni agricole e non ha mai smesso di pungolare con la nostra riflessione con i suoi contributi, che ci ricordano che la scuola politica italiana ha sempre una visione più profonda e lungimirante. Mentre Marco Formentini porta nel gruppo la sua serena laboriosità.

Il Parlamento Europeo è già oggi un'istituzione cruciale per la vita quotidiana dei cittadini, e questo è un ruolo destinato a rafforzarsi ulteriormente in futuro. Per questo è fondamentale che la nostra forza politica sia presente con autorevolezza per assicurare la supremazia dell'interesse collettivo dell'Europa sugli egoismi nazionali, il rispetto della legalità e dei principi fondamentali della democrazia, la visione di un'Europa che sappia mettersi in discussione senza perdersi in continue auto-glorificazioni.

Per questo, i Liberal-democratici lavorano per assicurare la vittoria politiche progressiste all'interno del Parlamento Europeo, dove il nostro voto fa spesso la differenza tra la sinistra e la destra.

Vorrei darvi qualche esempio. Sono fiero nel dire che sotto la mia leadership e insieme ai membri della Margherita i Liberal-democratici hanno preso posizione opponendoci alla guerra contro l'**Irak**. La nostra posizione è stata chiara - nessuna guerra senza l'autorità delle Nazioni Unite, e comunque va considerata come ultima risorsa di fronte a tracce evidenti fornite dagli ispettori di armi di distruzione di massa.

A guerra iniziata ho invitato il Parlamento Europeo a coalizzarsi contro l'uso della forza ed in particolare l'uso di uranio e bombe a grappoli. Da allora, abbiamo chiesto la presenza delle Nazioni Unite nella ricostruzione dell'Irak sottolineando che i colpevoli di abusi sui diritti umani e i crimini di guerra andassero portati di fronte ad un tribunale internazionale.

Attualmente abbiamo molte perplessità sulle prospettive dell'occupazione americana in Iraq. Le notizie degli ultimi giorni confermano che il programma iniziale pecca per ottimismo.

Sugli **OGM**, abbiamo formato una coalizione vincente per ottenere una tracciabilità ed una etichettatura trasparenti per l'uso di OGM nell'alimentazione e nei mangimi animali, in modo da garantire ai consumatori una libera scelta tra alimentazione a base di OGM oppure no. La prossima settimana, si cercherà di raggiungere un accordo su un compromesso dei Liberal-democratici che assicurerà agli Stati Membri misure per proteggere le coltivazioni organiche dai raccolti di OGM.

Nel campo economico, abbiamo sostenuto l'invito di Romano Prodi alla **riforma del Patto di Crescita e Stabilità** in modo da garantire alla Commissione un miglior controllo sui conti di quei governi che agiscono in modo irresponsabile nella politica fiscale. Per quanto riguarda la nostra politica sul commercio internazionale siamo forti sostenitori di una politica commerciale che tenga conto delle esigenze dei paesi in via di sviluppo e che rifletta l'importanza dello sviluppo sostenibile.

Sull'**immigrazione** e la richiesta di asilo, abbiamo dibattuto più volte sulla necessità per l'Unione Europea di una politica comune più umana, severa sul razzismo e la xenofobia, ma che tenga conto dell'importanza di un sistema migratorio legalizzato. Credo che possiamo affermare che in quanto a lotta all'antisemitismo, alla xenofobia e al razzismo, il nostro gruppo è il più avanzato nel Parlamento Europeo.

In particolare ci siamo distinti per la riflessione sul rapporto con l'**Islam**. Tra poche settimane pubblicheremo un libro che contiene numerosi contributi su questo tema, compresa una ricca riflessione del Presidente del Senegal, Maitre Wade, e due articolati interventi che Leoluca Orlando e Fouad Allam hanno esposto in occasione di un convengo da noi organizzato al Parlamento Europeo a gennaio.

Approfitto per ricordare l'amico Orlando, al quale il gruppo ELDR ha attribuito anni fa il "Civic Prize" per il suo straordinario impegno come sindaco di Palermo a favore della legalità.

Sul futuro dell'Europa, siamo stati forti sostenitori, in seno alla **Convenzione**, di una Europa più federale, con una Commissione più affidabile e forte, un maggior uso del voto a maggioranza e più poteri di controllo democratico al Parlamento Europeo.

Il nostro Gruppo ELDR in seno alla Convenzione, animato dal collega Andrew Duff e dal Presidente Dini (che qui saluto con particolare affetto), ha svolto un ruolo pionieristico nel pungolare costantemente la presidenza della Convenzione affinché una prospettiva federale restasse centrale nel disegno di costituzione. Ancora più di altri abbiamo assicurato una visione comune fra posizioni di stati fondatori, stati membri e nuovi paesi dell'Unione.

Il comitato Liberal-democratico ha lasciato il suo segno all'interno della Convenzione, dando vita ad idee innovative e soprattutto mantenendo una porta aperta alla Presidenza integrata dell'Unione Europea, qualcosa in cui Lamberto Dini e il mio collega inglese Andrew Duff meriterebbero maggior credito nel raggiungerla.

Le **analisi dei voti** parlano chiaro. L'ELDR vota più spesso con i socialisti che non con il PPE, oltre a concordare molto spesso, in circa il 65% dei voti, con i Verdi.

In particolare convergiamo in primo luogo con la sinistra nelle materie costituzionali, di bilancio, ambiente, giustizia, libertà e diritti della persona, affari esteri, politica regionale, trasporti; le convergenze maggiori con il PPE sono invece in materia economica.

Ciò non toglie che il nostro è un gruppo composito, come tutte le famiglie politiche europee. Ma per noi la ricerca del consenso interno è sempre svolta sulla base di un profondo rispetto reciproco, animato da una forte aspirazione europeista.

Non vi nascondo che una riflessione è in corso per riflettere sia sulla nostra identità, sia sulle prospettive future di una famiglia riformista ed europeista che si richiami esplicitamente ai termini di Democrazia e Libertà - le due parole della Margherita.

Già oggi la maggior parte dei partiti membri dell'ELDR non si chiamano "Liberali" e l'allargamento costituisce un'occasione preziosa per presentarci all'Europa più aperti e più ricchi.

Ben tredici osservatori dai nuovi paesi hanno scelto l'ELDR. Ma oggi mi rivolgo a voi, amici della Margherita.

Certo, l'Italia di oggi ha un disperato bisogno di Europa, e soprattutto di un'Europa che sappia mettere un freno all'avidità di Berlusconi, allo stravolgimento delle regole di fondo della democrazia che questo governo sta attuando, alle costanti minacce nei confronti della coraggiosa magistratura italiana.

Per noi amici dell'Italia è doloroso vedere questo continuo spettacolo che, credetemi, in Europa ha quasi dell'incredibile: un ministro della Repubblica che dichiara di volere prendere a cannonate le barche derelitte di poveri emigrati, un vice-presidente del consiglio che ancora pochi anni fa andava insieme a Le Pen a trovare Saddam Hussein, un ministro degli esteri che non ha ancora spiegato nulla della presidenza italiana, e un Primo Ministro che ferma a forza di leggi i procedimenti giudiziari contro di lui. È doloroso dirlo, ma come ha scritto il Financial Times, questa Italia, se fosse un paese candidato, non potrebbe entrare in Europa, perché ai nuovi membri chiediamo standard più esigenti.

Ma sono anche amareggiato di vedere una parte dell'Europa fin troppo tollerante con Berlusconi, trattato come un amico col quale si passa volentieri un fine settimana nella sua villa in Sardegna, quasi che la sua minaccia sia una caratteristica che riguarda solo gli italiani.

Ma è soprattutto l'Europa che ha bisogno dell'Italia. C'è infatti il rischio che l'Europa intraprenda la strada di una visione eccessivamente "amministrativa" della politica, e che si lasci prendere dal cinismo. Lo spazio che oggi Berlusconi trova in Europa è infatti una conseguenza di questo cinismo dirompente.

Rispetto a questi pericoli l'Italia è un paese che nella storia politica è sempre riuscito a conciliare i più alti valori della cultura cattolica-riformista (penso in particolare a un grande europeista come De Gasperi) e del pensiero laico, una sintesi che oggi vive felicemente nella Margherita. Un paese che ha rifiutato fanatismi e ha saputo primeggiare per generosità e capacità di visione. Rispetto all'egoismo e alle derive del consumismo più bieco, un paese come l'Italia può riportare al centro dell'Europa il dibattito sui valori della solidarietà e della coesione sociale, ma anche quelli dell'importanza della dimensione culturale e della difesa dell'ambiente del nostro continente. E di una politica estera che non sia né provincialismo e neppure un nuovo imperialismo.

Come tutti sappiamo il lavoro da compiere è tanto.

La nostra campagna su questi temi proseguirà nei prossimi mesi, durante la Presidenza italiana fino alle elezioni europee del prossimo anno. Insieme a Francesco Rutelli terremo sotto stretta sorveglianza la Presidenza italiana, a cominciare dall'incontro con Berlusconi che ho questo pomeriggio e dal dibattito di mercoledi prossimo a Strasburgo durante il quale sia io che Francesco ci rivolgeremo a Berlusconi.

Magari gli chiederemo se è disposto a firmare con gli europei un contratto meno demagogico e più serio di quello che ha sbandierato agli italiani in campagna elettorale.

Noi siamo ottimisti, amici della Margherita, come lo siete voi, soprattutto dopo il successo alle recenti amministrative.

Questo perché dietro le nostre idee c'è un forte impeto che ci permette di guardare alle prossime elezioni con grande fiducia. Abbiamo però bisogno del vostro aiuto, dei vostri consigli, della vostra ricchezza culturale e politica, delle vostre critiche.

Abbiamo infatti molti avversari, e solo se sapremo tutti metterci in discussione e rafforzare le ragioni del nostro comune impegno, l'Europa sarà più solidale e più democratica.

# Information and Addresses

## Graham Watson MEP
www.grahamwatsonmep.org

## Constituency Office
Bagehot's Foundry
Beard's Yard
Langport
Somerset TA10 9PS
UK
euro_office@cix.co.uk

## Liberal Democrats
4 Cowley Street,
London
SW1P 3NB
UK
www.libdems.org.uk

## Liberal Democrat MEPs:
http://www.libdemmeps.org.uk/

## ELDR Party
www.eldr.org

## ALDE Group in the European Parliament
European Parliament
Rue Wiertz
B-1047 Brussels
tel: +32 2 284 21 11
fax: +32 2 230 24 85
e-mail: aldegroup@europarl.eu.int
www.alde.eu

## European Parliament
www.europarl.europa.eu

## European Union
www.europa.eu